"What I love most about this book is how it speaks directly to the heart of what we do as school counselors—building relationships that lead to real change. It goes beyond surface-level collaboration and shows us how to form strong, intentional coalitions that can tackle the deep, systemic issues our students face. I haven't seen another book that so clearly connects our daily work to broader advocacy in such a practical and inspiring way. If you're a counselor who wants to do more than support students one-on-one—if you want to change the systems around them—this book is a must-read."

Gabe Villanueva, *School Counselor, School Counselor Coordinator, Illinois School Counselor Association Board Director*

"With both clarity and compassion, this book offers a compass for school counselors navigating the complex terrain of leadership and advocacy. It redefines what true leadership looks like—bold, authentic, and rooted in collective power."

Loretta Whitson, EdD, *Executive Director, California Association of School Counselors*

"*Equity-Driven Leadership in School Counseling: How to Champion Justice for All Students* is a remarkable book for all school counselors. This book is a valuable resource for school counselors in the field and school counseling master's students. Drs. Lopez-Perry and Mason break down the aspects of Leadership through an equity lens which guides leadership development and implementation for school counselors to advocate for all students in P-12 schools. This is a dynamic book to inform those who are seeking, learning, or refining their skills and voices in school counseling leadership spaces."

Malti Tuttle, PhD, LPC (GA), CPCS (GA), ATS, NCC, NCSC, *Associate Professor and School Counseling Program Coordinator, Auburn University*

Equity-Driven Leadership in School Counseling

Drawing from the authors' experience as former school counselors, their research on school counselor leadership and advocacy, and their professional advocacy work, this book provides insights and strategies to develop school counselors' leadership skills.

This book is divided into two parts. The first part focuses on self-reflection and critical consciousness for school counselors. It challenges their understanding of leadership and urges them to critically examine whether their personal definition of leadership aligns with the needs of diverse students and the broader educational context. Chapter topics include leadership and liberation, the limits of traditional leadership theories, leading with emotional intelligence, and the courage to confront systems of oppression. The second part calls the reader toward critical action and engagement in social and political activity and advocacy with the intent to disrupt and change perceived inequalities. Specific topics include developing political skills, addressing resistance to change, and developing collaborative relationships.

School counselors will find this book filled with the necessary knowledge and skills to effect change in schools, districts, and the public arena for the benefit of P-12 students, particularly those from historically marginalized populations.

Caroline Lopez-Perry is an Associate Professor and Program Coordinator of the School Counseling Program at California State University, Long Beach in Long Beach, CA.

Erin Mason is an Associate Professor in the School Counseling Program and Coordinator of the Counselor Education and Practice Doctoral Program at Georgia State University in Atlanta, GA.

Equity-Driven Leadership in School Counseling

How to Champion Justice for All Students

Caroline Lopez-Perry
and Erin Mason

Routledge
Taylor & Francis Group

NEW YORK AND LONDON

Designed cover image: Getty Images

First published 2026
by Routledge
605 Third Avenue, New York, NY 10158

and by Routledge
4 Park Square, Milton Park, Abingdon, Oxon, OX14 4RN

Routledge is an imprint of the Taylor & Francis Group, an informa business

© 2026 Caroline Lopez-Perry and Erin Mason

ISBN: 978-1-032-67919-8 (hbk)
ISBN: 978-1-032-67772-9 (pbk)
ISBN: 978-1-032-67917-4 (ebk)

DOI: 10.4324/9781032679174

Typeset in Times New Roman
by codeMantra

To those who inspired it and will not read it.

Caroline and Erin

For the two souls who shaped my heart, Mama and Abuelo—your love is my foundation.

For Steven whose love, patience, and humor have been my greatest gifts.

To my children, may you lead with purpose and compassion.

Caroline

For every student who teaches my soul.

For my mom, who teaches my spirit.

For Chris, who forever teaches my heart.
Erin

Contents

Foreword

This book invites the reader to embark on a journey; this journey marks a subtle transformation, if transformation could ever be subtle. This invitation is a request to re-evaluate, re-assess, reconsider, and redistribute. It offers us what we need today, tomorrow, and forevermore: a pathway to do better as educators and as human beings.

Envisioning a journey that wraps the voyager in the warmth of possibilities is the plight of the following eight chapters. Participation is voluntary; though this text reminds us that change in education is inevitable, whether we wish to use our roles to influence that change or not. The depths of our professional souls notify us of the necessity of this journey. We have to choose the journey, and Drs. Lopez-Perry and Mason provide the tools to soul-search while navigating difficult times. Each educator has to decide what kind of future they choose to imagine and enact. School counselors, we are given what we need to make informed decisions, think critically, and act according to what is best for the world.

Part 1 of this book strengthens our critical reflection. We make sense of our educational worlds and come to terms with the decisions that have brought us to this state of circumstances so that we consider other possibilities; better possibilities. What makes us eager, hopeful, saddened, and angered influences how we engage with the work of school counseling. William Ayers reminds us that when schooling exists for children as a site of harm, our response to the children and the system can reflect humanity or inhumanity.

Historical accounts of wickedness follow nefarious patterns and seemingly simplistic explanations. This book peels back the layers of intentional disguise to uncover what school counselors must find underneath: authenticity. When communities are taught who to fear, who to fight, and who to disempower, the wicked are assigned and unmourned. Drs. Lopez-Perry and Mason, intellectually and insightfully, resist the notion of wickedness's single story. They examine power and privilege. The impact of society on school counseling is analyzed, and historical accounts are evaluated for the improvement of education.

Finally, in Part 2, school counselors are empowered to break the cycle of inaction and harmful repetition of antiquated behavior. Education has never been apolitical. Schooling has always served a purpose for the community, the state, and the nation. The alarm to wake up has been set, and snoozing will do all of us no good. Through meticulous and compassionate redefining, this text outlines the various pathways of critical action because to act, in general, is to assume one's action leads to power and peace. The authors possess an acute understanding of the types of actions that produce justice, encouraging school counselors to adopt a different, more humane, and realistic approach to engaging with the systems designed to keep groups divided. This final part of a clear and decisive text rejects division and instead promotes unity and solidarity in the name of educational and social justice, working toward the betterment of all people.

Equity-Driven Leadership in School Counseling: How to Champion Justice for All Students is meant to be read, studied, annotated, and practiced throughout school counselors' graduate studies and the entirety of their careers. Steve Sharpe, a middle school counselor in Pennsylvania, often reminds American school counselors that we are uniquely positioned to enact the change we wish to see in schools and the world. This book provides us with a roadmap to truly be who we claim to be.

By Alicia Oglesby

Preface

The idea for this book grew out of many heartfelt conversations between Erin and me about the state of school counseling. During one of these conversations, our discussion turned to the self-aggrandizing persona of the Great and All-Powerful Wizard of Oz and the need to distinguish between false leaders and authentic ones. It was at that moment that we realized a resource like this text was urgently needed—one that helps school counselors challenge the illusions of power while stepping into their own authentic leadership.

There is a lot happening locally, nationally, and internationally, and the school counseling profession is not immune to the complexities of the world. School counselors are at a critical juncture, and as a profession, we must re-evaluate our priorities, values, purpose, and next steps. Carl Jung once said, "The world will ask who you are, and if you do not know, the world will tell you." How we lead ourselves, who we decide to lead us, and the ways in which we lead during these times will have a profound impact on shaping who we become as school counselors and, most importantly, our students' educational experiences. Given this, we have a lot to say about the state of school counseling and the urgent need to rethink leadership in our profession. We don't expect to appeal to everyone or even to the masses. Those who know us best know we have zero goals to be in the mainstream. Instead, this book centers on equity, social justice, leadership, and the role of school counselors in addressing disparities in the P-12 educational system.

After spending years in the field, training hundreds of school counselors nationwide, positioning ourselves to lead and advocate in various ways, and looking to other disciplines for alternatives, we're here to share some ideas. Our knowledge is not restricted to the walls of the ivory tower or academic spaces. Rather, our leadership and advocacy work is deeply informed by the wisdom, experiences, and practices of grassroots organizers, community leaders, and student and practitioner activists who have long been at the forefront of advocacy and systemic change. It is also informed by counseling leaders who came before us, whose leadership and advocacy continue to shape our work. Our aim is to connect you to many key thought leaders in our past who have helped move the needle of progress, as well as hidden leaders who are currently shaping the profession in profound yet unrecognized ways. Leadership is not synonymous with popularity, productivity, or position. Our concern is that the legacy of their work is being lost in favor of superficial fame over authentic impact. As such, in this book, we do more than merely cite these leaders. We provide brief highlights to honor their contributions and ground future efforts.

This book is not meant to be the starting point for your leadership abilities. Instead, it should function as a mirror and a map, helping you recognize and refine the skills you already possess while providing direction for where to go next. This text is intended to support reflection on the state of leadership in your work, schools, districts, and professional organizations while expanding your ideas on the qualities and process of effective leadership. We believe leadership is about the *redistribution* of power. Yet, education and school counseling have historically relied on a top-down approach to leadership, centralizing decision-making to a few while marginalizing the voices of others.

We recognize that the topic of school leadership can involve complex dynamics and power structures, which can make the very idea of stepping into leadership feel overwhelming. However, we believe school counselors already possess many of the skills needed to lead. They just need to recognize their own power. We also recognize that leadership can be a complicated experience for many marginalized groups (BIPOC, LGBTQIA+, disabled, etc.), especially when so many models of leadership don't reflect our identities or values. For marginalized groups, claiming leadership can mean challenging long-standing norms and expectations about who is "fit" to lead. Our approach is rooted in liberatory leadership, which centers on expanding our understanding of *who* gets to lead and *how* that leadership gets to happen.

This book offers both a perspective and a pathway to help school counselors find their way home to leadership. Just as Dorothy Gale navigated an unfamiliar world, school counselors, too, must navigate the dynamics of a system often built to exclude their voices. To guide this journey, we draw inspiration from *The Wonderful Wizard of Oz*. Like Dorothy, embarking on a journey of self-discovery and navigating unfamiliar territory, school counselors must navigate the complexities inherent in leadership and advocacy.

Discussing school leadership, educational inequities, and related politics can be daunting and overwhelming, often involving complex dynamics and power structures. However, we hope to alleviate some of this apprehension and provide hope to those who want to do right by students by drawing parallels to the story of Dorothy in the Land of Oz. Throughout our book, we draw connections from the school counselor leadership journey to that of Dorothy Gale, exploring new and unfamiliar territory in Oz.

We believe many core counseling skills (e.g., active listening, collaboration, group facilitation skills) translate to leadership skills. In each chapter, we teach the reader how to use these skills when leading for equity. Because systemic change can be highly political, we use Dorothy's encounters with each new person (i.e., Glinda, the Wicked Witch, the Great Wizard) as a way to think critically about possible alliances you can form and the potential saboteurs you may meet.

This book is divided into two parts.

Part 1: Down the Yellow Brick Road

Chapters 1–4 focus on self-reflection and critical consciousness for school counselors. It challenges traditional notions of leadership and urges school counselors to critically examine whether their personal definition of leadership aligns with the needs of diverse students and the broader educational context. School counselors must examine their identity as leaders as the first step. This step requires understanding how they arrived at their notion of "leadership" and what it means in the context of today's school counselor role. From here, we ask the reader to critically examine whether this personal definition is not only sufficient for the times but will help bring justice for all students and the school and community settings in which they work.

Part 2: Facing Oz

This section calls the reader to take critical action and engage in social and political activity and advocacy, with the intention of disrupting and changing perceived inequalities. Chapters 5–8 focus on developing the political skills and tactics needed to challenge systems of injustice and organize individuals in social justice work. It is in this section that we focus on content primarily outside the counseling discipline.

We hope to have given you a tool that has been a long time coming, but also well-timed for the circumstances many school counselors are facing.

Note: On January 23, 2025, Donald Trump initiated an Executive Order that led to the removal and archiving of hundreds of guidance documents, reports, and training materials related to equity and justice within the educational system from the Education Department website, including materials from the Office for Civil Rights. The Education Department has historically played a critical role in protecting civil rights and promoting equity for all students, including marginalized communities. Some of the documents that were removed included articles that we have referenced in this book. While the links to these documents are no longer active, we have used archival links in our references to preserve access for historical and posterity reasons. These references should serve as a reminder of the standards and protections that were once in place and honor the efforts of Department of Education staff who, despite being terminated, worked tirelessly to promote equality and justice.

Acknowledgments

We would like to express our deepest gratitude to our families and friends for their unwavering support and encouragement throughout this journey. To those we advocate with and for—our partners in purpose—thank you for your unwavering commitment to equity and justice. This work is richer because of you. To those who contributed their leadership stories, thank you for your vulnerability, wisdom, and generosity. We are deeply grateful for your perspectives, may your leadership inspire others.

Thank you to Amanda Savage and the entire editorial and production team for your support on this project.

Basic Assumptions

The following basic principles serve as a guiding framework and shape our perspectives. The purpose is to establish a common understanding and shared mindset with our readers. It introduces you to our core values and beliefs that form the basis of our work in leadership and advocacy. These basic assumptions include:

1 *All school counselors are leaders and must lead:* Regardless of the stage in your career, your age, the number of school counselors in your district, etc. ... you are a leader. This book is intended to enhance and strengthen your leadership skills, but by virtue of being a school counselor you are already a leader.
2 *Core counseling skills translate to leadership skills:* Many of the core counseling skills you learned in your graduate program are valuable leadership skills.
3 *All schools are systems and are a part of other systems:* Trying to do your job on behalf of all students often means working against multiple systems, not just one. Working against multiple systems can require more than one approach. There is no singular approach.
4 *All school counseling is political:* Because school counseling happens in the context of multiple systems, there are always many relationships to navigate and issues to negotiate. Leadership requires compelling others and taking stands for the sake of students.
5 *Leading isn't saviorship:* You aren't meant to lead alone. While school leaders can significantly impact the success and direction of their organization, they cannot single-handedly solve the problems of P-12 education. True liberation recognizes that the power lies within students and their families.
6 *You will make mistakes:* Leaders make mistakes. This is partly because they are often faced with complex and ambiguous situations with no clear-cut solution. Sometimes in these situations, the political dynamics or the environment is changing rapidly as decisions are being made. Despite this, leaders are willing to acknowledge their mistakes, grow from them, and keep focused

on the goal. Systems of oppression (racism, sexism, heterosexism, ableism, classism, ageism, etc.) will gaslight you and lead you to believe that your mistakes make you inadequate for leadership.

7 *Nothing, and no one is above critique:* Systems of oppression, like institutionalized racism, are maintained by the practices, policies, and beliefs within a system. Schools and school counselors are part of multiple systems (schools, districts, professional associations). To lead for equity, the practices, policies, and beliefs of these systems must be critiqued. Rather than asking why a system is under scrutiny, ask yourself why it should be immune to criticism. We must critique the things we hold dear. Much like a plant, we tend to the weeds to ensure its growth. If we hold something dear, we must nurture its care. This includes the people, practices, groups, and systems that uphold our profession.

8 *Children are children, and every child should be treated as OUR child, to be loved and protected as one of the most valuable members of our society:* Children are an essential part of our world and deserve the space to experience their youth with joy, freedom, and community. However, in a society rooted in capitalism, children are too often disregarded because they cannot produce. If we truly claim to love children, then that must be reflected in our actions and behaviors. They deserve to be protected in mind, body, and spirit. To be able to explore, grow, make mistakes, and define who they are in a safe and supportive environment that affirms their humanity. Our love for them must be translated into solidarity when their rights and agency are stripped from them.

Glossary of Characters and Key Symbols

Throughout the chapters, readers will encounter our use of The Wonderful Wizard of Oz characters and storyline as a metaphor for school counseling, leadership, and advocacy. Below, we provide a list of the primary characters and symbols in alphabetical order.

Dorothy Gale   Dorothy represents the school counselor or school counselor leader.

Emerald City   The Emerald City generally represents any institution or system operating on power and oppression (e.g., racism, heterosexism, ableism, capitalism).

Flying Monkeys   The flying monkeys represent those who are lackeys or who may be exploited for someone else's agenda.

Good Witch   The Good Witch represents white feminism, toxic positivity, or saviorism.

Hot-Air Balloon   The hot-air balloon represents privilege or an easy way out.

Lion   The Lion represents the value or skill of courage.

Munchkinland   Munchkinland represents a part of Dorothy's support system along with Lion, Scarecrow, and the Tin Woodman.

Oz   The Wonderful Wizard of Oz generally represents any individual or group that initially appears to hold desirable power and privilege but in reality, is an agent of oppression.

Scarecrow   The Scarecrow represents the value or skill of intellect.

Tin Woodman   The Tin Woodman represents the value or skill of compassion.

Toto   Toto represents the core social justice values of a school counselor leader.

The Wicked Witch   The Wicked Witch represents resistance or obstacles faced by leaders.

The Brick Road   The brick road represents a path or journey.

The Poppy Fields   The poppy fields represent anything that lures us into ease, comfort, or familiarity, and away from our leadership goal.

Definitions

Language is fluid and ever-changing, and terminology is being redefined regularly by social justice movements. Being a life-long learner means having the ability to change how you see yourself, the world, and your actions. As such, new language is needed to account for those shifts over time. We recognize that the vocabulary and definitions we use below may evolve over time, and we remain open to growth, learning, and honoring our collective progress.

Activism: Action taken to challenge those in power to bring about change in society and benefit the greater good.

Activist: A person who engages in intentional and sustained efforts to promote, challenge, or transform social, political, economic, or cultural systems.

Advocacy: Speaking or acting on behalf of an individual or group to uphold their rights, explain their point of view, or support their interests, either independently or in collaboration with them. This can occur at the micro and macro levels (Toporek & Daniels, 2018).

BIPOC: Refers to Black, Indigenous, and People of Color. It is used to acknowledge the collective group and distinguishes Black and Indigenous communities because of their distinct histories of oppression in the United States and within education (e.g., slavery, colonization, genocide). It recognizes that not all people have the same experience regarding systemic oppression. It includes the following groups:

- Asian, South Asian, or Asian American
- Black, African, or a part of Africa's Global Diaspora
- Latino/a, Latine/x, Hispanic, or Afro-Latino/a
- Multi-racial, multi-ethnic, bi-racial, or mixed
- Native American, American Indian, or Indigenous
- Pacific Islander, Samoan, or Hawaiian Native
- Persian, Arab, Middle Eastern, or North African

Note: While BIPOC is meant to be inclusive, it is imperfect and imprecise. Some individuals do nt see themselves in this acronym. Another term ALAANA (also ALANA)—African, Latinx, Asian, Arab, and Native American—is used as an alternative. Unlike BIPOC, which centers on these communities' experiences with oppression, ALAANA centers on their distinct racial and ethnic identities. Ultimately, honoring the way someone chooses to identify themselves is *always* preferable.

Carceral Logic: A punishment mindset, describing how our ideologies, practices, and structures have been shaped—often unconsciously or invisibly—by a commitment to punishment, imprisonment, exclusion, and disposability (Shalaby, 2021).

Collectivism: A worldview that emphasizes the interconnectedness of individuals within a group, where social relationships and mutual obligations shape personal identity. It prioritizes group cohesion, shared responsibilities, and collective well-being over individual autonomy (Oyserman et al., 2002).

Collective Liberation: Recognizes that systems of oppression are interconnected, creating a web of structural inequality that must be challenged collectively (Combahee River Collective, 1977/2017).

Copaganda: The range of strategies and narratives used by police, unions, and governments to secure funding, spread misinformation, and influence public perception alongside media portrayals that legitimize and normalize policing. It also works to counter negative perceptions of police and normalize their practices, serving as "propaganda favorable to law enforcement" (Kaba & Ritchie, 2022, p.183).

Critical Action: Engagement in social and political activity and advocacy with the intent to disrupt and change perceived inequalities (Diemer et al., 2014).

Critical Awareness: The ability to identify oppressed status and oppression, including one's relationship between self and society (Friere, 1970; Houser & Overton, 2001).

Critical Reflection: The ability to perceive inequalities and recognize dominant culture privilege (Diemer et al., 2014).

Cultural Humility: A life-long commitment to self-evaluation and self-critique, to recognizing and redressing the power dynamics and imbalances that affect marginalized groups, and to developing mutually beneficial partnerships with communities on behalf of individuals and defined populations. It involves engaging with others, particularly those of marginalized identities, humbly, authentically, and from a place of learning (Tervalon & Murry-Garcia, 1998, p.117).

Discrimination: The differential treatment of different ages, genders, racial, ethnicities, religions, national, ability identity, sexual orientation, socioeconomic, and other groups at the individual level and the institutional/structural level. Discrimination is usually the behavioral manifestation of prejudice and involves negative, hostile, and injurious treatment of rejected group members (American Psychological Association, n.d.).

Ideological Oppression: The promotion of beliefs by society, institutions, systems, or individuals that justify inequality, making unfair systems seem normal or acceptable. It spreads through culture, media, education, and policies, reinforcing power imbalances and influencing how people see themselves and others. These beliefs, which support various forms of discrimination (like racism, sexism, and classism), are deeply rooted in history and culture, shaping how people understand the world (Bell, 2013).

Individual Liberation: The process by which a person frees themselves from internalized oppression, limiting beliefs and practices, and systems of domination that restrict their full potential. It is a crucial step toward collective liberation.

Individualism: A worldview that emphasizes personal autonomy, self-fulfillment, and individual goals over collective or social considerations. It prioritizes personal rights over obligations, values uniqueness and self-control, and defines identity based on personal accomplishments rather than group affiliation (Hofstede, 1980; Oyserman et al., 2002).

Institutional Oppression: Discrimination of certain groups by societal structures and institutions where laws, policies, and practices favor some groups over others (Bell, 2013).

Internal Oppression: Involves how individuals absorb belief systems that lead them to feel superior or inferior to others, shaping their sense of self-worth based on these perceptions (Bell, 2013).

Interpersonal Oppression: The idea that one group is better than another and has the right to control the other, which gets structured into institutions, gives permission and reinforcement for individual members of the dominant group to personally disrespect or mistreat individuals in the oppressed group (Bell, 2013).

Intersectionality: A framework for conceptualizing how systems of oppression overlap to create distinct experiences for people with multiple identity classifications (i.e., race, class, gender identity, sexual orientation, religion, and other identity markers) (Crenshaw, K., 1989, 1991).

Oppression: The combination of prejudice and institutional power that creates a system that discriminates against some groups (often called "target groups") and benefits other groups (often called "dominant groups"). Examples of these systems are racism, sexism, heterosexism, ableism, classism, ageism, and anti-Semitism (Chinook Fund, n.d.).

Organizing: A process in which individuals and groups build the skills and power to influence social, political, and educational decisions that matter to them (Speer & Han, 2018).

Paternalism: The practice of making decisions for others rather than letting them take responsibility for their own lives.

Power: The ability to control or influence the behavior of people or resources (Murray et al., 2020). Society and schools within society are affected by many different power structures: patriarchy, white supremacy, heterosexism, cissexism, and classism are only a few (Powell, 2022).

Prejudice: The formation of attitudes toward persons, groups, and situations before there is any experience with or study of them.

Privilege: Unearned advantages or benefits that individuals or groups receive based on aspects of their identity, such as race, gender, class, or ability, often without awareness. These advantages give privileged groups a greater ability to navigate and succeed in society compared to marginalized groups, often maintaining social inequalities (McIntosh, 1989).

Race: A system of structuring opportunity and assigning value based on phenotypic properties (e.g., skin color and hair texture associated with "race" in the United States), which ranges from daily interpersonal interactions shaped by race to racialized opportunities for good education, housing, employment, and other resources, and unfairly disadvantages people belonging to marginalized racial groups. Racism is a form of prejudice that generally includes negative emotional reactions to members of the group, acceptance of negative stereotypes, and racial discrimination against individuals; in some cases, it leads to violence (American Psychological Association, n.d.).

School Counselor Educator (SCE): Counselor Educators with school counseling work experience, who encompass a school counseling professional identity and teach future school counselors (McMahon et al., 2009; Milsom & Moran, 2015).

Social Justice: The use of systems awareness, empowerment, cultural affirmation, and advocacy that ensures that oppressed persons have access to resources and opportunities that have historically been reserved for those in privileged life spaces (Sue & Sue, 2016).

Stereotype: An exaggerated or distorted belief that attributes characteristics to members of a particular group, simplistically lumping them together and refusing to acknowledge differences among group members.

Systemic Barriers: The laws, policies, procedures, and practices embedded into systems that disproportionately impact or exclude marginalized groups based on race, class, gender, ability, etc.

Systems Advocacy: Changing policies, laws, procedures, or rules that impact how someone lives their life. These efforts can be targeted at a local, state, or national level. The focus can be changing laws or simply written or unwritten policies. What is targeted depends on the type of problem and who has authority over the problem (Brain Injury Resource Center, 1998).

White Supremacy Culture: A set of behaviors, characteristics, and values that are normalized and institutionalized in our organizations, communities, and homes, where whiteness and white cultural norms dominate (Okun, 2021).

Part 1

Down the Yellow Brick Road

Chapter 1

We're Not in Kansas Anymore
Leadership and Liberation

These are undeniably complex times, with many feeling uneasy about the direction our society is moving toward. There are more intersecting crises in the world today than most of us have ever witnessed in our lifetimes and our social, political, economic, and educational systems are being tested in unprecedented ways. The dizziness of it all can leave one feeling directionless. In the face of such uncertainty, it is easy to feel powerless. Yet, through it all, school counselors must continue to look forward, believe in something bigger, and take small but significant steps forward.

For a moment, imagine a world that recognizes the humanity and agency of every child. A country that prioritizes the needs, interests, and voices of children and youth. Schools that operate from love rather than domination. Educators, staff, families, and students who protect, care for, and affirm the most marginalized. This vision for the future is not some imaginary world found in fantasy books but a reality that can be built if we work toward this common goal. To make this vision possible, schools need leadership that is grounded in equity and social justice, and school counselors are at the forefront of this work. Taking a whole-child approach to education, they are uniquely positioned to challenge oppressive systems, foster inclusive school communities, and ensure that every student is seen, heard, and supported. In these trying times, who better to lead through a crisis than school counselors? We are often the steady force through times of uncertainty for all those in our school communities.

The need for leadership isn't just theoretical but plays out in real and urgent ways in our schools every day. Caroline learned this firsthand early in her career as a school counselor. During the first week of the school year, as she and her co-counselor worked to solve a schoolwide scheduling disaster that had the entire school on edge, the math coach walked into her office to check in and said, "You are the litmus test for all of us. If you [the school counselors] freak out, we know things are bad!" It was at that moment Caroline realized the critical role she played, not just as a school counselor, but as a leader and stabilizing force at her site. Likewise, Erin was called to a neighboring middle school in her first year to help provide crisis support after the Valujet Flight 592 crash into the Florida Everglades.

DOI: 10.4324/9781032679174-2

The school lost several soccer players and their parents on the flight. Erin learned how vital her leadership skills were to contributing to a climate of safety and calm, and to being prepared for future crises. Educators and staff often look to school counselors for reassurance, problem-solving, and leadership. The most important work we can do as educators is to work together to build a world where children and youth are protected, nurtured, and supported to live expansive lives.

In the theme of *The Wonderful Wizard of Oz*, many school counselors are familiar with the idea that we are skilled at helping mitigate the damage during and after tornadoes. However, as authors, we embrace the idea that our leadership skills can contribute to being more prepared for, redirecting, channeling, and even quelling them. Historically, social movements and educational movements have been deeply intertwined. Whether at the local, state, or national level, social movements have influenced education curriculum changes, policy reforms, and funding shifts. In fact, many educational movements arose from the perceived failures or injustices in the current structure, and educators and students alike have reaped the benefits of the fight for diversity, equity, and inclusion. The Women's Rights Movement advocated for gender equality in education, including equal access to higher education and sports programs. The Civil Rights Movement led to the desegregation of schools, increased funding for Black colleges and universities, and the creation of affirmative action programs. The LGBTQ+ Rights Movement brought about the inclusion and protection of LGBTQ+ students and educators in schools, and the Special Education Movement fought for inclusive education and resulted in laws such as the Individuals with Disabilities Education Act (IDEA), ensuring access to special education services.

While some may debate the role of school counselors in politics, the truth is our profession has never been value-neutral. The history of our profession reminds us that counseling is deeply embedded in social, political, and historical realities (Katz, 1985). At present, economic instability, public health concerns, climate change, and geopolitical tensions are shaping our students' educational environment, their personal and postsecondary future, and our working conditions. Dr. Kristen Monroe, professor and director of UC Irvine's Interdisciplinary Center for the Scientific Study of Ethics and Morality, says, "… remember that almost all narratives addressing how we deal with others should be defined as political" (2023, p.34). The school counseling profession has always shifted in response to social movements, but at this moment, we have a unique opportunity to redefine our roles and lead a movement toward love and liberation.

Finding Our Way Home

Before we begin to lead such a movement, we must first look inward. In a world that feels increasingly uncertain, we have an opportunity to be anchors of hope and advocates for justice. We are in the eye of the storm. Budget cuts, increasing student needs, political polarization, and unjust policies at the state and federal level, are testing our commitment to equity. Finding our way home is a call to remembering who we are, reconnecting with our values and purpose, and transforming school counseling into a liberatory practice. It may be tempting to respond to injustice with immediate action, however to make this work impactful and sustainable it begins with deep reflection of our values, biases, and motivation. This kind of self-examination is a critical aspect of both leadership and self-care that we explore more fully in Chapter 8. To lead with purpose one must study the foundations of social justice, learn from the rich legacy of organizing, and study the systems we aim to transform.

We use the term "we" throughout this book because both Erin and I consider ourselves school counselors at heart and view ourselves as part of the collective "we." While our roles have shifted to counselor educators, training the next generation, we believe we cannot teach the work of school counselors without grounding our practice in the same principles. Although our setting has changed, the essence of the work has remained constant. Throughout the readings, we help you step into your ruby shoes, tap into your leadership potential, and rediscover the skills you possess. Like Dorothy Gale, who realized she had the power all along to solve her problems, we encourage you to leverage the unique leadership strengths you bring to schools. School counselors are skilled relationship builders and, thus well positioned to engage in liberatory leadership practices. Many core counseling skills (e.g. active listening, collaboration, group facilitation skills) translate directly to leadership skills. In each chapter, we teach you how to use these skills when leading for equity. We use Dorothy's alliances with each member of her community (e.g., Toto, Scarecrow, Tin Woodman, the Lion) to help you think critically about your own community and how vital they are to your journey for liberatory leadership.

Pause and Reflect

1 What does it mean to lead for equity and justice?
2 Who has historically been recognized as a leader in school counseling, and who has been excluded?
3 How do power and privilege shape leadership opportunities?
4 Is leadership something you develop or something you embody?

The Black and White History of Education and School Counseling

Before we begin this leadership journey, it is important to consider the historical origins of both education and school counseling. During the colonial period, schooling was not mandatory and only about 10% of the colonies' wealthiest children went to school (Urban et al., 2019). After the Revolutionary War, textbooks were written to standardize language and instill patriotism and religious beliefs. At this time, compulsory education emerged to further national unity and teach immigrants "American" values (Urban et al., 2019). While this was an important development in making education accessible, it was rooted in ethnocentrism and was in part, aimed at preventing immigrants from corrupting "American" values (Bowles & Gintis, 2002; Cole, 2008). This pattern of using education to enforce white Christian Eurocentric cultural norms has continued and historical records have documented how schools have been used for cultural assimilation, particularly through the Native American boarding school system and punitive and exclusionary schooling practices toward racially and ethnically diverse students. We expand on these historical practices more in Chapter 4. At the same time, education has long been criticized for its focus on preparing youth to be obedient workers.

Bowles and Gintis (2002) assert that schools function to socialize youth into hierarchical structures and condition them to follow rules without complaint. These social interactions and reward systems replicate the work environment, serving to praise discipline and obedience to authority. The very structure of schooling emphasizes routine and the development of skills necessary for economic productivity. It is essential to point out that guidance counseling emerged within this framework and began with vocational guidance conducted by administrators in the early 1900s (Gysbers, 2010). This meant that the primary function of guidance counselors was to orient students to career paths available to them, assess their suitability, give them information on how to pursue the career, and place them in programs or jobs best suited for their skills. In the 1920s, school counseling began to change, shaped by the mental hygiene, psychometric, and child study movements (Lambie & Williamson, 2004). As a result of these influences, a more clinically oriented approach to school counseling emerged. For example, during the 1930s E.G. Williamson created the first guidance and counseling theory, suggesting school counselors adopt a more directive administrative approach to working with students (Lambie & Williamson). The title "guidance counselor" reflects the role and function of the time, one that views children as unidimensional and offers them little agency in shaping their futures. A critical shift occurred later in the 1930s when Carl Rogers, the "Father of Counseling" introduced the humanism movement. With this shift, the term *guidance* was replaced with counseling in the literature and counselors conceptualizing clients as "people rather than problems" (Super, 1955, p.4). The role continued to evolve with the launch of Sputnik in 1957, when school counselors were primarily positioned to guide select students to math and science fields and over time, the profession continued to develop in response to societal shifts.

Yet, even as our profession has progressed and adapted to new understandings of human development, public perception of our role has struggled to keep pace. Despite the title change decades ago from guidance counselor to school counselor, we continue to fight for our appropriate title- school counselor. Why is it so hard for people to understand this shift? We believe the answer lies in the origins of both education and our profession. Schools were designed to produce compliant and workforce-ready individuals and that system is working as it was intended. Those who subscribe to this approach want *guidance counselors*. We are seeing the resurgence of this philosophy play out in real-time across various states as both violations of child labor laws and proposals to roll back protections are on the rise and students' constitutional rights are being challenged across various states in this country (Sherer & Mast, 2023, March 14). Don't get lost in the semantics. Words shape expectations, and the term guidance counselor reinforces the idea that our role is to move students through a production line, actively shaping their futures with little consideration for their agency and identity. We believe the very presence of a school counselor disrupts this model. This is why we are seen as optional and not essential and why the fight for both title and role continues today. By seeing students as full human beings with emotional, social, and personal complexities, we challenge the current system built on control rather than care.

Ultimately, it will take more than our mere presence to disrupt this black-and-white model of education. To step into a full-color world, Renae Mayes and Kara Ieva, thought leaders in the field of school counseling suggest that school counselors must actively work to build environments that center humanity, resistance, and joy (Mayes et al., 2024). The first 100 years of the profession were about what school counselors do. From 2000 to 2020, our professional focus was on how students are different as a result of the school counseling program. Now, we must look to the horizon and ask ourselves, how are students' school experiences more equitable when school counselors advocate for social justice in the building and beyond (Mason, 2023)? While we very much recognize that education is in the midst of a tornado, we must weather this storm together to reach the vibrant horizon we dream of.

Reflection

What question would you write for the next 20 years of school counseling?

The Tornado of Upheaval and the Perfect Storm

As we consider the next chapter of our profession, it is clear that the path forward is being shaped by the storms we have recently faced. The COVID-19 pandemic and the Black Lives Matter movement, particularly following the murder of George Floyd created the perfect storm of social upheaval. Both of these events exposed systemic inequities that disproportionately impact marginalized communities, and the structural racism embedded in healthcare, criminal justice, and education. By mid-July 2020, COVID rates for non-Hispanic Black persons and Hispanic or Latino youth ages 0-17 were 4.6 and 7.5 times the rate among non-Hispanic white persons, respectively (CDC, 2020). Among marginalized communities, the pandemic exacerbated children's exposure to racism and xenophobia (Marron, 2021). Between 2019 and 2021 socioeconomic disparities in education widened, particularly among elementary children, due to limited access to quality remote instruction, quality instruction, and supplemental supports (Gee et al., 2023). While schools have returned to in-person instruction, the lasting impact of a worldwide pandemic compounded by structural inequalities cannot be overlooked. Pediatric experts warn that these effects will disproportionately impact children (Oberg et al., 2022). At the same time, the Black Lives Matter and immigration protests forced schools to re-evaluate how they serve Black students and marginalized communities sparking debates over budgets and policing.

In the words of Dorothy, "We're not in Kansas anymore." And yet, most schools went back to doing business as usual. Social justice issues are complex and nuanced and school counselors can no longer live in a black-and-white world where choices are simple. In an effort to advance equity and racial justice in education, school counselors must understand the intricacies of systems and develop new skills for leading and advocating within them. Education is becoming more layered and difficult to navigate. There has been a surge in anti-Critical Race Theory (CRT) legislation across numerous states in response to coordinated campaigns. Between 2021 and 2022, 563 anti-"CRT'" measures were introduced across 49 states with 241 enacted (Alexander et al., 2023).

The majority targeted P-12 education and regulated classroom teaching and curriculum materials (Alexander et al., 2023). Thousands of books that expand students' worldviews and understanding of one another were removed from classroom shelves and libraries (U.S. Department of Education, 2023). Policies are restricting gender-diverse students from participating in sports, using bathrooms, and being addressed by their preferred pronouns (Rezal, 2021). School counselors have not been immune to this backlash. Those attempting to lead anti-racist practices, implement social-emotional learning curricula, and support LGBT+ students have found themselves at the center of attacks from white supremacy groups (Voght, 2022).

The results of the 2024 election ushered in a new whirlwind of uncertainty and panic for many educators. Trump's appointment of Linda McMahon, former WWE executive, as Secretary of Education, and the dismantling of the Department of Education, have been untenable. Black individuals, including college and school-aged students, almost immediately after the election, received text messages about being "selected to pick cotton" (The Guardian, November 8, 2024). A later report from the FBI indicated that discriminatory texts were also sent to LGBTQ+ and Hispanic communities (Federal Bureau of Investigation,

November 15, 2024). Many of the students school counselors serve, their families, and their rights to a free appropriate public education (FAPE), have been increasingly threatened. How the new administration and a 2nd Trump presidency will impact school counseling overall as a profession is a big question mark. This tornado of upheaval places us at a critical crossroads, challenging how we respond and revealing our core beliefs about what all children deserve in a democratic education. Yet it also creates a perfect storm of opportunity, one that calls on us to step up as leaders and actively shape the path forward.

The Overton Window

The fight for education is also the fight over which voices and ideas are allowed to be heard. We are witnessing the last-ditch efforts to hold on to the old world of education, rooted in control and dominance. If we are to shape a new more equitable path, we must understand the forces at play. The educational landscape is changing rapidly, with numerous pressing issues, from debates over LGBTQ+ rights to the teaching of race and racism to concerns about school violence and mental health. Navigating these shifts can feel as disorienting as if your house had dropped from the sky and landed in strange new territory. In a season of many political changes and hot-button issues, even the most experienced school counselor can have difficulty keeping track of it all. However, understanding these shifts and the conversations that shape them is essential to leadership. Educational policies can have far-reaching effects, impacting students, educators, and administrators alike. With the weight of the current realities and the unknown of what lies ahead it's easy to wonder, like Dorothy, "How did we get here?"

The Overton Window, developed by Joseph Overton, a U.S. policy analyst, provides a model for understanding how public opinion and policy shift over time. It illustrates the spectrum of policy ideas deemed acceptable by the public at any given moment. Figure 1.1 illustrates how policy options on a given issue can be plotted on a spectrum of public acceptability, from unthinkable to fringe to acceptable to common sense. Policymakers do not move the Overton Window; they observe its boundaries and adjust their positions within it. Ideas within the window are those that the public and political landscape are ready to accept, while those outside the window might be considered too radical. As the public's perception shifts, what falls within the window of acceptability can change as well. For example, school-based mental health resources were once considered an extra resource rather than a necessity. Increasing awareness of student anxiety, depression, and trauma has shifted the narrative to a more holistic approach to education. It is no longer about whether schools provide mental health supports but how they can ensure equitable access to these services.

As society changes, the advocacy work school counselors engage in related to equity, inclusivity, or social justice may become easier or more difficult because of

Range of Politically Acceptable Ideas

Unthinkable   Radical   Acceptable | **Sensible   Popular   Policy   Popular   Sensible** | Acceptable   Radical   Unthinkable

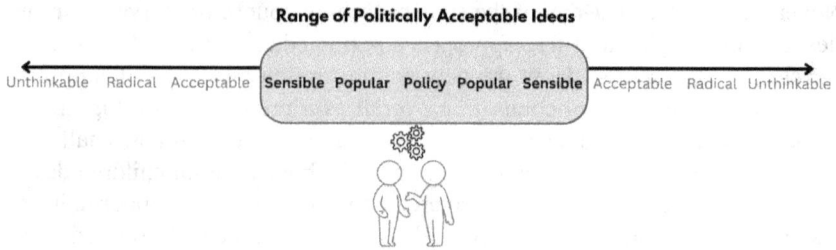

Figure 1.1 The Overton Window

shifts in the Overton Window. The window is not just a reflection of societal norms but an actively managed space where leaders and advocates work to redefine what is considered acceptable discourse and, by extension, policy. Effective leaders understand that shifts in the Overton Window present both opportunities and challenges. This is because introducing bold or radical positions on an issue into public discourse can shift the window and create room for others' views to appear more moderate in comparison. For instance, abolishing police may seem radical, but this stance can shift public perceptions and make reforms such as reducing police presence in schools or banning qualified immunity seem like reasonable compromises. Rather than reacting to shifts in the window, school counselors must proactively work to move the window in the direction of policies and practices that create equitable, inclusive, and caring environments for all students. The chapters that follow will help school counselors become not just responders to change but true agents of change. The storm is here. You can choose to stare out the window and passively watch it, like Dorothy getting swept away by its force, or you can study its changing winds and actively work to shape the landscape that will come after.

School Counselor Advocacy

The call to leadership requires us to engage in critical conversations and shape policies that will best support our students. If school counselors are not actively shaping policy, decisions will be made without their voices and often to the detriment of the students they serve. School counselors frequently express frustration with new policies that negatively impact students, yet these policies do not emerge in isolation. Too often, warning signs (e.g., legislative proposals, board meetings, or public discourse) signal impending change. School counselors with political leadership and advocacy skills are better positioned to identify these signs and respond accordingly.

While the importance of leadership in school counseling is not a new concept, there remains a gap between theory and practice. Numerous frameworks, professional standards, and position statements have described the role of school counselors in advocacy, systemic change, and schoolwide leadership efforts (Cheatham & Mason, 2021; Dowden et al., 2021; Ratts & Green-leaf, 2018). Yet much of the discourse on school counseling leadership has largely centered on school counselors' ability to design, implement, and evaluate a comprehensive school counseling program. Leading for equity is more than individual program implementation or the delivery of direct services. It involves engaging in systems change and navigating the politics inherent in this work. To be effective leaders, school counselors must understand the political forces that shape our educational system. Unfortunately, school counselors have not historically been trained or encouraged to engage in the political arena. This gap in preparation is particularly concerning given that P-12 education in the United States is largely governed at the state level rather than through federal oversight (McDermott, 2009).

While the American School Counseling Association (ASCA) establishes a foundation for counseling programs and the role of the school counselor, these guidelines cannot account for state-specific priorities, policies, and legislative mandates that shape the day-to-day realities of students' lives and the work of school counselors. Because policy is shaped at the state and district level, school counselors cannot solely rely on ASCA to drive systemic change. School counseling leaders are needed at every level to ensure that educational policies are student-centered and equity-driven.

To meet this need, school counselors must recognize the power they already possess to enact change. Like Dorothy, we are often socialized into believing we are insufficient instead of that who we are, what we know, and what we can do are enough to meet the moment. It's no surprise that the imposter phenomenon can be a real barrier for many (Cokley, 2024). Rather than looking for someone "great and powerful" to give us the answer and to lead the way, we encourage school counselors to understand the knowledge and power they possess within themselves. One way that we give away our power is to believe and behave as if those with status, success, or money have more valuable thoughts, ideas, or ways of being than we do. At this critical juncture in education and our profession, we cannot afford to give automatic deference to people in positions of authority. We must return power to the people, our students, and our communities rather than to those who pontificate at the podium.

Effective leadership in school counseling requires political engagement, however, existing frameworks have not addressed this critical need. For example, the ASCA National Model conceptualizes leadership using the traditional Bolman and Deal four-frame model (2021), which encourages leaders to approach organizational issues from four perspectives or frames: structural, human resource, political, and symbolic. One limitation of this model is the assumption that school counselors know when to apply a given frame to a situation and have the skills to do so. While Bolman and Deal (2021) identify political leadership as an essential skill; they also note it as a neglected area of focus in leadership programs. Dollarhide (2003) contends that school counselors lack political leadership aptitude because these skills are not typically a part of school counselor training.

This lack of political training is evident in how counselors approach advocacy efforts, particularly when relying on data alone. School counselors have been heavily trained in the use of data to drive their advocacy efforts, and many find themselves puzzled and frustrated when their efforts to highlight data do not result in meaningful change. Often missing is an understanding of the leadership and advocacy skills necessary to influence decisions. According to Buckley (2010), "effective advocacy requires long-term and short-term thinking, an understanding of the points of resistance and the means to gain traction, the readiness to form alliances, and the flexibility to seize windows of opportunity" (p.2). Data alone is not enough and sometimes it isn't even a part of the equation. School counseling leaders seeking to engage in social justice advocacy must gain knowledge and skills in political leadership.

Social justice advocacy which involves challenging systematic barriers that impede students' academic, social-emotional, and career development (Ratts, 2009) requires more than good intention. It requires concrete strategies and skills. The American Counseling Association (ACA) Advocacy Competency Domains (Figure 1.2) offer a means for determining when situations call for advocacy with or on behalf of an individual and when interventions call for

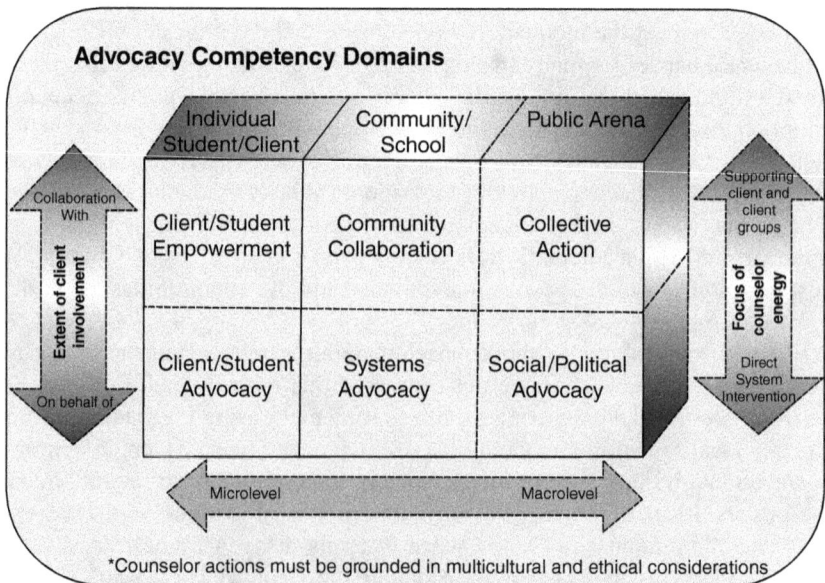

Original model by Lewis, Arnold, House & Toporek (2002) updated by Toporek & Daniels (2018)

Figure 1.2 ACA Advocacy Competency Domains

microlevel and macrolevel approaches. Yet, it fails to clarify how to put social justice advocacy into practice. Sue and Sue (2008) have suggested that many enter the counseling profession to work one-on-one with students and may not be equipped to engage in social justice advocacy. While some school counselors may understand how educational policies and systems impact students and have a desire to improve conditions, the desire to influence policy at the local, state, or national level is not the same as actualizing change (Mcnutt, 2011). Within these pages, you will find strategies for effective advocacy and ways to transform individual power into collective action.

Stepping into a Full-Color World: Leadership for Liberation

Much like Dorothy, school counselors must step out of the black-and-white binaries that constrain our work and into a full-color world beyond program management. In Chapter 4, we ask school counselors to look at leadership from a liberatory perspective that involves both individual and collective liberation. Harper and Kezar (2021) define liberation as "an individual and collective process in which one becomes aware of their true selves, their political circumstances, and works to upend oppressive structures and systems" (p.9). In the context of school counseling, individual liberation involves learning and unlearning what school counselors know about themselves and traditional ideas of leadership. This process is integral not only to their development but to the practice of school counseling. School counselor leadership must also focus on collective liberation, which involves understanding the systems of oppression that impact their work and the students they serve. It focuses on changing systems, structures, and cultural norms that allow oppression to continue. Leadership is not about the charismatic "edu-celeb," the social media likes and followers, or climbing institutional ladders. It isn't even about adhering to traditional frameworks or the increasingly compliance-driven approaches to school counseling. It is about building collective power and creating systems that center equity, justice, and the opportunity to thrive.

To engage in this work, school counselors must take an anti-oppressive approach and examine the systems they are situated in (e.g., schools, districts, and professional organizations) and their role in upholding or disrupting inequity. Bemak and Chung (2005) called for school counseling that acknowledges broad, systematic societal inequities and oppression through social justice counseling. For decades, critics have argued that counseling prioritizes individualism, reinforces existing societal structures, and overlooks the social and political challenges faced by clients and students (Arredondo et al., 2020; Bemak & Hanna, 1998; Holcomb-McCoy, 2022; Kantrowitz & Bailou, 1992). Recent events such as the Black Lives Matter, the Free Palestine Movement, anti-LGBTQ+ legislation, and the COVID-19 pandemic have highlighted the interconnectedness of school counseling and social issues. While each of us brings our own positionality into these issues and is impacted differently, we are all embedded within a larger system that perpetuates inequality and exclusion toward marginalized groups.

One of the most prominent ways systems of oppression are upheld is through silence. Bemak and Chung (2008) assert that a major obstacle to social justice advocacy and change in schools is the *nice counselor syndrome* (NCS). Individuals who exhibit NCS prioritize maintaining harmony and being perceived as agreeable over engaging in systemic change efforts. Although they may believe in equity, their desire to avoid conflict leads them to support the status quo. While NCS has been characterized primarily as silence and inaction, we believe that the drive for harmony can also result in silencing those who challenge the status quo. In an effort to maintain harmony, some school counselors disengage from difficult conversations, while others actively discourage critique. This dynamic has played out in school counseling spaces where BIPOC school counselors who advocate for systemic change have been met with resistance, dismissal, and even hostility in social media discussions and professional committees.

If we prioritize comfort over justice, the systems that harm our students will continue to fester unchecked in our classrooms, hallways, and playgrounds. School counseling is at a defining moment in history, one that presents a critical opportunity to radically reimagine the role of school counselors and how schools function. To seize this moment, school counselors must recognize their power to lead and push the boundaries of what school counseling and education can be. This change does not happen overnight, but it begins with brave leaders who are willing to challenge dominant narratives and shift the Overton Window. If we want to create learning environments that honor the humanity and brilliance of everyone, then it starts with our willingness to challenge, disrupt, and advocate for a more just system. Only then can we move ideas that center love and humanity from the margins to the mainstream.

Following the Yellow Brick Road

Dorothy's leadership journey began when she bravely took her first step down the yellow brick road. If you recall, her first steps were slow and spiral, but as she pushed forward, the path became clearer, and she became more confident in her stride. In many ways, leadership follows a similar path, uncertain at first but gradually becoming more defined with experience and growth. The yellow brick road is more than just a path. It symbolizes a course of action that a person takes with the belief that it will lead to good things. Everyone's journey is unique, and you do not need to occupy a formal leadership position to exercise leadership. Some of the most effective leadership occurs behind the scenes and isn't always visible to others. As such, we invite you to take a journey down the yellow brick road toward greater self-awareness and create a roadmap for the type of leader you would like to become.

While the leadership journey may be a personal one, the path itself is shaped by broader systems of privilege and oppression. The yellow brick road also serves as a metaphor for the social and institutional barriers that many, particularly those from marginalized backgrounds, face in their pursuit of liberation. It is not a straightforward journey to success. Sometimes the bricks on the path are uneven, broken, or missing altogether. In this book, we examine leadership within these obstacles and offer you the tools you need to use your power and positionality to drive systemic change. Our goal is to show you that like Dorothy, you have the skills necessary to lead.

Navigating the Leadership Path

Leadership in school counseling demands a deep commitment to equity and the courage to challenge systemic barriers. Unfortunately, traditional leadership frameworks often overlook how systemic inequities can shape access to leadership, particularly for women and racially and ethnically diverse groups. The *glass ceiling* long characterized the slow advancement of women leaders (Hymowizt & Schellhardt, 1986), but for women of color, racism, and sexism intersect to create additional barriers described as the *concrete wall* or *sticky floor* (Bell & Nkomo, 2001; Betters-Reed & Moore, 1995). Alternatively, the *labyrinth* metaphor describes how women must navigate complex and uneven paths to leadership while managing discrimination, caregiving responsibilities, and exclusion from networks of power, more commonly known as the "good ol' boys club" (Eagly & Carli, 2007). Without strong mentorship or structural support, many face these challenges in isolation (Haslam & Ryan, 2008). Yet, for women, particularly BIPOC women, to acknowledge any of these barriers is often perceived as weakness rather than a critique of organizational inequity. In contrast, the *glass escalator* refers to the structural advantages cis-hetero white men receive in female-dominated occupations, where they are assumed to be more competent leaders than women (Keynton & Lee, 2023).

These realities require us to reexamine leadership through an equity lens. This book situates school counselor leadership within these contexts. We offer strategies to challenge traditional hierarchies and create inclusive leadership pathways that uplift marginalized voices. Whether you identify as a woman, BIPOC, LGBTQ+, able-bodied, a white woman, a cis-hetero white male, or any other identity, this book is for you. In a profession that is predominantly white and female, diversifying school counseling leadership has become a moral imperative for all. Leaders must examine how their privileged identities uphold systems of oppression. A barrier to progress is the unwillingness of some school counselors to acknowledge their role in perpetuating harm to marginalized groups. Consider this an opportunity to engage in deep reflection and examine not only your behaviors but the systems you uphold. As leaders, each of us has a responsibility to understand the lived experiences of those most impacted by these inequities.

Reflection

1   What role do charisma, appearance, or confidence play in your perception of a leader's competence? Have you ever been swayed by these over substance?
2   Who are the leaders in your life, both formal and informal? Do they reflect diverse perspectives, or do they mostly come from similar backgrounds?

Holding Tight to Toto: Walking in Your Core Values

In today's political climate, where leaders at every level are being pressured to follow unjust policies and where equity and inclusion are increasingly under attack, staying anchored in your values is essential. Leadership is built on the foundation of ethics, values, and morals. As you begin this journey, being firmly rooted in your core values will help guide your decisions and actions. Leadership, like school counseling, is not value-free and is deeply connected to your beliefs. Toto's constant presence grounds Dorothy in the familiar while navigating an unfamiliar world. Like Dorothy carrying Toto, leaders must carry their core values with them, especially as they navigate challenges that will test their principles. Toto's protective bark alerts Dorothy to danger. Similarly, our core values serve as an internal warning system, signaling threats to our beliefs and principles. While school counselors are trained in laws and ethics as part of their graduate program and through ongoing professional development, leadership requires a deeper exploration of the values and morals that guide decision-making. True leadership lies in a leader's character, not charisma, with integrity, trust, and moral literacy driving their vision and actions (Sankar, 2003). Who you are and what you believe will impact how you lead. Values, what we believe is most important, shape what we consider right and wrong. While it is easy to identify several things you value, leaders should narrow these down to their core values, those that drive and shape their leadership approach.

Reflection

Our values shape our interactions with students, families, and colleagues. Identifying your core values can ensure that your leadership behaviors are in alignment with your core values. Take a moment to reflect on your personal and professional beliefs and list five values that are central to your work as a school counselor.

1 _____

2 _____

3 _____
4 _____
5 _____

Our values form the foundation of morality. While values reflect individual and societal priorities, *morals* guide individual beliefs about right and wrong and are shaped by culture, religion, or society. *Morality* refers to the broader system or framework of moral beliefs and practices of a culture, community, or religion. Lawrence Kohlberg's theory of moral development (1981) provides insight into how individuals form their sense of right and wrong. This framework outlines three levels and six stages of moral reasoning. He suggests that moral thinking begins with a focus on personal consequences (like a child following rules to avoid punishment) and gradually develops into higher-level thinking for adults, who may weigh their personal values against societal expectations or principles such as justice and equality (Table 1.1). Leaders who advocate for equity must engage in this advanced moral reasoning, championing policies that support marginalized

Table 1.1 Kohlberg's Stages of Moral Development

Level and Age	Stage
Pre-conventional Up to age 9	**Stage 1: Punishment-avoidance/ Obedience** Obey rules to avoid punishment **Stage 2: Self-interest** Get regards and have factors returned
Conventional Most adolescents and adults	**Stage 3: Good boy/Good girl** Conforms to avoid disapproval or dislike by others. Right and wrong are determined by social approval. **Stage 4: Authority & social order** Behavior is driven by obeying authority and conforming to social order. Obey laws without questions and show respect for authority. Most do not progress past this stage.
Post-conventional 0%–15% of Adults over 20	**Stage 5: Social contract** Rules are a social agreement, as opposed to a strict order and can be changed when necessary. **Stage 6: Universal ethical principle** Right and wrong are driven by moral principles which are seen as more important than laws of the land. Based on the ability to put oneself in other people's shoes.

students while challenging inequitable systems. Understanding moral development can help leaders recognize how they form their sense of right and wrong and how it influences their approach to advocacy and systemic change.

Jonathan Haidt (2012) described two different ways moral systems can be structured. The first, *vertical morality* is a top-down system where morality is based on authority, tradition, or a higher power (e.g., religious or government institutions). Those who operate within this system view morality as hierarchical, with their deity or moral authority at the top, those they disagree with below them, and themselves and everyone else ranked somewhere between. Leaders who emphasize vertical morality prioritize compliance and discourage questioning authority or rules. In contrast, *horizontal morality* asks us to look around at each other from a side-by-side perspective and recognize that nobody is inherently better or worse than anybody else. It requires us to assess the impact of our actions based on how they affect those around us, and to adjust based on the individuals and circumstances.

Leaders who embrace horizontal morality encourage democratic decision-making, shared responsibility, and collective action. Horizontal morality asks, "Is this fair to my fellow humans?" while vertical morality asks, "Does this align with the authority above me?" In education, these frameworks influence leadership approaches. A leader operating within vertical morality may focus on enforcing policies and maintaining traditional structures, while a leader grounded in horizontal morality seeks to implement practices that equitably serve all students. Consider the issue of pronouns. Vertically, I impose my own perspective on what I think your pronouns should be based on what I think is right. Horizontally, I learn about your preferences because our encounters are more productive when you are comfortable. These two moral frameworks can shape our approach to authority, power, and decision-making. They can influence how leaders interact with their followers and shape organizational culture. In the next section, we propose a core set of values that align with liberatory leadership and horizontal morality. More is discussed about morals and moral courage is introduced in Chapter 3.

Reflection

This reflection will help you examine how your values influence your decision-making.

1 Think about a time when you had to make a difficult decision in your role as a school counselor. What values guided you in that moment?
2 You are part of a school committee that is deciding whether to support a new policy that will benefit some but disadvantage others. What values and moral framework will guide you in this situation?

Justice: The #1 Core Value of Liberatory Leadership for School Counselors

In the overarching discipline of counseling, one of the five meta-ethical principles is "justice." As described by ACA, justice, at its most basic, refers to counselors providing clients with what they need where their needs vary and equally otherwise. Implied in this definition is the idea that clients come into counseling with specific needs and exist within systems (e.g., society, work, family) that may or may not serve them. In the case of school counseling, we translate this to mean that students come to school with specific needs and that this system may or may not serve them. School counselors then should provide students with what they need where their needs vary, and equally otherwise. The already and increasingly diverse demographic of school-aged students demands that we lead with justice. Justice then is the core value that is the driver toward equity.

This diverse student demographic is in U.S. schools built on historically white supremacist beliefs, that uphold racist, misogynistic, xenophobic, homo and transphobic, colonialized, Christian, and ableist structures, practices, and policies. What these students are owed, schools will not or cannot provide unless there are dramatic changes. Too many students have been shortchanged by schools already. The first Trump presidency, followed by the pandemics of 2020, the January 6th insurrection, global conflicts and genocides, and the second Trump presidency all highlight numerous and deep racial, ethnic, cultural, and economic disparities in society, including education, along with the public's love/hate relationship with educators. The fact that societal messages are at odds about what educators and educational systems should prioritize is cause for grave concern.

School counseling, as a profession, has been and continues to be predominantly white and historically has not committed to decentering whiteness. White centering in school counseling ranges from admissions practices of school counseling graduate programs to hiring decisions of school districts to curricular choices of school counselors. This lack of decentering whiteness has further embedded school counseling practice in white supremacy cultural norms that are pervasive in education. As a result p-12 school counseling programs can become systems that uphold an inequitable status quo.

On a large scale, the school counseling profession is pitting the "how" and "what" against the "why" and "who" of the work of school counseling. There are various sources for the "how" and "what" of the work of school counseling and sadly many of these sources commercialize, commodify, and oversimplify the practice. But the "why" of the work of school counseling has gotten lost at great expense of the "who"—students. "Why" may be described in as many different ways as our individual stories of how we got into the profession, but the bottom line "why," the "why" at the end of the day when we go to bed exhausted and when we get up again in the morning (hopefully recharged)—should be an ideal we all believe is important.

School counseling has never proposed a widely held philosophy or guiding principles, though some may point to a particular theoretical orientation or educational philosophy for counseling. What follows is for consideration for school counselor leaders as the profession grapples with how it will evolve post-COVID-19, amid national sociopolitical divisions, and global genocides and conflict. It is not meant to be a model or a framework for programming but rather a proposed central belief system or set of core values.

A Justice Philosophy for the School Counseling Profession

School counseling is a justice-oriented profession, meaning that it is driven by an overarching aim of achieving justice for students. When justice is a core value then equity is the most important goal. All students are owed basic things from the educational system but it is often the case that some students benefit from policies and practices while others do not. When students do not receive what they need from the educational system (i.e., injustice), school counselors must serve as justice agents. *The philosophy is comprised of two purposes of school counseling, three promises to students, and four principles for school counseling practice.*

The **two purposes** of school counseling are to seek justice by:

1 empowering students through direct service (e.g., counseling, curriculum, etc.)
2 challenging systems through advocacy (e.g., data leveraging, policy change, etc.)

The philosophy defines **three promises** to students. Although these may seem similar to the original three domains of school counselor functioning (academic, social/emotional, college/career), they are different. These three areas are considered what students are *owed* in the educational system and the areas in which school counselors should intervene if there is injustice. These three areas are fluid with regard to level of urgency. For example, when there is a data-based need to attend to students' mental health and wellness in a district, this becomes the justice priority. The educational system may minimize this as a priority over other issues, in which case, school counselors must engage more in challenging the system. Likewise, we may need to do this as a whole at the state level or the national level (ASCA) when something is not a priority that should be. The first letter of the last word in each of these promises spells out *"owe"* as a reminder that students are our "why" when working from this justice philosophy.

Educational Safety and **O**pportunity
Mental Health and **W**ellness
Postsecondary Access and **E**quity

Four Justice Principles of Practice

Along with the two purposes of school counseling and three promises to students, are **four principles of practice**. These principles are intended as daily guides for how school counselors engage in their work. Like the *"owe"* of the promises, these principles are also intentional in their spelling out of *"risc,"* similar to "risk." In essence, the justice philosophy contends that school counseling requires taking risks if we are truly going to advocate for what our students are owed by the educational system, and if we are really about seeking justice.

1 **Reparations:** School counseling professionals publicly acknowledge the historical and current inequities in the educational system, including sometimes within the school counseling program. School counseling seeks to contribute to repairing past and present harm from the system by influencing change to inequitable policies and practices and embracing and celebrating students' culture so they thrive. School counseling also prioritizes the prevention of future harm.

2 **Interrogation:** Interrogation is a process of deep and sometimes difficult questioning about true purpose. Professionals in school counseling commit to the persistent challenging of self about whether one's work and program are centered on justice for students (e.g., "Am I more committed to earning RAMP recognition than I am to challenging a district policy that negatively impacts students?"). Likewise, school counseling professionals commit to similar persistent challenging of systems about student-centered goals vs. system-centered goals (e.g., "How do all students have equal opportunities for learning if some have access to devices and others do not?"). When student-centered goals are not the true purpose, professionals in school counseling then use interrogation to create dialogue about how to refocus the purpose and accountability practices to stay on track.

3 **Solidarity:** This is not performative gestures or lip service from social media. Solidarity means engaging in daily personal and programmatic actions that demonstrate support for marginalized students and ongoing dedication to justice. Solidarity is grounded in anti-racist, antibias, and anti-oppressive practices including learning about the unique identities of students and ways these identities can be supported, the compounded oppressions of intersecting identities, and the ways in which the educational system presents barriers. School counseling professionals find ways to demonstrate solidarity with marginalized students even when the system does not.

4 **Connectedness:** Justice work cannot and should not be done alone. Connectedness provides accountability, momentum, and affirmation. Challenging the system and advocacy requires school counseling as a profession to engage all roles (e.g., practitioners, counselor educators, supervisors and directors, associations) and others (e.g., school staff, district administration, legislators, community members) in the purposes, promises, and principles of justice.

References

Alexander, T., Clark, L., Reinhard, K., & Zatz, N. (2023). *CRT forward: Tracking the attack on critical race theory.* UCLA School of Law Critical Race Studies.

Arredondo, P., D'Andrea, M., & Lee, C. (2020). Unmasking white supremacy and racism in the counseling profession. *Counseling Today, 63*(3), 40–42.

Bell, E., & Nkomo, S. (2001). *Our separate ways: Black and White women and the struggles for professional identity.* Harvard Business School Press.

Bemak, F., & Chung, R. C. Y. (2005). Advocacy as a critical role for urban school counselors: Working toward equity and social justice. *Professional School Counseling, 9*(3), 196–202.

Bemak, F., & Chung, R. C. Y. (2008). New professional roles and advocacy strategies for school counselors: A multicultural/social justice perspective to move beyond the nice counselor syndrome. *Journal of Counseling & Development, 86*(3), 372–381.

Bemak, F., & Hanna, F. J. (1998). The twenty-first century counsellor: An emerging role in changing times. *International Journal for the Advancement of Counselling, 20,* 209–218. https://doi.org/10.1023/A:1005394927213

Betters-Reed, B. L., & Moore, L. L. (1995). Shifting the management development paradigm for women. *Journal of Management Development, 14,* 2–24. https://doi.org/10.1108/02621719510078876Bolman, L. G., & Deal, T. E. (2021). *Reframing organizations: Artistry, choice, and leadership.* John Wiley & Sons.

Bowles, S., & Gintis, H. (2002). Schooling in capitalist America revisited. *Sociology of Education, 75*(1), 1–18. https://doi.org/10.2307/3090251

Buckley, S. (2010). *Advocacy strategies and approaches: Overview paper.* Association for Progressive Communications. https://www.apc.org/en/advocacy-strategies-and-approaches-overview

Centers for Disease Control and Prevention. (2020, July 24). *COVID view: A weekly surveillance summary of U.S. COVID-19 activity https://web.archive.org/web/20200724223128/https://www.cdc.gov/coronavirus/2019-ncov/covid-data/covid-view/index.html*

Cheatham, C. B., & Mason, E. C. M. (2021). Using the ACA advocacy competencies as a guide to group work for supporting the career development of school-aged African American males. *The Journal for Specialists in Group Work, 46*(1), 62–74. https://doi.org/10.1080/01933922.2020.1856253

Cokley, K. (2024, March 14). *It's time to reconceptualize what "Imposter syndrome" means for people of color.* Harvard Business Review. https://hbr.org/2024/03/its-time-to-reconceptualize-what-imposter-syndrome-means-for-people-of-color

Cole, M. (2008). *Marxism and educational theory: Origins and issues.* Routledge.

Dollarhide, C. T. (2003). School counselors as program leaders: Applying leadership contexts to school counseling. *Professional School Counseling, 6*(5), 304. https://bit.ly/3wFqyvP

Dowden, A., Anderson, N., & McCloud, L. (2021). School counselors' use of Multicultural and Social Justice Counseling Competencies (MSJCC) leadership framework in title I school settings. *Journal of School Counseling, 19*(51), 1–16.

Eagly, A. H., & Carli, L. L. (2007). *Through the labyrinth: The truth about how women become leaders.* Harvard Business School Press.

Gee, K. A., Asmundson, V., & Vang, T. (2023). Educational inequities related to race and socioeconomic status deepened by the COVID-19 pandemic. *Center for Poverty and Ine-*

quality Research. https://poverty.ucdavis.edu/post/educational-inequities-related-race-and-socioeconomic-status-deepened-covid-19-pandemic

Gysbers, N. C. (2010). *Remembering the past, shaping the future: A history of school counseling.* American School Counselor Association.

Haidt, J. (2012). *The righteous mind: Why good people are divided by politics and religion.* Vintage.

Harper, J., & Kezar, A. (2021). *Leadership for liberation: A leadership framework and guide for student affairs professionals.* USC Pullias Center for Higher Education.

Haslam, S. A., & Ryan, M. (2008). The road to the glass cliff: Differences in the perceived suitability of men and women for leadership positions in succeeding and failing organizations. *Leadership Quarterly, 19,* 530–546. https://doi.org/10.1016/j.leaqua.2008.07.011

Holcomb-McCoy, C. (2022). *School counseling to close opportunity gaps: A social justice and antiracist framework for success.* Corwin Press.

Hymowitz, C., & Schellhardt, T. C. (1986, March 24). The glass ceiling: Why women can't seem to break the invisible barrier that blocks them from the top jobs. *Wall Street Journal, 1*(4), 1D-24D.

Kantrowitz, R. E., & Ballou, M. (1992). A feminist critique of cognitive-behavioral therapy. In L. S. Brown & M. Ballou (Eds.), *Personality and psychopathology: Feminist reappraisals* (pp. 70–87). The Guilford Press.

Katz, J. H. (1985). The sociopolitical nature of counseling. *The Counseling Psychologist, 13*(4), 615–624. https://doi.org/10.1177/0011000085134005

Keynton, R., & Lee, K. (2023). Taking the glass escalator theory to school. *Socius, 10.* https://doi.org/10.1177/23780231231217828 (Original work published 2024)

Kohlberg, L. (1981). *The philosophy of moral development: Moral stages and the idea of justice.* Harper & Row.

Lambie, G. W., & Williamson, L. L. (2004). The challenge to change from guidance counseling to professional school counseling: A historical proposition. *Professional School Counseling, 8*(2), 124–131. https://www.jstor.org/stable/42732614

Marron, J. M. (2021). Structural racism in the COVID-19 pandemic: Don't forget about the children! *The American Journal of Bioethics, 21*(3), 94–97.

Mason, E. C. M. (2023). Transformation of school counseling. In Schimmel, C. J., Springer, S. I., Grant, K. L., & Ieva, K. (Ed.S.), *#IRL School Counseling: An Introduction to the Profession.* (pp. 3–13). Cognella.

Mayes, R. D., Kearl, B., & Ieva, K. (2024). Introduction to the special issue: Homeplace and Black joy in K-12 education. *Theory Into Practice, 63*(1), 1–6. https://doi.org/10.1080/00405841.2023.2287760

McDermott, K. A. (2009). The expansion of state policy research. In G. Sykes, B. Schneider, & D. N. Plank (Eds.), *Handbook of education policy research* (1st ed., pp. 749–766). Routledge.

Mcnutt, J. (2011). Is social work advocacy worth the cost? Issues and barriers to an economic analysis of social work political practice. *Journal of Policy Practice, 21*(4), 397–403. https://doi.org/fntqps

Monroe, K. R. (2023). *When conscience calls: Moral courage in times of confusion and despair.* University of Chicago Press.

Oberg, C., Hodges, H. R., Gander, S., Nathawad, R., & Cutts, D. (2022). The impact of COVID-19 on children's lives in the United States: Amplified inequities and a just path to recovery. *Current Problems in Pediatric and Adolescent Health Care, 52*(7), 101181.

Ratts, M. J. (2009). Social justice counseling: Toward the development of a fifth force among counseling paradigms. *Journal of Humanistic Counseling, Education & Development, 48*(2), 160–172. https://doi.org/fz2rb5

Ratts, M. J., & Greenleaf, A. T. (2018). Multicultural and social justice counseling competencies: A leadership framework for professional school counselors. *Professional School Counseling, 21*(1b), 1–9.Rezal, A. (2021, December 1). *States restricting how transgender students play sports*. U.S. News & World Report. https://www.usnews.com/news/best-states/articles/2021-12-01/these-states-restrict-how-transgender-students-participate-in-school-sports

Sankar, Y. (2003). Character not charisma is the critical measure of leadership excellence. *Journal of Leadership & Organizational Studies, 9*(4), 45–55. https://doi.org/10.1177/107179190300900404

Sherer, J., & Mast, N. (2023, March 14). *Child labor laws are under attack in states across the country: Amid increasing child labor violations, lawmakers must act to strengthen standards*. Economic Policy Institute. https://www.epi.org/publication/child-labor-laws-under-attack/

Sue, D. W., & Sue, D. (2008). *Counseling the culturally diverse: Theory and practice* (5th ed.). Wiley.

Super, D. E. (1955). Transition: From vocational guidance to counseling psychology. *Journal of Counseling Psychology, 2*(1), 3–9.

United States Department of Education Office of Civil Rights. (2023, May 19). *U.S. Department of Education's Office of Civil Rights resolves investigation on the removal of library books in Forsyth County Schools*, Georgia. https://web.archive.org/web/20230520050737/https://www.ed.gov/news/press-releases/us-department-educations-office-civil-rights-resolves-investigation-removal-library-books-forsyth-county-schools-georgia

Urban, W. J., Wagoner, J. L., Jr., & Gaither, M. (2019). *American education: A history.* Routledge.

Voght, K. (2022, April 24). '*Really scary and sad': How school counselors got caught in the GOP's culture-war dragnet*. Rolling Stone. https://www.rollingstone.com/politics/politics-features/dont-say-gay-school-counselors-students-mental-health-1342328/

Walkar, A. (2024, November 8). Racist text messages sent after Trump's win under investigation. *The Guardian.*https://www.theguardian.com/us-news/2024/nov/08/racist-text-messages-trump-win

Chapter 2

The Basic Bricks of Leadership

We believe traditional models and theories of leadership, which have often centered on the experiences and perspectives of men, predominantly white, Eurocentric, and cisheteronormative culture, can be problematic for several reasons. By focusing only on men, these theories can perpetuate harmful stereotypes and biases about what leadership looks like and who can be a leader. Many of these theories have been incorporated into educational contexts and shaped the version of leadership that was integrated into school counseling through the early ASCA Model. These theories have often failed to recognize the unique challenges and experiences of women and other marginalized groups. Therefore, they may not provide the most effective strategies for promoting diversity and inclusion in leadership. While older models have contributed to our understanding of leadership, they also have limitations and should be used with caution.

Leadership does not occur in isolation, yet traditional leadership models often focus on the traits, styles, and behaviors that define leaders. When leadership centers on whiteness, it ignores how race and power operate within organizations. Leading for equity requires understanding the racialized spaces in which leadership occurs and the role of followers in sustaining or challenging these dynamics. Racialized organization theory provides a holistic approach to understanding how leaders navigate organizational structures. Next, we introduce the idea of followership, a lesser-researched concept but one that is necessary to understand in relation to leadership. We then suggest that the old bricks of the day have given way, and school counselors must step out onto a new brick road, one with bricks better designed for the current challenges. A more holistic and nuanced approach to leadership is needed that considers the complexities of both individual and organizational contexts. Leadership for school counseling in today's world calls for more than what we have known.

DOI: 10.4324/9781032679174-3

Pause and Reflect

1   We invite you to consider the various leadership examples from your professional path.
2   Which leaders have been memorable and why?
3   How did the effective ones do their jobs well?
4   How did the ineffective ones fall down on the job?
5   Which ones did you respect and why?
6   Which ones did you like and why?
7   If there was a difference between those last two, why?
8   Who do you hope to be as a leader?

Finding Your Leadership Path

Leadership is the most researched and written-about topic, and an expected outcome of counselor training programs (Paradise et al., 2010). Upon reviewing more than 20 years of leadership research, Kezar et al. (2006) posited that "no single way exists to be a "good" leader or that a universally "appropriate" leadership process exists. Thus, we need to consider leadership as a multi-dimensional phenomenon" (p.176). Leadership is a complex concept and has always been that way. As school counselors change schools, positions, and career stages, and as society and education evolve, it is essential to maintain flexibility in leadership, allowing room for growth and learning.

Traditional Leadership Models

Leadership models of the early 20th century claim that leadership is a set of innate traits associated with public figures, often referred to as "great men," such as Churchill, Gandhi, Lincoln, or Napoleon (Northouse, 2020). According to Northouse, the trait approach emphasizes personal characteristics such as intelligence, self-confidence, determination, integrity, and sociability. Bennis (1989) had a similar model of leadership, which included qualities such as humility, dedication, and creativity. However, despite the amount of research that has investigated a trait approach, no definitive, static list of leadership traits exists. Northouse (2020) claims that the trait approach still has popular appeal but that it constrains society to the belief that some are meant to lead and others are not.

Another model was the skill-based theory of leadership, which originated with Katz's three skills: conceptual, interpersonal, and technical aspects of leadership (1955). In Katz's model, leadership was about a set of skills that could be learned. Mumford et al. (2000) later expanded Katz's work and developed a model that essentially combined the skills theory with the trait theory. Skill theories emphasize the competencies and knowledge of the leader. Skill theories also assume that leadership is accessible to many because knowledge can be acquired and competencies can be improved upon (Northouse, 2020). In Chapter 1, we mentioned Boleman & Deal's four frames of leadership, another skills-based theory. Skills theories can be helpful, but also leave much to be desired.

Greenleaf (1977) introduced servant leadership, which emphasizes leading to help others, especially those who are marginalized by society. In their book, *Professional Counseling Excellence through Leadership and Advocacy*, editors Chang and Barrio-Minton (2022) emphasize the role of service as part of leadership, given that it is a complementary fit for many counselors, especially if they were part of Chi Sigma Iota, the International Counseling honor society, during their graduate program. Greenleaf's model also underscores the importance of trust, vision, ethics, and long-term, big-picture thinking. Service leadership (SLT) originated in China with Dr. Po Chung, the CEO of DHL International, the courier company (Shek et al., 2018). SLT focuses on the three Cs of competence, character, and care, but sets itself apart from the earlier model of servant leadership (Greenleaf, 1977). Service leadership involves leading oneself (through ongoing reflection and self-improvement) and dedicating energy to benefit others and systems (Shek et al., 2018). Service and servant leadership have much appeal but may be perceived by some groups as "savior" leadership because the focus is on the individual.

A final traditional, popularized leadership model is that of transformational leadership, which originated with Burns in 1978 and was later expanded upon by Bass as late as 2006. Bass's version of transformational leadership included the "Four Is" or skills of the leader:

1 idealized influence
2 intellectual stimulation
3 inspirational motivation
4 individualized consideration

There is a substantial amount of literature on transformational leadership in education and related fields, such as school counseling. Some of this literature aligns historically with the Transforming School Counseling Initiative (TSCI) of the late 1990s, which called for dramatic changes to the preparation and training of school counselors. The TSCI ushered in the addition of leadership as a core aspect of future training (House & Martin, 1998; Martin, 2002) and what later became a theme of the ASCA Model (2003). Transformational leadership was an important bridge to leadership possibilities for school counselors at a critical point in our professional history. However, other models are a better fit for the work that needs to be done to champion justice for students.

Racialized Organization Theory

As leaders in schools, school counselors play a critical role in challenging systems of inequity. Their effectiveness can be enhanced by their ability to understand how systems of oppression operate. Leadership books often describe organizations, such as districts, schools, and professional associations, as race-neutral bureaucratic structures. Racialized organization theory (Ray, 2019) describes how an individual's beliefs and schemas about race influence the formation of organizations, including structural hierarchies, policies and practices, resource distribution, and the personal agency of racial groups. While racialized organization theory is not a leadership theory, it can help leaders gain insight into how institutions, such as districts, schools, school boards, and professional associations, are structured to centralize and maintain power. Ray maintains that in organizations, race is more than a demographic variable, but serves as a mechanism for reproducing racial inequality and outlines four key tenets of racialized organizations:

1 Organizations shape the power and choices available to different groups
2 Organizations distribute resources unfairly
3 Whiteness is treated as a qualification for leadership and advancement
4 Gaps between official policies and everyday practices reinforce racial inequality

---

Reflection

Consider how these tenets operate in your school, district, or professional organizations.

1 Are there practices and policies that impact marginalized groups' ability to lead and advocate for change?
2 Who has access to resources (e.g., funding, leadership opportunities) and who is overlooked?
3 How can you disrupt the way whiteness is treated as a credential in your organization?
4 How does your organization ensure that policies and practices that promote racial equity are consistently enforced?

Recognizing how these tenets operate across various levels of the school's ecosystem (macro, meso, micro) is essential for equity-focused leadership. Rather than operating within these racialized systems, leaders must identify and disrupt these organizational patterns. These dynamics are not new, but have played out for generations within our schools, districts, communities, and professional spaces, shaping power, decision-making, and opportunity gaps. In light of this, school counselors must consider leadership models that critically challenge these dynamics.

Modern Leadership Models

As authors, we write this book as a critique of the current definition of school counselor leadership and as a challenge to what has previously been taught. While some ideas may still be relevant, we believe that the way we conceptualize leadership must be broader and bolder to meet today's students' needs and the challenges of today's society. What we propose may sound different or inconsistent from what some think of the role of "counselor." It is important to remember that we can hold multiple identities at once, and more than one thing can be true at a time. Just as Dorothy discovered things she did not know about herself, so have our leadership journeys revealed much more about ourselves than we thought they could.

Modern leadership models focus less on the leader as a person and more on leadership as a set of conditions or shared context which people facilitate or in which they operate and interact. The following more modern leadership theories are worth reading up on as more valuable ones for the challenges of school counseling in today's world:

1 Transformative Leadership by Dr. Carolyn Shields
2 Liberation Leadership by Dr. Sean Ruth
3 Leadership for Liberation by Drs. Harper and Kezar

Dr. Carolyn Shield's Transformative Leadership model (2011) has considerable application for school counselors in the current sociopolitical landscape. Shields worked from an international perspective, having lived and studied in several countries. She defined a "VUCA" world—volatile, uncertain, complex, and ambiguous—a term from the Cold War period (Shields et al., 2018, p.1). The applicability of the VUCA world to today's climate is evident, as are Shields' eight core tenets (Shields, 2011, p.24):

1 A mandate for deep and equitable change
2 The need to deconstruct knowledge frameworks that perpetuate inequity and injustice and to reconstruct them in more equitable ways
3 The need to address the inequitable distribution of power
4 An emphasis on both private and public (individual and collective) good
5 A focus on emancipation, democracy, equity, and justice
6 An emphasis on interconnectedness, interdependence, and global awareness

7   The necessity of balancing critique with promise
8   The call to exhibit moral courage

Dr. Shields wrote with school counseling leaders Dr. Collette Dollarhide and Dr. Anita Young in 2017 to apply the eight tenets to the context of school counseling and the ASCA National Model. Of the modern leadership theories presented here, it is the only one we know of that has been published explicitly with an application to school counseling so far.

Dr. Seán Ruth introduces us to liberation leadership (2006), which resonates well with counselors due to its foundations in Psychology and its role as a force for social change. Social change is what we believe school counselor leadership should work toward; leadership is a means, not an end. Ruth claims that authentic leadership is about liberating leadership in others while honoring the full context of power and oppression in which this work happens. Ruth suggests there are four levels on which a leader must think about the members of a group (pp.5–7):

1   individually
2   collectively
3   the wider situation that has implications for individuals or the group
4   individuals and the group over time

These levels are consistent with the American Counseling Association's 2018 Advocacy Competencies, which call for counselors to advocate in individual, community, and public arena domains. Ruth goes on to explain that leadership is wholly relationship-based. Many of the conflict resolution strategies suggested by Ruth will be discussed in Chapter 6 and are noted to be very much in congruence with the counseling skills taught in many school counselor preparation programs.

Ruth's model of leadership liberation differs from leadership *for* liberation, which is Harper and Kezar's (2021) expansion of the Social Change Model of Leadership (HERI, 1996). Harper and Kezar's model also fits well for the version of school counselor leadership we believe is necessary today. This model emphasizes the role of power dynamics and oppression and adds components such as storytelling, fellowship, system challenging, and inclusivity of the experiences of racially marginalized persons. Ruth, Harper, and Kezar note that traditional models of leadership did not address the importance of identities, especially race (Figure 2.1).

Shields, Ruth, Harper, and Kezar, along with other modern leadership theorists, recognize several critical aspects key to school counselors. First, they acknowledge privilege and oppression in society. Second, they understand the role of power dynamics in systems, supporting our argument for school counselors understanding racialized organization theory. Third, they greatly value the distribution of leadership and the interaction between leaders and followers. For these theorists, leadership goes beyond a lone leader with basic traits, skills, or providing service; it is a full-on picture of community.

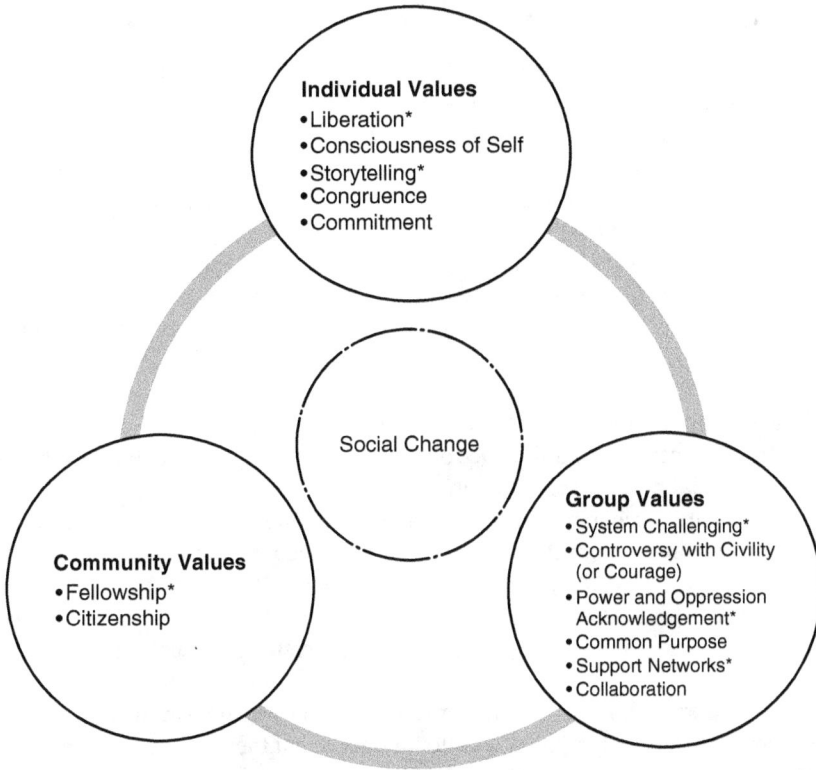

Figure 2.1 Harper & Kezar New Configuration of Social Change Model for Leadership

Starting Where You Are...

Consider your Advisory Council or whatever group provides input into your school counseling program. If you don't have one yet, this may be a great starting point to consider what leadership can look like. If you do, it may be a time to re-assess. Are they there in name only or do they truly care about championing justice for all students? What would the ideal community look like that would support school counseling for students in your school?

Who would be involved?

What are its primary functions?

How can you work toward it?

Followership

The topic of followership is less studied, though it has gained much more traction in recent years. Over a 19-year period from 1990 to 2008, in *The Leadership Quarterly,* only 14% of the articles included some version of the word' follower' in the abstract or title (Bligh, 2011). Scholars now make an obvious case: without followers, there are no leaders, and without followership, there is no leadership (Ul-Bien et al., 2014).

In 2014, Ul-Bien et al. published a comprehensive review of the available followership literature, attempting to categorize existing theories and set pathways for future research. These researchers broadly group existing followership ideas into these areas:

1 Leader-centric: how the leader influences followers.
2 Follower-centric: the significance of the follower, role (trait or behavior-based), or as a social process (constructionist).
3 Social identity leadership: "people (leaders and followers alike) derive a part of their self-concept from the social groups and categories to which they ascribe belongingness—i.e., their collective self" (Hogg & Reid, 2006) (p.87).
4 Relational: process-oriented, "constructions can take the form of a stable hierarchical role relationship or a shifting leadership structure" (p.95).

When considering how Dorothy, Toto, the Scarecrow, the Tin Woodman, and the Lion worked together, there was no hierarchy, but they gained meaning from spontaneously coming together. Each one contributed their skills to the goal of getting to Oz, removing his cover, and defeating the Wicked Witch. In this way, we might categorize their followership dynamic as follower-centric or social identity leadership. We can also look to the Munchkins as another type of follower. In *The Wonderful Wizard of Oz,* the Munchkins are one of several groups of followers who have their own land but are ruled by a witch. The Munchkins appear to align with a leader-centric or relational followership dynamic. As a group, they were quite deferential to figures outside of themselves, such as Oz, the Wicked Witch, and Glinda. The Munchkins lived under the mystique of Oz for a long time. Dorothy was not there for very long, but they still deferred to her and trusted her quickly enough to help and provide her with hospitality.

School counselors must reflect on their positions as both leaders and followers and consider the dynamics at play when they assume each role. Taking the time to understand the leader-follower dynamic is one of the most valuable things we can do to reveal unhealthy or destructive patterns or gain insights into our insecurities or biases. For example, school counselors who grew up in households that did not engage in open conflict often struggle with confrontational conversations, either as followers or as leaders. Conversely, some who did grow up in households with open conflict may not have found it productive. Rather than conflict being a vehicle for decision-making, it may have been an

impediment. However, the social justice and advocacy nature of school counseling and education settings generally requires that various perspectives be
shared frequently for idea generation and decision-making; some conflict, as
long as it is healthy, is a norm.

Both leadership and followership can go to extremes that are not productive.
When this happens, one model is called the Toxic Triangle (Padilla et al., 2007).
See Figure 2.2. The Toxic Triangle is composed of destructive leaders, susceptible followers, and conducive conditions. Destructive leaders tend to have five
core characteristics: charisma, personalized need for power, narcissism, negative
life themes (e.g., childhood adversity, abuse, family chaos), and an ideology
of hate. We can think of prominent historical or political leaders who fit this
description and are known most for their destructive actions. Still, the five core
characteristics can be present in leaders of many roles in many settings, including schools and their connected systems. The reach and impact of a leader can
influence the magnitude of their destruction or liberation.

Susceptible followers are either conformers or colluders. Conformers follow
the directives of destructive leaders, trying to stay out of the way and minimize

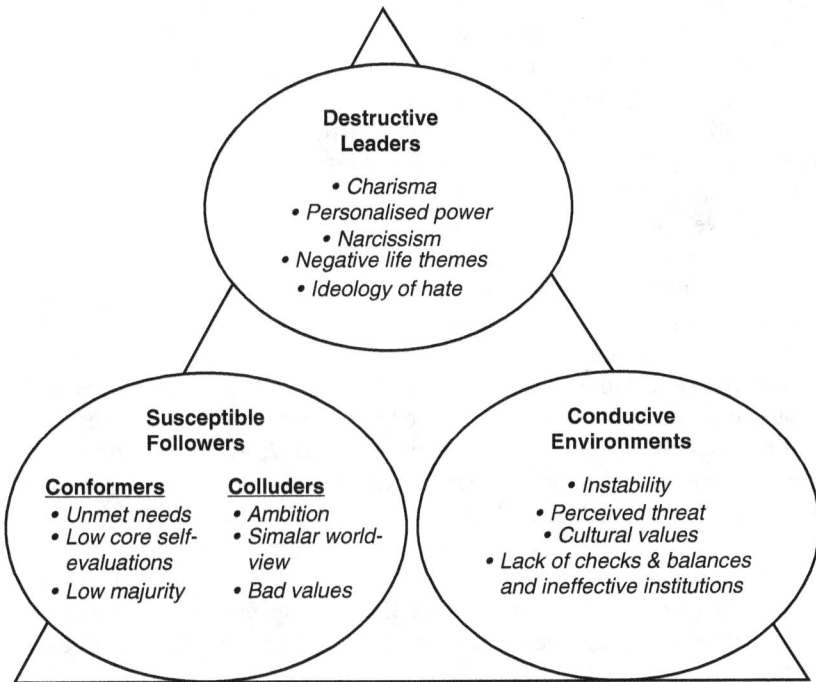

Figure 2.2 The Toxic Triangle: Elements in Three Domains Related to Destructive Leadership

(Padilla et al., 2007)

any negative consequences for themselves. Colluders, on the other hand, join destructive leaders, hoping to gain their favor and benefit from showing their allegiance. Conducive environments are those that are unstable, meaning there are imminent threats of some kind (e.g., economic, environmental), a culture of distinct power dynamics between high- and low-status groups, and a lack of institutional checks and balances (Padilla et al., 2007).

Given the ecological and systemic nature of schools and educators' work within them, including that of school counselors (McMahon et al., 2014), it is easy to understand how toxic triangles can emerge. For example, in today's climate, this happens when allegiances emerge between school board members and local elected officials who promote book banning. There are multiple cases of this happening in both school and public libraries, especially in the Southern United States, where divisive concepts legislation passed in recent years (Southern Poverty Law Center, 2025).

Leadership in School Counseling

Prior to and at the time of the first editions of the ASCA Model, there was minimal research on school counselors and leadership (Bemak, 2000; Dollarhide, 2003; Lieberman, 2004; Schwallie-Giddis et al., 2003). The TSCI out of The Education Trust, in the late 1990s, gave rise to the significance of leadership as a necessary element for school counselors to embrace (House & Martin, 1998; Martin, 2002; Paisley & Borders, 1995; Paisley & Hayes, 2003; Paisley & McMahon, 2001; The Education Trust, 1996). The TSCI was a national, multi-university movement that reshaped school counselor preparation, incorporating five core tenets: leadership, advocacy, teaming, collaboration, and data use (House & Martin, 1998; Martin, 2002; The Education Trust, 1996). From there, the ASCA Model and other published training texts highlighted the role of leadership in school counseling (DeVoss & Andrews, 2006; Erford, 2003; Pérusse & Goodnough, 2004; Stone & Dahir, 2006).

Since that time, more literature has been written and more research published about school counselor leadership, and at least two instruments have been developed to measure this construct (Gibson et al., 2017; Young & Bryan, 2015). Empirical studies in the past 20 years on school counselor leadership have covered topics such as school counselor leadership during COVID (Hilts & Liu, 2023), leadership in MTSS (Goodman-Scott & Ziomeck-Daigle, 2022), school counselor leadership and emotional intelligence (Hilts et al., 2022; Mullen et al., 2018), which is covered more in Chapter 3, leadership, values, and service delivery (Shillingford & Lambie, 2010), and leadership and professional development (Strear et al., 2018).

Leadership in the ASCA Model

It is essential to note the history of leadership's position in *The American School Counselor Association National Model*. In the first three editions of the ASCA

Model (2003, 2005, 2012), leadership is represented in the model graphic as one of the four core themes, along with advocacy, collaboration, and systemic change. These were identified as necessary skills for the school counselor to implement the model and influenced by the TSCI mentioned earlier (House & Martin, 1998; Martin, 2002). In the fourth edition of the model (2019), leadership, along with the other themes, was removed from the graphic. Within the text the themes are referenced and the following is stated:

> The four themes of leadership, advocacy, collaboration and systemic change no longer appear around the edge of the ASCA National Model diamond but instead are woven throughout the ASCA National Model to show they are integral components of a comprehensive school counseling program.
> (American School Counselor Association, 2019, p.116)

As authors of this book and school counseling professionals with a considerable history in our field, we viewed the removal of the themes from the graphic as a critical mistake. Not only is it vital to underscore the leadership role of school counselors in relation to program functioning, but also to visually highlight, for ourselves and others, how leadership connects to our roles as advocates, collaborators, and systemic change agents. In a single image, previous graphics succinctly tied our necessary identity and skills to our essential responsibilities. While this visual alteration may seem minimal to some, we believe it may impact the zeitgeist of the profession at a pivotal time (Figure 2.3).

Even I, Erin, have conducted my investigation into leadership in school counseling, and things have changed dramatically over the years. Initially, when I examined the relationship between school counselor leadership and comprehensive program implementation in 2009, using the Leadership Practices

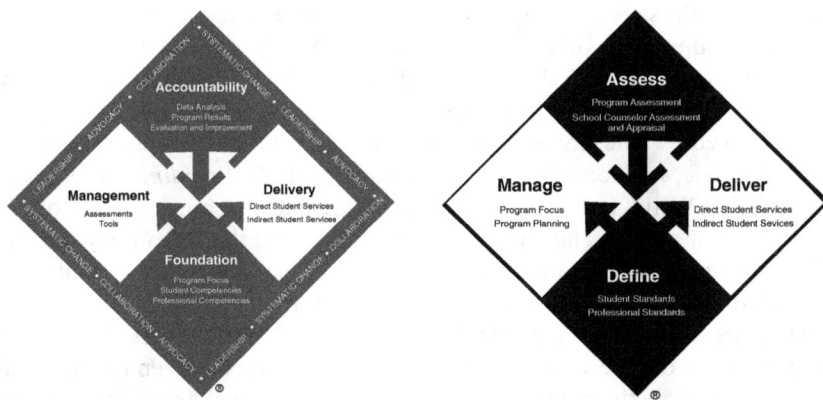

The ASCA National Model diamond graphic is a registered trademark of the American School Counselor Association and may not be reprinted or modified without permisision.

Figure 2.3a,b Comparison of ASCA National Model Diamonds

Inventory (LPI) by Kouzes and Posner (2003) with a relatively small sample, school counselors scored moderate to high on some subscales but not all. Notably, older and more experienced school counselors scored higher on leadership practices. More recently, when colleagues and I replicated the original study with a larger national sample, the results demonstrated how prevalent and influential the ASCA Model has been in the profession (2023). We used multiple leadership measures, including two specifically designed for school counselors mentioned earlier (Gibson et al., 2017; Young & Bryant, 2015), and the items on these measures were correlated. That is to say, school counselor leadership has evolved into a more developed and identifiable construct over the years. But no more are demographics like age and experience predictors of leadership. Instead it is training in the ASCA Model and working in a RAMP school (Mullen et al., did find a relationship between age and leadership experience in 2018). In some ways, this was not surprising as the proliferation of the model came very far between 2009 and 2023. However, the change in results gave me significant pause. Is an understanding of leadership in the context of the ASCA Model sufficient? Who are school counselors without the ASCA Model? Do they see themselves as leaders without it? What about the kind of leadership required in these times? Can school counselors take leadership beyond the way they understand it in the ASCA Model? If we don't have a clear answer to these questions, our school counseling programs, and especially our students, may be on an uncertain and tenuous path.

What Comes Next?

Models help conceptualize how we accomplish our work, as well as our leadership. And yes, there are leadership skills and practices to learn and hone. We explore in this book those that are natural for most school counselors and those that may take you out of your comfort zone. How, what, and who school counselors are leading may not be the same as it was even five years ago; leadership *must* evolve. Suppose we are to keep up with rapid changes in society, and push for changes in education for the benefit of students, especially those who are pushed to the margins. Shouldn't leadership be a principle, a core value, something one must hold central to professional identity as a whole, not something that is manualized? In *Braiding Sweetgrass*, author Robin Wall Kimmerer shares that indigenous teachings are "an orientation, but not a map. The work of living is creating that map for yourself" (p.7). The same can be said about leadership for school counselors, it is an internal guiding force. Is leadership something that you do or essential to who you are as a school counselor (Mason et al., 2023)? Leadership is a path you are always on, the very bricks beneath you. What is to keep us from getting swept away in the next cyclone if we aren't grounded firmly in our sense of leadership? These are some of the questions we hope you'll grapple with as you read these pages.

Sample Leadership Instruments

There are several leadership instruments that school counselors can use to begin examining their approach to leadership, whether assessing style, practices, or skills. We recommend completing instruments that have been researched and can give you reliable and valid results. Specifically, we suggest the two explicitly designed for school counselors and developed by school counselor educators. The authors can be contacted at their universities about their instruments.

1 The School Counselor Leadership Survey by Young and Bryan (2015).
2 The School Counselor Transformational Leadership Inventory (SCLTI) by Gibson et al. (2017).

Other instruments like The Leadership Practices Inventory by Kouzes and Posner (2025) are proprietary ($22) and set up to be taken by groups at an organizational level.

Another approach to keep costs low is to coordinate a book study using any of the texts or articles mentioned in this chapter on leadership, and to have regular discussions about school counselor leadership. Assessments can be part of the discussion, but they should not be the only activity involved in developing a leadership identity. We encourage all school counselors to take a reflective and community approach to exploring leadership at *all* stages of career development and to engage in continuous assessment and evaluation.

Stepping into Your Ruby Shoes: Use of School Counseling Skills

Regardless of the models you learned for school counseling programs in your graduate training, you will learn that leadership is a critical part and that your leadership skills are worth sharpening over time. School counselors know how to collect and use data, work with and facilitate various groups of people. They understand cultural competence and social justice, as well as career and lifespan development, and have insight into intrapersonal and interpersonal relationships. All of these are skills that are incredibly valuable on the path of leadership. Just as leadership as a concept has changed over time, so too has our understanding of leadership and our leadership skills.

References

American School Counselor Association (2003). *The ASCA national model: A framework for school counseling programs* (2nd ed.). Author.
American School Counselor Association (2012). *The ASCA national model: A framework for school counseling programs* (3rd ed.). Author.
American School Counselor Association (2019). *The ASCA national model: A framework for school counseling programs* (4th ed.). Author.

Bass, B. M., & Riggio, R. E. (2006). *Transformational Leadership.* (2nd ed.). Lawrence Erlbaum Associates Publishers. https://doi.org/10.4324/9781410617095

Bemak, F. (2000). Transforming the role of the counselor to provide leadership in educational reform through collaboration. *Professional School Counseling, 3,* 323–332.

Bennis, W. (1989). *On becoming a leader.* Arrow Books.

Bligh, M. (2011). Followership and follower-centered approaches. In A. Bryman, D. Collinson, K. Grint, B. Jackson, & M. Uhl-Bien (Eds.), *The sage handbook of leadership* (pp. 425–436). London: Sage.

Burns, J. M. (1978). *Leadership.* Harper & Row.

Chang, C. Y., & Barrio Minton, C. A., (Eds.). (2022). *Professional counseling excellence through leadership and advocacy.* Routledge.

DeVoss, J. A., & Andrews, M. F. (2006). *School counselors as educational leaders.* Houghton Mifflin.

Dollarhide, C. T. (2003). School counselors as program leaders: Applying leadership contexts to school counseling. *Professional School Counseling, 6*(5), 304–308.

Erford B. T. (Ed.). (2018). Transforming the school counseling profession.

Gibson, D. M., Dollarhide, C. T., Conley, A. H., & Lowe, C. (2017). The construction and validation of the school counseling transformational leadership inventory. *Journal of Counselor Leadership and Advocacy, 5*(1), 1–12. https://doi.org/10.1080/2326 716X.2017.1399246

Goodman, S. E., & Ziomek, D. J. (2022). School counselors' leadership experiences in multi-tiered systems of support: Prioritizing relationships and shaping school climate. *Journal of Counseling & Development, 100*(3), 266–277. (John Wiley & Sons, Inc.). https://doi.org/10.1002/jcad.12426.

Greenleaf, R. K. (1977). *Servant leadership: A journey into the nature of legitimate power and greatness.* Paulist Press.

Harper, J., & Kezar, A. (2021). Leadership development for racially minoritized students: An expansion of the social change model of leadership. *Journal of Leadership Education, 20*(3), 156–169.

Higher Education Research Institute. (1996). *A social change model of leadership development: Guidebook version III.* National Clearinghouse for Leadership Programs.

Hilts, D., & Liu, Y. (2023). School counselors' perceived school climate, leadership practice, psychological empowerment, and multicultural competence before and during COVID-19. *Journal of Counseling & Development, 101,* 193–203. https://doi.org/ 10.1002/jcad.12464

Hilts, D., Liu, Y., & Luke, M. (2022). School counselors' emotional intelligence and comprehensive school counseling program implementation: The mediating role of transformational leadership. *The Professional Counselor, 12*(3), 232–248. https://doi.org/ 10.15241/dh.12.3.232

Hogg, M. A., & Reid, S. A. (2006). Social identity, self-categorization, and the communication of group norms. *Communication Theory, 16*(1), 7–30.

House, R. M., & Martin, P. J. (1998). Advocating for better futures for all students: A new vision for school counselors. *Education, 119,* 284–291.

Kezar, A. J., Carducci, R., & Contreras-McGavin, M. (2006). Rethinking the "L" word in higher education. *ASHE Higher Education Report, 31*(6), 1–207.

Kouzes, J. M., & Posner, B. Z. (2003). *The leadership practices inventory: Self instrument* (3rd ed.). San Francisco: Jossey-Bass.

Kouzes, J. M., & Posner, B. Z. (2025). *The leadership practices inventory: Self instrument* (5th ed., revised) Wiley, ISBN: 978-1-394-33167-3.

Lieberman, A. (2004). Confusion regarding school counselor functions: School leadership impact role clarity. *Education, 119,* 552–558.

Martin, P. J. (2002). Transforming school counseling: A national perspective. *Theory Into Practice, 41,* 148–153.

Mason, E. C. M., Michel, R., Young, A., Olsen, J., Tillery, C., & Chang, M. K. (2023). School counselor leadership and program implementation revisited: Findings from a national sample. *Professional School Counseling, 27*(1), 1–11. DOI: 10.1177/ 2156759X231182144

McMahon, H. G., Mason, E. C. M., Daluga, G. N., & Ruiz, A. (2014). An Ecological Model of Professional School Counseling. *Journal of Counseling & Development, 92*(4), 459–471. (John Wiley & Sons, Inc.), https://doi.org/10.1002/j.1556-6676.2014.00172.x

Mullen, P. R., Gutierrez, D., & Newhart, S. (2018). School counselors' emotional intelligence and its relationship to leadership. *Professional School Counseling, 21*(1b), 1–12. https://doi.org/10.1177/2156759X18772989Mumford, M. D., Zaccaro, \S. J., Harding, F. D., Jacobs, T. O., & Fleishman, E. A. (2000). Leadership skills for a changing world. *The Leadership Quarterly, 11*(1), 11–35. https://doi.org/10.1016/s1048-9843(99)00041-7

Northouse, P. G. (2020). *Introduction to leadership: Concepts and practice* (5th ed.). SAGE Publications, Inc.

Padilla, A., Hogan, R., & Kaiser, R. B. (2007). The toxic triangle: Destructive leaders, susceptible followers, and conducive environments. *The Leadership Quarterly, 18*(3), 176–194.

Paisley, P. O., & Borders, L. D. (1995). School counseling: An evolving speciality. *Journal of Counseling and Development, 74,* 150–153.

Paisley, P. O., & Hayes, R. L. (2003). School counseling in the academic domain: Transformations in preparation and practice. *Professional School Counseling, 6S,* 198–204.

Paisley, P. O., & McMahon, H. G. (2001). School counseling for the 21st century: Challenges and opportunities. *Professional School Counseling, 5,* 106–115.

Paradise, L. V., Ceballos, P. T., & Hall, S. (2010). Leadership and leader behavior in counseling: Neglected skills. *International Journal for the Advancement of Counselling, 32*(1), 46–55. https://doi.org/10.1007/s10447-009-9088-y

Pérusse, R., & Goodnough, G. E. (2004). *Leadership, advocacy and direct service strategies for professional school counselors.* Brooks/Cole.

Ray, V. (2019). A theory of racialized organizations. *American Sociological Review, 84*(1), 26–53.

Ruth, S. (2006). *Leadership liberation: A psychological approach.* Routledge.

Schwallie-Giddis, P., Maat, M. t., & Pak, M. (2003). Initiating leadership by introducing and implementing the ASCA national model. *Professional School Counseling, 6,* 170–173.

Shek, D. T. L., Chung, P. P. Y., & Zhu, X. (2018). Service leadership in the service era. In D. C. Poff, & A. C. Michalos (Eds.), *Encyclopedia of business and professional ethics* (pp. 1–7). Springer International.

Shields, C. M. (2011). *Transformative leadership : A reader /.* Peter Lang.

Shields, C. M., Dollarhide, C. T., & Young. A. A. (2018). Transformative leadership in school counseling: An emerging paradigm for equity and excellence. *Professional School Counseling, 21*(1–11). https://doi.org/10.1177/2156759X18773581.

Shillingford, M. A., & Lambie, G. W. (2010). Contribution of professional school counselors' values and leadership practices to their programmatic service delivery. *Professional School Counseling, 13*(4), 208–217.

Southern Poverty Law Center. (2025, March 14). *Struggle for control of public libraries in full swing across the Deep South.* https://www.splcenter.org/resources/stories/book-challenges-laws-deep-south/

Stone, C. B., & Dahir, C. A. (2006). *The transformed school counselor.* Boston: Houghton Mifflin. https://doi.org/10.5330/PSC.n.2010-13.208

Strear, M. M., Van Velsor, P., DeCino, D. A., & Peters, G. (2018). Transformative school counselor leadership: An intrinsic case study. *Professional School Counseling, 22*(1). https://doi.org/10.1177/2156759X18808626

The Education Trust. (1996). *National initiative to transform school counseling* [Brochure]. Author.

Uhl-Bien, M., Riggio, R. E., Lowe, K. B., & Carsten, M. K. (2014). Followership theory: A review and research agenda. *The Leadership Quarterly, 25*(1), 83–104. https://doi.org/10.1016/j.leaqua.2013.11.007

Young, A., & Bryan, J. (2015). The school counselor leadership survey: Instrument development and exploratory factor analysis. *Professional School Counseling, 19*(1), 1–15. https://doi.org/10.5330/1096-2409-19.1.1

Chapter 3

Leading with Heart and Brain
Emotional Intelligence and Leadership

Emotional intelligence (EI) is the ability to understand and manage one's own emotions as well as the emotions of others (Goleman, 2005). It involves being aware of and able to express one's own emotions, as well as understanding and empathizing with the emotions of others. Daniel Goleman is a leading researcher and writer on EI, who identifies five skills as part of EI: self-awareness, self-regulation, motivation, empathy, and social skills (Goleman, 2020). We will address each of these here. EI is important in various contexts and can be particularly helpful to school counselors when navigating the complex social situations that arise in leadership and advocacy work. Accordingly, we explain how readers can develop and strengthen their EI and establish a culture of EI in the organizations they lead.

There are several ways that school counselors' use of EI can be operationalized on a day-to-day basis. For example, a school counselor with EI will know which data to present to which audience, providing a compelling and persuasive argument. While many school administrators or school boards may respond better to outcome data, statistics, and numbers, some legislators, school partners, and families may respond more to qualitative data, such as themes from student feedback or individual stories. Secondly, a school counselor with EI will consider what is needed to set the stage for using one's leadership to challenge a policy or pitch a new idea.

EI can help advocates build strong relationships with others in the community, such as fellow advocates, policymakers, and community leaders, leading to more effective equity work. By understanding and managing their own emotions, as well as the emotions of others, school counselors can foster more effective collaboration and cooperation. EI can help leaders create inclusive and equitable environments that empower individuals and communities.

Advocacy often involves the leadership skill of persuading others to support a particular cause or issue, and EI can help advocates connect with their audience on a deeper level. For example, an advocate with high EI can recognize when their audience feels skeptical or resistant to their message and adjust their approach accordingly. They might use empathy to understand their audience's

DOI: 10.4324/9781032679174-4

perspective and EI to tailor their message to speak to their audience's lived experiences. In *The Wonderful Wizard of Oz*, we watch Dorothy do this with the Scarecrow, the Tin Woodman, and the Lion, relating uniquely to each one until she eventually has a team to support her in achieving her goal of getting to Oz.

Knowing Your Emotional Intelligence

Research demonstrates that counselors and those in training possess moderate to high levels of EI (Constantine & Gainor, 2001; Gutierrez & Mullen, 2016; Gutierrez et al., 2017; Hilts et al., 2022; Mullen et al., 2017, 2019; Wahyuni et al., 2019). However, school counselors may not necessarily consider EI as a tool for leadership.

Pause and Reflect

Consider the following ideas when it comes to your own EI:

1 How aware are you of your patterns of thoughts, emotions, and reactions?
2 How aware are you of others' patterns of reactions?
3 How do you set and manage boundaries with others?
4 How do you encourage and influence others?

Internal vs. External Self-Awareness

Self-awareness is a key component of EI. Eurich (2018) suggests that there are two types of self-awareness, one internal and one external. The internal type is one we are more familiar with, the idea that we have a sense of ourselves, including our strengths and flaws. External self-awareness is the idea that we know how others perceive us. Furthermore, when there is congruence between leaders' external self-awareness and their constituents' ideas of the leader, there is generally a better relationship and more satisfaction with the leader. If we consider that one may range from low to high on either internal or external self-awareness, then Eurich and colleagues provide this framework of four possible archetypes (Figure 3.1).

From these four archetypes, we can imagine that no progress will be made if a school counselor always operates from the "pleaser" position and never addresses issues of equity to maintain peace. Likewise, we can imagine how a school counselor may be fighting a lone battle if they always operate from the "introspector" position and never seeks out or only challenges alternative views. A "seeker" may appear unprepared to engage, vulnerable, or possibly very open to ideas. Most of all, what we learn from Eurich's work is that self-aware leaders have both internal and external self-awareness. They actively work on both by investing in understanding themselves better and inviting feedback from others.

The Four Self-Awareness Archetypes

This 2×2 maps internal self-awareness (how well you
know yourself) against external self-awareness (how
well you understand how others see you).

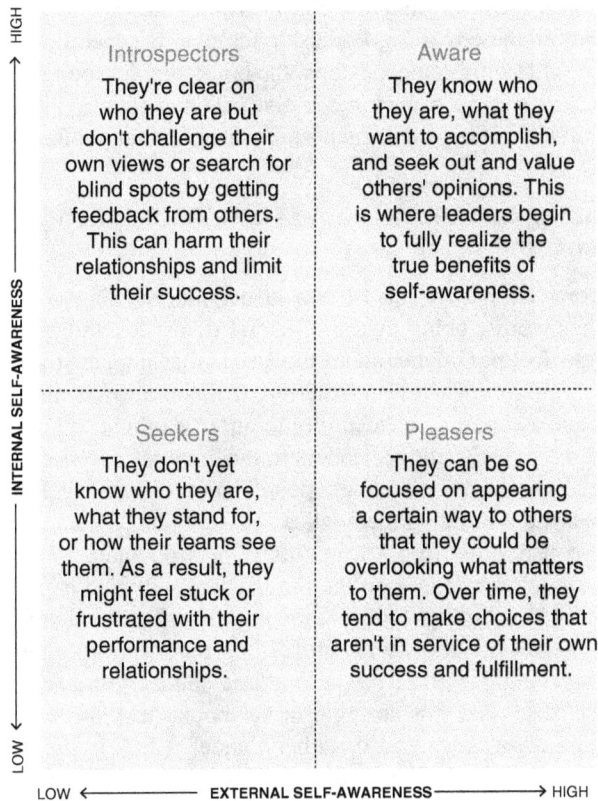

	Introspectors	Aware
INTERNAL SELF-AWARENESS (HIGH → LOW)	**Introspectors** They're clear on who they are but don't challenge their own views or search for blind spots by getting feedback from others. This can harm their relationships and limit their success.	**Aware** They know who they are, what they want to accomplish, and seek out and value others' opinions. This is where leaders begin to fully realize the true benefits of self-awareness.
	Seekers They don't yet know who they are, what they stand for, or how their teams see them. As a result, they might feel stuck or frustrated with their performance and relationships.	**Pleasers** They can be so focused on appearing a certain way to others that they could be overlooking what matters to them. Over time, they tend to make choices that aren't in service of their own success and fulfillment.

LOW ←———— EXTERNAL SELF-AWARENESS ————→ HIGH

Figure 3.1 Eurich's Four Self-Awareness Archetypes

Lacking Self-Awareness as a Barrier to Leadership

A lack of self-awareness can be a barrier to leadership when the leader cannot self-regulate, cannot depersonalize a situation, holds the majority of the privilege and power, or for other reasons. Interestingly, Eurich (2017) notes that introspection, which we typically associate with self-awareness, does not necessarily equal insight. In other words, a leader may be very introspective but not have as much insight into themselves as one would expect. Leaders can have blind spots in their knowledge, emotions, and behavior, which can be addressed through feedback. If not sought and integrated, these can lead to a loss of objectivity (p.86).

Eurich (2017, p.52) says experienced leaders are more likely to overestimate their skills than newer leaders. Researchers also refer to this as the Dunning-Kruger effect, where people are generally less skilled than they think they are and are often oblivious to it (Kruger & Dunning, 1999). This effect is an important trend to keep in mind when working with those in leadership positions, such as administrators, and when considering tenure in a leadership role. She also notes that narcissism in leaders is a rising trend. For all these reasons, leadership turnover is generally positive. Sometimes, we've been leading someone down the brick road for too long, and it's time to let someone else step up. Sometimes, we've been too comfortable hanging at the back, and it's time to get out front and position ourselves for a different role.

Understanding Social Awareness and Relationship Management

Part of the connection between EI and leadership is being able to "read the room," in other words, being aware of social dynamics and navigating them. It is your job to feel passionate about the issues that impact students and communities, *and* you do not work in isolation. Collaboration is also your job and necessary. Social awareness is the ability to observe others and understand their behaviors and motives. It allows leaders to make better decisions about how to respond to behaviors and connect with people more effectively. Burning bridges is quick and easy, but building them takes skill and time. There will be potential allies and co-conspirators (e.g., Scarecrow, Tin Woodman, Lion) who can be very helpful to you as a leader on the road. There will also be wicked witches whom you shouldn't think of twice. Knowing the difference between these two will help you save time and energy in reading the room and the relationships that are worth saving. Loretta Ross, a longtime educator and activist for reproductive justice, discusses this struggle in her book, *"Calling In: How to Start Making Change with Those* You'd Rather Cancel" (2025). She describes how, in our efforts to confront the real sources of injustice, we can end up "punching sideways" (p.79) and lose valuable support. As authors, we each have our experiences of making mistakes and celebrating the big and small wins that come with navigating what Ross refers to as calling in, calling out, and calling it off. Relationships have complex dynamics within schools and school systems where people may play more than one role to each other and where individuals may have varying levels of self and social awareness.

We've often heard colleagues refer to these dynamics as the "politics" of education, which they disdain or feel ill-equipped for. Braddy and Campbell (2020) define political skill as the ability to maximize and leverage relationships to achieve organizational, team, and individual goals. Their research found that leaders who use political skills are less likely to face setbacks, such as stagnation, dismissal, or demotion, that could disrupt their career (Braddy & Campbell, 2020). Yes, there may be benefits in giving yourself time in a new space to get to know the characters and the lay of the land. However, we would argue that school counselors are at an advantage due to their training in basic skills and sensitivity to body language, tone of voice, and other nonverbal cues. These communications, as well as verbal ones, are essential to attend to in both counseling and leadership contexts. Crossed arms, body distancing, a sudden change in vocal tone, glaring, or rolling eyes are likely signs that the other party in your interaction is put off by what you're saying. If it's an interaction you want to nurture, it may be time to stop, call yourself out, and say, "Let me stop and hear from you" before continuing with your agenda. If you find yourself emotional or questioning the value of the interaction, it may be better to slow down, breathe, and say, "I hear you, and I need some time. I'll get back to you." Ross says that in her many years of activism, she had to learn that "power over" was never as strong or as strategic as "power with" (p.80).

School Counselors, Emotional Intelligence, and Leadership

There is minimal research specific to school counselors and EI (Constantine & Gainor, 2001), but thankfully, there are several recent studies that examine EI and leadership (Hilts et al., 2022; Mullen et al., 2019, 2018). Not surprisingly, Mullen and colleagues found that school counselors (2018) and those in training (2019) have moderate to high EI. In addition, the findings of these studies indicated a relationship between aspects of EI and leadership. Specifically, management of others' emotions predicted leadership experience for school counselors (2018), and awareness of others' emotions predicted self-leadership in school counselors in training (2019). Other researchers (Hilts et al., 2022) found a positive relationship between school counselors' EI and transformational leadership (measured with Gibson et al.'s SCLTI mentioned in Chapter 2). Importantly, in this study, researchers concluded that "through leadership practice, school counselors' EI may offer an indirect effect on their CSCP implementation" (p.242). Overall, school counselors are pretty well suited for situations in which they use EI and leadership based on the ways we have to measure them. What remains to be seen is whether our current definitions of EI and leadership hold up for what it means to champion justice for students today and into the future.

Regulating Emotion in Leadership

Don't be Afraid of Fear

Numerous times in *The Wonderful Wizard of Oz,* we see Dorothy as fearful, when she lands in Oz and learns the house has landed on the Wicked Witch of the East, when she encounters the Wicked Witch of the West, and in the initial moments of meeting the Wizard of Oz. In all of these instances, the unknown was more fear-inducing than the thing itself. In these instances, Dorothy was more focused on her fear than on her power. Our emotions influence how information is processed. Fear improves ethical choices (Kligyte et al., 2013). Anger inhibits ethical decision-making and sense-making (Kligyte). Fear leads people to learn more and become better educated about a topic compared to anger (Marcus et al., 2000; Parker & Isbell, 2010; Valentino et al., 2008). Anger can lead to a self-focused interpretation of the situation, which has the potential to result in retaliatory or self-serving behaviors (Lenhart & Rabiner, 1995).

School counselors may be fearful of leadership, either of those in leadership positions in their schools or of taking on leadership roles themselves. This is because the culture of white supremacy built into the hierarchy of schools is designed to imbue fear. Many recognize situations that feel like "being sent to the principal." When it comes to school counselor leadership, we, as authors, and we suspect Dorothy, would stand by the motto, "Do it scared." Let fear fire you up. Use fear as a valid, powerful, and motivating emotion rather than trying to eliminate it. One of Goleman's (2020) five factors of EI, after all, is motivation. Passion and drive to end injustice are usually the easy part. Fear can be part of your EI because it will give you heightened awareness, a keen radar for reading others, and a sharp sense of protecting yourself and those who need protection. Furthermore, as a leader who "does it afraid," you will be less likely to make hasty decisions, and in a time of crisis, you will understand how and why others will operate out of fear (Parkin, 2020).

Recognizing Fight, Flight, Freeze, and Fawn

While fear can be a powerful motivator, unprocessed trauma can have deleterious effects on how we navigate our personal and professional spaces. You are likely aware of humans' biological responses when feeling physically or psychologically threatened. We see several characters in *The Wonderful Wizard of Oz* respond to threats and danger through various fight, flight, freeze, and fawn responses. The Wicked Witch uses aggression and intimidation (fight), the Tin Woodman becomes rusted and unable to move (freeze), the Lion runs and cowers (flight), and the Scarecrow prioritizes and appeases others (fawn). While the fight or flight responses are the easiest to understand, the freeze and fawn responses are less so and have been discovered only through more research into animal and human behavior. The freeze response can be recognized even in highly productive people who exhibit temporary behaviors such as task paralysis, signs of perfectionism, or procrastination. This response is a way of pausing the nervous system so it can attempt to recover. Peter Walker (2013) added the fawning response to capture the type of response that includes people-pleasing behaviors used to avoid further trauma; these can include over-apologizing, being overly agreeable, having difficulty saying no, prioritizing the needs of others, or having weak boundaries. Fawning is harder to detect because it is often mistaken for genuine connection, and systems that maintain the status quo often normalize and even reward fawning behavior, as it reinforces compliance and avoids conflict. From a very young age, women are taught to prioritize harmony over conflict, which can shape how we navigate equity work. There is an old Spanish phrase said to young girls and women, "calladita te ves mas bonita," which translates into "You look more beautiful when you're quiet." Steeped with misogyny, it suggests that you do better when you keep your head down and stay quiet. We believe that patriarchy and misogyny are significant sources of trauma for women, children, and marginalized genders. School counselors benefit from recognizing how they respond to environmental stressors. Are we acting in service to our values, or are we conflating niceness with justice? Recognizing fawning behaviors in ourselves and our systems is key to identifying when compliance is driven by fear or a trauma response. Alternatively, you may have heard an Old English saying that is similar: "Children should be seen and not heard," which is in total contrast to the listening aspect of the school counselor's job. However, it can still be perpetuated by school counselors who encourage fawning in students by asking them to "play nice" or "just ignore it."

Understanding Humility, Privilege, and Ego

As school counselors, we work for and with many marginalized populations, so it is important to stay keenly aware of the positions of privilege we hold; this is especially the case for white (74%) female (87%) school counselors who still make up the majority of the profession (ASCA, 2023). When serving as leaders, operating from a place of humility is vital. Recognizing privilege and having humility help keep the ego in check, which are skills related to EI, such as self-awareness and empathy.

Humility can apply to all aspects of a school counselor's work, populations, and settings. Cultural humility was defined early in the medical literature as "a lifelong commitment to self-evaluation and self-critique, to redressing the power imbalances in the patient-physician dynamic, and to developing mutually beneficial and nonpaternalistic clinical and advocacy partnerships with communities on behalf of individuals and defined populations" (Tervalon & Murray-Garcia, 1998, p.117). Experts on cultural humility suggest that we aspire to this as it is more significant than mere cultural competence. School counselors with cultural humility may have high EI, including empathy and social skills. They will be able to avoid or minimize microaggressions and macroaggressions, or identify them quickly, and work to repair interpersonal ruptures when they occur.

Intellectual humility is another form of humility desirable for school counselor leadership because it can also be connected to EI (e.g., self-awareness, social skills). Multiple researchers reviewed numerous works on intellectual humility and the various ways it has been defined (Porter et al., 2021). In the end, Porter and colleagues concluded their analysis by presenting a framework

Internal

QI

QII

Awareness of one's ignorance
"Although I have particular views about _____ ,
I realize that I don't know everything that I need to know about it"

Awareness of value in other people's intellect
"I recognize the value in opinions that are different
from my own"

Awareness of one's fallibility
"I accept that my beliefs and attitudes may be wrong"

Recognition of One's Intellectual Limitations

Self

Other

Public

Admitting one's ignorance and fallibility
"I am willing to admit it if I don't know something"

Listening to other people's ideas
"I am willing to hear others out, even if I disagree
with them"

Private

Redressing one's ignorance and fallibility
"I search actively for reasons why my beliefs might
be wrong"

Openness to corrective feedback
"I am willing to accept feedback from others, even if it
is negative"

QIII

Expressed

QIV

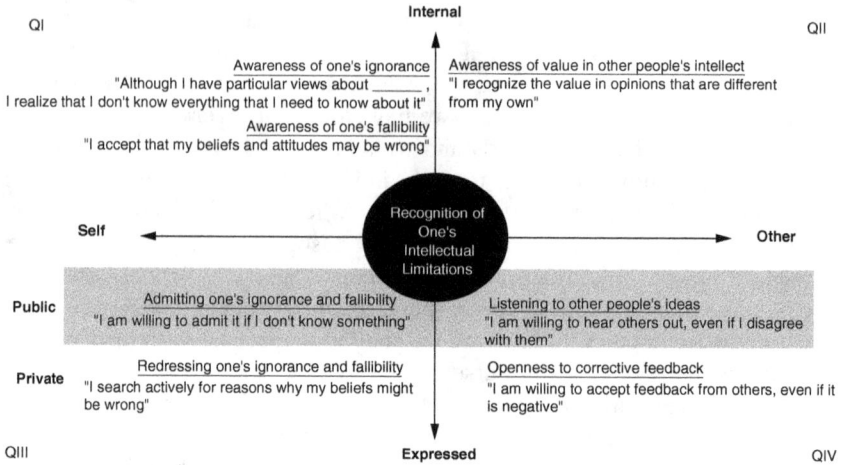

Figure 3.2 Porter et al. Intellectual Humility Framework

of intellectual humility that defines it as having both internal and externally expressed elements (Figure 3.2).

Notably, the researchers describe intellectual humility this way,

> In our view, recognition of one's intellectual fallibility and ignorance are necessary but not sufficient for intellectual humility because it would not be intellectually humble to realize that you are incorrect or ignorant but act as though you were correct or knowledgeable. Yet, expressed awareness of one's intellectual limitations is insufficient because it would not be intellectually humble to realize that you are incorrect or ignorant, express the fact that you are incorrect or ignorant, but dismiss other people's knowledge or feedback that could redress your ignorance.
>
> (p.580)

Internally, school counselors may experience cognitive dissonance when they act out of knowledge they know they don't have. For example, if there is a routine decision we are accustomed to making based on our past experience at school, we may make the same decision as last year without considering changes in school demographics or the community at large. Externally, we may confess we know where our knowledge falls short, but we don't incorporate new information to modify our actions. Convenience wins out over intentionality. The classic line, "We've always done it this way," is a sure sign of a lack of intellectual humility. Another simple example of this is admitting we don't know how to pronounce student names, but defaulting to having students say them rather than learning them ourselves.

Ego and Privilege

A fundamental definition of "ego" from *Merriam-Webster* is "the self, especially as contrasted with another self or the world." Ego, in this basic sense, is necessary for, at minimum, the self-awareness and self-regulation factors of EI. As a leader, one must be able to engage in reflection and self-assessments to make adjustments for intrapersonal and interpersonal reasons. Likewise, a leader must recognize signs (from themselves or others) if they are not acting in a way that is congruent with their morals, values, or reality. When there is a lack of congruence in behavior, we might recognize it as cognitive dissonance (in ourselves), as hypocrisy (in others), or, in more extreme terms, as someone who has broken with reality. The ego is neither good nor bad; it helps us to make sense of the world and our relationship to it, but it is also vulnerable to influences. Dorothy's ego was influenced by her family enough that she internalized what she could and couldn't do as a young woman from Kansas. It took a natural disaster and being among radically different people who supported her to let go of her ego. Liberation from ego is what we encourage school counselors to consider as leaders before they can engage in collective liberation.

Liberating Your Ego

1 How might your ego be holding you back?
2 What do you need to let go of being right about so you can be free?
3 What were you taught about *others* that is wrong and doesn't fit with who you are now or need to be?
4 What were you taught about *yourself* that is wrong and doesn't fit with who you are now or need to be?
5 Who do you need to help you be free?

In collective liberation, there is no space for ego or privilege. No one is out for themselves, so EI is about the greater good. Erik Erikson (1963) believed the ego was a driving force in human development and identity. While we are most familiar with Erikson's ego identity development during K-12 developmental stages, the stage of Intimacy vs. Isolation reminds us that developing loving relationships is a primary task in adulthood. Effective leaders can check their egos and recognize when they are wrong, shift their perspectives when needed, and accept constructive criticism. They recognize that leading for collective liberation prioritizes the needs of the team over the needs of the ego. Successfully managing one's ego can lead to strong relationships, while failure to do so can result in isolation. However, ego creeps in or bursts through when humility is in short supply and privilege is readily available.

Remember in *The Wonderful Wizard of Oz* when Oz flies off in a hot-air balloon? Think of the balloon like privilege; it is our easy exit, the opportunity to say, "This situation doesn't apply to me." If school counselors are to be leaders who invest in collective liberation, they must set aside their ego and privilege. Most often, we think of racial privilege, such as white privilege, which is prominent in the school counseling profession. Still, we must also consider the privilege of language, socioeconomic status, education, gender identity, sexual orientation, religion, immigration status, and much more. We can also recognize when others, including other leaders, show ego or privilege and know they are not worth our time or energy. If they are part of the root cause of injustice, we will need the support of our community to take them on.

Moral Courage

Although this is a chapter on the heart (Tin Woodman) and brain (Scarecrow), it wouldn't be truly complete without a dedicated section on courage (Lion) too. Moral courage is a complex concept. We bring it up in this chapter because it is intertwined with EI and because school counselors do work that requires courage, especially in these times. School counselor leaders can be morally courageous and are often called to moral courage. If you recall from Chapter 2, moral courage is one of the eight tenets of Shields' Transformative Leadership model (2011). Monroe (2023) provides a comprehensive definition of moral courage, which has nine elements (p.176–177). Moral courage:

1 Necessitates having empathy for others, which leads to connecting with shared humanity
2 Involves gratitude for what one has
3 Identifies core values that usually come from the family
4 Core values include (a) respect for well-being; (b) everyone is equal under the law; (c) commitment to justice and fairness; (d) dignity for all, even opponents
5 Is about living one's values, usually justice, fairness, human worth
6 Is about advancing the well-being of all people, not just the groups one belongs to
7 Includes having significant restraint
8 Includes small and large acts, often building on each other
9 Is not viewing oneself as heroic, and is characterized by everyday people and accessible to each of us

Reflection

Using Monroe's (2023) 9-point definition, who would you point to that has exhibited moral courage? Based on point 9, this could be someone in your own life, someone you have just known of, or someone you identify based on their public profile. They may not exhibit every point but perhaps most of them.

1 What would you ask them if you had a chance to interview them?
2 Do you imagine that they identify themselves as having moral courage?
3 How might you also exhibit the 9 points of Monroe's definition?

Courage is what it takes to continue the campaign for the professional identity of school counselors, to increase their numbers where they are in short supply, and to use school counselors properly based on their training. More so, moral courage is what some school counselors are calling upon today as the rights of students, their families, and others in schools are being targeted. We believe school counselors must champion the human rights of their students; these rights have a deep impact on students' ability to learn in a safe environment that respects who they are. As leaders, our moral courage is a form of advocacy on behalf of students, especially in the P-12 arena. Our developmental knowledge and training, along with keeping up with research, can help us understand what positively and negatively impacts the populations we work with, allowing us to speak truth to power. With our power we can fight for everything from keeping African American, Hispanic/Latinx, and Indigenous history courses and texts in schools, resources for undocumented and refugee families, policies that provide access and safety to LGBTQ+ students and those with disabilities, hiring and retaining diverse staff, and much more.

In *The Wonderful Wizard of Oz*, we witness the Munchkins at a somewhat tumultuous time. A strange house has fallen from the sky, and an unknown being called "Dorothy" appears as a witch but is not. She has inadvertently killed a major oppressor of the people. The Munchkins share their joy and relief that their oppressor is gone by centering Dorothy as an accidental hero. Fortunately, Dorothy doesn't seem to take to this deference and sticks to her need for help to get home. Dorothy's handling of the scene with the Munchkins shows she has a fair amount of EI (e.g., self-awareness, empathy, motivation). At the tale's beginning, Dorothy, the Scarecrow, the Tin Woodman, and the Lion are not what we would ascribe as having moral courage, but by the end, the party has taken on some significantly formidable foes and acted to protect each other. Dorothy makes some decisions she's never had to make before. She confronts the all-powerful Oz and calls him out on his abuse of power. Why? We argue that we witness a shift in Dorothy's moral development in real time. Recall Kohlberg's (1981) stages of moral development that we reviewed in Chapter 1. Moral reasoning does not necessarily result in moral behavior, so thoughts may not always equal behavior—remember cognitive dissonance and hypocrisy? Kohlberg's theory of moral development states that people who respect rules are capable of immoral behavior in the name of authority (Kohlberg, 1981). According to Kohlberg, such behavior is most likely among adults in the "conventional" ranges of ego development, which includes between 60% and 75% of Western adults (Cook-Greuter, 1999; Loevinger, 1976). If Dorothy had continued to respect the rules (conventional level), she would not have defended the others who joined her or confronted Oz for the harm he was doing to so many. Thus, *psychological maturity is needed to oppose destructive authority* (Padilla et al., 2007, p.184).

Catherine Sanderson (2020) suggests that moral rebels exemplify moral courage in action. Moral rebels tend to have high self-esteem, feel confident about their judgment, values, and ability, and are less socially inhibited than others (Sanderson, 2020). They are willing to take a principled stand and refuse to comply, stay silent, or simply go along when this would require them to compromise their values. While the term may sound cool, being a moral rebel is far from easy. Moral rebels stand in opposition to unjust systems, even when doing so may lead to negative social consequences such as disapproval, ostracism, and career setbacks (Monin et al., 2008). Leaders such as Martin Luther King Jr., Nelson Mandela, Tarana Burke, and Greta Thunberg courageously led movements of resistance that were initially unpopular. We are not asking school counselors to break rules or oppose authority at will. We are, however, encouraging school counselor as leaders to strategically challenge systems, policies, and people of power or the sake of justice for students.

Strategies

Dorothy does none of what she does alone. Although she is a primary character, the tale of *The Wonderful Wizard of Oz* is of the group working for collective liberation. This is perhaps the most important strategy alone but it is also a necessary feature of leading with heart and brain; having a community. Goleman (2020) is clear to say that EI can be improved with age but not with basic professional development. EI and other constructs presented here must be learned over time via skills practice and feedback, much like you learned basic counseling skills. Similar to what was encouraged with leadership, revisit EI in the same way, in community, along the way as you experience job changes and hit various milestones in your career path.

Leading with Heart *and* Brain

What does it mean to lead with heart *and* brain? School counseling leadership unquestionably requires both. To return to EI, we might say that of the five factors, motivation, and empathy are the heart (i.e., innate passion for the work), while self-awareness, self-regulation, and social skills (i.e., cognitive skills we work on) are the brain. Leading with heart and brain is messy, confusing, exhausting, and it is never easy. This is because the morals and values (e.g., social justice, diversity, equity, inclusion, mental health) that lead us to and sustain us in this school counseling profession can often be at odds with the laws, rules, and regulations (e.g., state laws, district, and school board policies) that are required to do the job—especially in today's oppressive climate. Another way of looking at this is that the brain part of our job often requires us to rely on conventional principles of morality, whereas the heart part comes through a post-conventional morality lens. Most days we work from the heart and the brain, when others would have us work from one or the other. The school counselor's job is messy and hard because those who uphold the laws, rules, and regulations that oppressive systems need to operate (e.g., principals, school boards, district officials) would rather you disappear, "play nice," or "be a team player," particularly if moral courage is in the mix.

Many of us were never given the information we needed to understand this counterintuitive aspect of the job, let alone the tools to do it. One of my (Erin) favorite quotes to sarcastically express the heart-brain dynamic, which I have on a pin, is "Do no harm, but take no shit." School counselors often and easily get on board with skills that fit with the heart (e.g., helping, listening, caring), but in a leadership position, we have to know that others will manipulate those heart-related skills if we don't use our brains. Heart-related leadership is more of the norm in school counselor leadership; it's relational and helps you connect with others. Brain-related leadership is more in line with taking no shit; it's strategic and conveys what the goals are. Taking no shit looks like holding appropriate boundaries to protect your time and energy as well as those who are working with you. It also looks like not responding to or with emotion so as not to distract from the goals. Balancing heart and brain leadership is a constant process, much like working on new groups of muscles versus old ones.

Stepping into Your Ruby Shoes: Use of School Counseling Skills

As a school counselor, many of us most likely came to the profession with EI. We may have been the calm "listening ear" to siblings or cousins or a reliable source of support and encouragement for young friends. Even if school counseling wasn't your first career, you may have been led here by key experiences in your life. School counselors often have a leaning toward helping. This helping is generally positive in nature. However, we can recognize that a more finely attuned EI can give us more information about how to help in humbly, courageous ways and in ways that allow us to preserve our own well-being. Leading with EI is leveling up to using these inherent or acquired skills in ways that gives us greater power and guides us more purposefully down the leadership path.

References

ASCA. (2023). *Comparison of ASCA Membership Data with Teachers, Students, and U.S. Census Data on Race/Ethnicity and Sex.* https://www.schoolcounselor.org/getmedia/9c1d81ab-2484-4615-9dd7-d788a241beaf/member-demographics.pdf

Braddy, P., & Campbell, M. (2020). *Using political skill to enhance leadership effectiveness.* Center for Creative Leadership. https://cclinnovation.org/wp-content/uploads/2020/03/usingpoliticalskill.pdf

Cook-Greuter, S. (1999). *Postautonomous ego development: Its nature and measurement.* Unpublished doctoral dissertation. Cambridge, MA: Harvard University.

Constantine, M. G., & Gainor, K. A. (2001). Emotional intelligence and empathy: Their relation to multicultural counseling knowledge and awareness. *Professional School Counseling, 5*(2), 131–137.

ego. (2025). In *Merriam-Webster Dictionary.* https://www.merriam-webster.com/dictionary/ego

Erikson, E. H. (1963). *Childhood and society* (2nd ed.). W. W. Norton.

Eurich, T. (2017). Insight. NY: Crown Business.

Eurich, T. (2018). What Self-Awareness Really Is and How to Cultivate It: It's not just about introspection. Harvard Business Review. https://hbr.org/2018/01/what-self-awareness-really-is-and-how-to-cultivate-it

Goleman, D. (2005). *Emotional intelligence.* Bantam Books.

Goleman, D. (2020). *Emotionally intelligent leader.* Gildan Audio.

Gutierrez, D., & Mullen, P. R. (2016). Emotional intelligence and the counselor: Examining the relationship of trait emotional intelligence to counselor burnout. *Journal of Mental Health Counseling, 38,* 187–200. doi:10.17744/mehc.38.3.01

Gutierrez, D., Mullen, P. R., & Fox, J. D. (2017). Exploring emotional intelligence among master's level counseling trainees. *Counselor Education and Supervision, 56,* 19–32. doi:10.1002/ceas.12057

Hilts, D., Liu, Y., & Luke, M. (2022). School counselors' emotional intelligence and comprehensive school counseling program implementation: The mediating role of transformational leadership. *The Professional Counselor, 12*(3), 232–248. https://doi.org/10.15241/dh.12.3.232

Kligyte, V., et al. (2013). The influence of anger, fear, and emotion regulation on ethical decision making. *Human Performance, 26*(4), 297–326. https://doi.org/10.1080/08959285.2013.814655

Kohlberg, L. (1981). *The philosophy of moral development: Moral stages and the idea of justice.* Harper & Row.

Kruger, J., & Dunning, D. (1999). Unskilled and unaware of it: How difficulties in recognizing one's own incompetence lead to inflated self-assessments. *Journal of Personality and Social Psychology, 77*(6), 1121–1134. https://doi.org/10.1037//0022-3514.77.6.1121

Lenhart, L. A., & Rabiner, D. L. (1995). An integrative approach to the study of social competence in adolescence. *Development and Psychopathology, 7,* 543–561.

Loevinger, J. (1976). *Ego development.* San Francisco: Jossey–Bass.

Marcus, G. E., Neuman, W. R., & MacKuen, M. B. (2000). *Affective intelligence and political judgment.* The University of Chicago Press.

Monin, B., Sawyer, P. J., & Marquez, M. J. (2008). The rejection of moral rebels: Resenting those who do the right thing. *Journal of Personality and Social Psychology, 95*(1), 76–93. https://doi.org/10.1037/0022-3514.95.1.76

Monroe, K. R. (2023). *When conscience calls: Moral courage in times of confusion and despair.* University of Chicago Press.

Mullen, P. R., Gutierrez, D., & Newhart, S. (2017). School counselors' emotional intelligence and its relationship to leadership. *Professional School Counseling, 21*(1b), 1–12. https://doi.org/10.1177/2156759X18772989

Mullen, P. R., Limberg, D., Tuazon, V., & Romagnolo, S. M. (2019). Emotional intelligence and leadership attributes of school counselor trainees. *Counselor Education & Supervision, 58*(2), 112–126. https://doi.org/10.1002/ceas.12135

Padilla, A., Hogan, R., & Kaiser, R. B. (2007). The toxic triangle: Destructive leaders, susceptible followers, and conducive environments. *The Leadership Quarterly, 18*(3), 176–194. Parker, M. T., & Isbell, L. M. (2010). How I vote depends on how I feel: The differential impact of anger and fear on political information processing. *Psychological Science, 4*, 548–550.

Parkin, D. (2020, March 27). *Emotionally intelligent leadership in a time of crisis: fear and reassurance*. Advance HE. https://www.advance-he.ac.uk/news-and-views/emotionally-intelligent-leadership-time-crisis-fear-and-reassurance

Porter, T., Baldwin, C. R., Warren, M. T., Murray, E. D., Cotton Bronk, K., Forgeard, M. J., Snow, N. E., & Jayawickreme, E. (2021). Clarifying the content of intellectual humility: A systematic review and integrative framework. *Journal of Personality Assessment, 104*(5), 573–585. https://doi.org/10.1080/00223891.2021.1975725

Ross, L. (2025). *Calling in : How to start making change with those you'd rather cancel / Loretta J. Ross*. Simon & Schuster.

Sanderson, C. A. (2020). *Why we act: Turning bystanders into moral rebels*. Harvard University Press.

Tervalon, M. & Murray-Garcia, J. (1998). Cultural humility versus cultural competence: A critical distinction in defining physician training outcomes in multicultural education. *Journal of Heath Care for the Poor and Underserved 9*(2), 117–125.

Valentino, N. A., Hutchings, V. L., Banks, A. J., & Davis, A. K. (2008). Is a worried citizen a good citizen? Emotions, political information seeking, and learning via the Internet. *Political Psychology, 29*, 247–273.

Wahyuni, F., Wiyono, B. B., Atmoko, A., Hambali, I. M. (2019). Counselor's burnout relationship between emotional intelligence, and positively school climate: A structural equal model. *Journal for the Education of Gifted Young Scientists, 7*(4), 1361–1374. DOI: https://dx. doi.org/10.17478/jegys.639397

Walker, P. (2013). *Complex PTSD: From surviving to thriving: A guide and map for recovering from childhood trauma*. Azure Coyote.

Chapter 4

The Courage to Confront
Challenging the Great and Powerful Oz

Collective liberation is an approach to leadership and advocacy that recognizes that multiple forms of oppression exist, that all our struggles are intimately connected by white supremacist capitalist patriarchy, and that we must work together to create the kind of world we know is possible. For school counselors, that world is P-12 schools. As leaders and agents of change, school counselors are well-positioned to challenge these systemic issues in their advocacy work (ASCA, 2021). Each of us has a stake in ending white supremacy and all related systems of oppression. Unfortunately, barriers to LGBTQ+ rights and representation, restrictions on Social and Emotional Learning (SEL), curricular censorship, and book bans are becoming all too common, and the grip of oppressive structures is tightening around schools. These policies harm all students by reducing the richness and depth of student learning, and limiting their opportunities to engage in critical thinking, empathy, and emotional growth. (First Books, 2023; McClure, 2022). The long-term effects of these policies can be harmful to the principles of democratic education and our society as a whole, diminishing students' ability to thrive in a complex, diverse, and interconnected world.

Given this, school counselors must adopt a systems-level perspective and examine their role in maintaining and dismantling oppressive structures. In her essay "There is No Hierarchy of Oppressions," Audre Lorde (1983) insisted that understanding a person requires looking at all aspects of their identity rather than isolating them to a single dimension (e.g., only their gender). She maintains that profound change requires considering the various aspects of people's identity that shape their experiences, including race, gender, socioeconomic status, and more. In school counseling, this concept can help us consider the multiple dimensions of students' identities when advocating for them and confronting the intersecting systems of oppression that affect students' lives. Effective leadership in school counseling requires moving beyond individual student needs and advocating for systemic change. Recognizing how a system impacts students involves understanding the whole of our students and the type of barriers they face, which can determine whether a student's problems are a function of individual, situational, or systemic factors. Seeing students in their entirety allows us to identify the root cause of their issues and the oppressive structures operating within their experiences.

DOI: 10.4324/9781032679174-5

School counselors tackling structural inequalities can draw from Dorothy's encounters in Oz. A great deal of her journey involved unpacking oppressive beliefs, becoming aware of the systemic realities in Oz, and discovering her own strength. When we are introduced to her companions, the Scarecrow, the Tin Woodman, and the Cowardly Lion, each grapples with feelings of inadequacy, powerlessness, and lack of direction. Be it intelligence, compassion, or courage, each one believes they are lacking something essential, and seek external validation from authoritative systems, the Wizard and the Emerald City. Once they are introduced to each other and begin supporting and affirming one another, they find the strengths they already possess. Despite repeatedly demonstrating these qualities, they continue to seek approval from those in power, thinking they need it to be whole. Whether it is the Wizard's power or the allure of Emerald City, systems of control can create beliefs that obscure people's true strength. Just as Dorothy and her friends lost sight of their inherent worth and capabilities, oppressive structures can cause school counselors and students alike to feel inadequate without institutional approval or validation, leading us to accept systemic inequities as they are. This dynamic allows systems to assert themselves as the ultimate authority on what is just and equitable.

Derald Wing Sue, a leading figure in multicultural counseling, has consistently called on counselors to confront how our profession inadvertently upholds systems of oppression. Nearly 50 years ago, he wrote, "Counseling is the handmaiden of the status quo," and reflected on how counselor educators, practitioners, and students are inextricably linked to perpetuating racism and white supremacy by remaining silent, non-committal, and inactive in the face of so many forms of structural and institutional racism (1977). Patricia Arredondo, Michael D'Andrea, and Courtland Lee, pioneers in multicultural counseling, warned that despite the changes in broader society, the counseling profession remains predominantly white and Eurocentric, with minimal progress in diversifying graduate students, counselor educators, theories, and research methods (2020). They called for transformative change and challenged leaders to unmask and address systemic racism within the counseling profession. Adopting anti-oppressive frameworks requires acknowledging and dismantling institutional barriers that have long upheld inequities. Instead of seeking validation from outdated models, it is time to pull back the curtain and challenge Oz.

Pause and Reflect

1   What oppressive structures have you observed in education?
2   How have dominant structures shaped your leadership practices?
3   In what ways have you sought validation from authority figures?
4   How might our long-standing practices and beliefs in counseling inadvertently contribute to systemic oppression?
5   In what ways might self-interest impact one's ability to challenge oppressive structures?

Collective Liberation Is the Goal

Collective liberation recognizes that systems of oppression are interconnected, creating a web of structural inequality that must be challenged collectively (Combahee River Collective, 1982). In schools, this means school counselors must examine not only the individual challenges students face but also the institutional forces that shape their experiences. The Combahee River Collective, a Black feminist group, suggests that systems of racism, capitalism, hetero-patriarchy, and ableism operate with and through each other. They stressed that freedom and equality cannot be achieved for some without liberation for all. Leaders who embrace collective liberation recognize that true justice can only be achieved when all people are liberated from systems of oppression. bell hooks expands on this idea through her essay "Love as the Practice of Freedom," emphasizing that we must operate from an ethic of love in our efforts toward justice. Without an ethic of love, we risk perpetuating systems of domination like imperialism, sexism, racism, and classism. She warns that by fighting against one form of oppression, we can inadvertently support other forms of domination. In a similar manner, seeing the whole child goes beyond their academic, career, and social-emotional development. It involves recognizing how students' identities (race, gender, socioeconomic status, ability, etc.) interact with and are constrained by societal structures. School counselors who fail to recognize how students' identities intersect may miss aspects of their experiences and reinforce the norms and practices of oppressive systems.

Collective liberation is rooted in love and the idea that our fate is bound up with each other and is the strongest weapon against divide-and-control (or "law and order") tactics that keep oppressed groups from uniting. White supremacy, capitalism, and other systems of oppression are designed to make almost everyone feel inadequate, isolated, and powerless. However, leadership that centers on an ethic of love emphasizes the importance of service to others. In traditional leadership models, leaders are often framed in terms of power, control, and authority. When leadership is driven by love and service, it transforms leadership from a top-down, authoritarian model to one that is relational, supportive, and focused on the collective empowerment of everyone. Leading through love is not a weakness. Instead, it is the foundation for building community and addressing both individual and collective needs. The sense of community and solidarity we build through collective liberation gives us the courage to challenge systems. Collective liberation and an ethic of love allow us to operate from horizontal moral systems. Whereas a vertical moral system operates from a place of authority and control, a horizontal moral system emphasizes mutual care and shared power. Leading through an ethic of love requires us to look around and recognize the interconnectedness of our lives. Lorde (1983) maintains,

> I have learned that oppression and the intolerance of difference come in all shapes and sexes and colors and sexualities; and that among those of us who

share the goals of liberation and a workable future for our children, there can be no hierarchies of oppression.

Unfortunately, not all leadership that claims equity is rooted in collective liberation. Sometimes power can complicate people's intentions and distort their impact. Leaders who model an ethic of love commit to collective well-being rather than individual or hierarchical success. A mistake of some aspiring equity leaders is to use their power and influence for personal gain rather than collective liberation. Leaders who identify more with their personal self are more likely to act selfishly, particularly when they have more power, while those who identify with a collective self (as part of a group) are less influenced by power and less likely to engage in self-serving behavior (Wisse & Rus, 2012). Smith (2015) maintains that within systems of white supremacy, individuals can be both victims and complicit, because the way we survive and resist is shaped by white supremacy itself. This can be seen in how individuals seduced at the prospect of participating in other pillars of power may inadvertently support the very system that oppressed them. In leadership, self-interest can mirror this dynamic when individuals acting out of personal gain may reinforce the oppressive system even while being marginalized by it. Leaders oriented toward collective liberation recognize that no one person or system is bigger than the community, while those oriented to the self prioritize personal interest over communal care. Unfortunately, leaders can mistakenly conflate self-interest with the pursuit of broader social justice. These types of leaders can dilute the integrity and impact of advocacy efforts, and school counselors must be able to recognize and challenge these behaviors.

In order to stay grounded in collective values, school counselors should understand the nuances between collective liberation, self-preservation, and self-interest. *Self-preservation* refers to protecting yourself in a way that enables long-term engagement in advocacy efforts. This can involve protecting your mental, physical, or emotional health so that you can remain an effective advocate. The goal is to preserve your ability to contribute to collective liberation over time without putting yourself in a position where you are unable to advocate for the issues that matter. Self-preservation allows leaders to navigate oppositional tactics and personal attacks, enabling them to continue challenging the system for collective liberation. *Self-interest* in leadership includes any action in which a leader uses their power with the intention to benefit the self (Williams, 2014). These actions include focusing on career advancement, seeking recognition or rewards, aligning with influential figures or exploiting others for personal benefit, or avoiding conflict or discomfort. Acts of self-interest are often done at the expense of marginalized groups and in a way that perpetuates the status quo. The difference between self-preservation and self-interest is subtle but significant; the distinction lies in the intent, impact, and consequences.

Systems of Oppression

Engaging in collective liberation requires understanding the ways in which racism, sexism, ableism, and other systems of oppression operate at the individual and systemic levels. Merriam-Webster (n.d.) defines oppression as an unjust or cruel exercise of authority or power. Oppression is more than the choices of a few people; rather, it can be structurally rooted in unchallenged norms and institutional practices (Young, 2008). At its core, it operates through structures of power limiting access to resources and opportunities. School counselors must be able to recognize how power structures in our society are reproduced in the educational spaces they lead. First, let us refer to Table 4.1, adapted from the Chinook Fund (n.d.), for a deeper exploration of the various forms of oppression; then, we will explain how oppression operates as a system through multiple levels.

The Four "Is" of Oppression is a helpful framework for understanding how systemic injustices can perpetuate in education over time (Bell, 2013). This framework outlines four overlapping and interdependent ways that oppression can manifest itself both in society and in education. *Ideological oppression* is rooted in value systems that allow people to dehumanize, exploit, or harm other individuals and groups. At its core, it is the belief that one group is somehow better than another and, in some measure, has the right to control the other group. These ideologies form the foundation for racism, sexism, ableism, and other "isms." These beliefs can have long-standing cultural and historical roots and serve as a way of understanding the world. *Internalized oppression* involves the way individuals absorb belief systems that then contribute to a false sense of supremacy or deficiency within themselves in relation to others. *Interpersonal oppression* occurs when those internalized beliefs are expressed between individuals or groups. It involves the actions, language, and behaviors that reinforce control or dominance over others.

Finally, *institutional oppression* is how policies, laws, and social practices are used to disadvantage certain groups. Even when a member of a marginalized group holds prejudices or anger toward dominant groups, their ability to act on them is limited by the lack of institutional power and often results in harsher consequences when they do. The concept of reverse racism, for example, fails to account for the ways in which power structures uphold and enforce dominant group control. As noted in Table 4.1, each ism involves a combination of prejudice and institutional power. Understanding the Four "Is" of oppression allows school counselors to recognize how these forces shape and maintain the barriers students face and a lens for challenging them.

Building on this framework, let us examine how these forms of oppression can manifest as barriers to students' success. Determining whether a student's problems are a function of individual, situational, or systemic factors can help school counselors address the root cause of their struggles. *Individual barriers*

Table 4.1 Forms of Oppression

Type of Ism	Definition	Formula	Power Structure
Racism	A system of oppression based on race. Includes prejudice, exclusion and discrimination of people of color. The category of race is a social/artificial construction based on physical differences and origin of ancestry, but has very real consequences.	Power + Racial Prejudice = RACISM	Dominant: White Subordinate: People of Color (Of Asian/African/Latin American/Indigenous/Multiracial backgrounds)
Sexism	A system of oppression based on sex & gender. It is based on the idea that there are only two "normal"/ biological genders—male and female, and that one (male) is superior. Includes prejudice, exclusion, and discrimination against women.	Power + Gender Prejudice = SEXISM	Dominant: Men, people perceived to be male Subordinate: Women, people perceived to be female
Cissexism	A system of oppression based on gender identity. It is based on the idea that there are only two "normal"/biological genders—male and female, and that your gender identity and expression must match your biological sex. Includes prejudice, exclusion, and discrimination of transgender, gender queer, intersex, and gender non-conforming people.	Power + Gender Prejudice – CISSEXISM	Dominant: Cisgender, gender conforming Subordinate: Transgender, gender queer, intersex, gender Non-conforming

(Continued)

Table 4.1 (Continued)

Type of Ism	Definition	Formula	Power Structure
Classism	A system of oppression based on economic status. Highly shaped by existing form of capitalist economy. Includes prejudice, exclusion, and discrimination of poor & low-income people based on real or perceived economic status.	Power + Class Prejudice = CLASSISM	Dominant: Middle & upper class people Subordinate: Poor, low-income & working class people
Heterosexism	A system of oppression based on sexual orientation. Includes prejudice, exclusion, and discrimination of people who are or who are perceived to be lesbian, gay, bisexual, transgender, or queer (LGBQ). Homophobia is the fear of LGBQ people.	Power + Sexual Orienta tion Prejudice = HETERO SEXISM	Dominant: Heterosexual or "Straight" people Subordinate: LGBQ people
Ableism	A system of oppression based on mental/ physical ability. Includes prejudice, exclusion, and discrimination of people who have mental or physical disabilities or differences.	Power + Ability Prejudice = ABLEISM	Dominant: Able-bodied people Subordinate: People with disabilities
Ageism	A system of oppression based on age, particularly targeting older or younger individuals. Includes prejudice, exclusion, and discrimination against people due to their age.	Power + Age Prejudice = AGEISM	Dominant: Younger or middle-aged people Subordinate: Older or younger individuals

are internal, vary between students, and can involve confidence, maturity, motivation, or self-perceptions. *Situational barriers,* on the other hand, refer to an individual's situation in life at a given time. They are external to the individual and can include mental or physical health concerns, personal life events (death, divorce, etc.), family obligations, or lack of time, support, or information. *Systemic barriers,* however, refer to the broader structures within institutions that affect entire groups of individuals similarly and are embedded in systems that shape students' opportunities and experiences. Opportunities in education consist of the programs and services designed to guide student development and support their advancement and success. When these opportunities are inaccessible or distributed unevenly due to systemic barriers (e.g., bias, discrimination), they become opportunity gaps. Institutional structures such as laws, regulations, resource allocations, and organizational cultures form the context in which pathways function as barriers or opportunities and are often rooted in systems of oppression (e.g., racism, sexism, cissexism, and ableism).

The Four "Is" of Oppression not only help us understand the different forms of oppression but also illustrate how these forms intersect, creating a cycle of oppression that reinforces systemic barriers in education (Figure 4.1). To illustrate this cycle in action, let us apply it to a scenario in a school involving advanced placement (AP) and honors classes. Let us take the policy requiring three teacher recommendations for enrollment in AP or honors classes. Mindsets rooted in exclusivity, deficit thinking, and paternalism, where biased assumptions about student motivation and readiness or capability suggest that students must "prove" their readiness through the approval of multiple teachers, are grounded in ideological oppression. These beliefs become formalized through the three-teacher signature policy (institutionalized oppression). Teachers and counselors then reinforce the three-signature rule without considering the barriers students from marginalized backgrounds face, reinforcing exclusionary practices (interpersonal oppression). When students are consistently denied access to advanced courses, they can begin to internalize these experiences, leading to a lack of self-confidence and motivation. They may start to believe that they are not "AP material," reducing their motivation to apply to these courses and resulting in low enrollment of marginalized students (internalized oppression). When looking at data, educators may unintentionally engage in blame reversal. In many ways, school counselor training has led us to prioritize data as a tool to identify students, but this deficit lens risks reinforcing the cycle of oppression by misinterpreting students' struggles as personal deficiencies, ignoring the broader structural factors contributing to their challenges. This approach leads to confirmation bias further entrenching educators and students alike in oppressive practices.

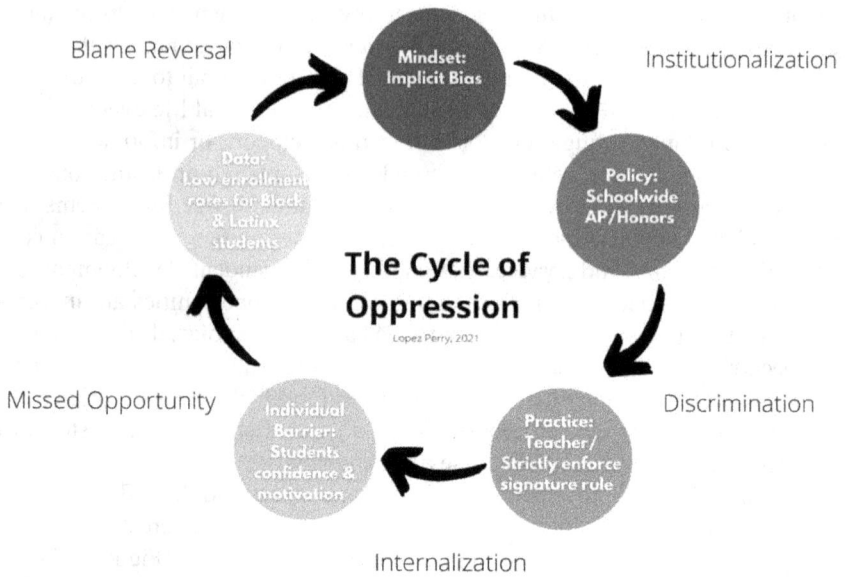

Blame Reversal

Institutionalization

Mindset: Implicit Bias

Data: Low enrollment rates for Black & Latinx students

Policy: Schoolwide AP/Honors

The Cycle of Oppression

Lopez Perry, 2021

Missed Opportunity

Individual Barrier: Students confidence & motivation

Practice: Teacher/ Strictly enforce signature rule

Discrimination

Internalization

Figure 4.1 The Cycle of Oppression

Melting the Wicked Forces

While this may seem discouraging, there is a silver lining. School counselors who embrace their role as leaders can disrupt this cycle of oppression at various points. Whereas other specialties focus on individual client needs, school counselors are well-positioned to influence broader institutional change. Our role extends beyond direct student support involving advocacy, systemic change, leadership, and collaboration (Mason et al., 2021). Just like Dorothy was able to melt the wicked forces, school counselors can disrupt the hold of oppressive forces (Figure 4.2). School counselors can dismantle institutional oppression by advocating for policy change that creates a more equitable environment for students that considers individual, situational, and systemic barriers that hinder opportunities. This requires relearning and expanding their knowledge base to identify alternative ways of functioning beyond traditional approaches. They can also disrupt interpersonal oppression by supporting students through school-wide programming that shifts power dynamics. Through student-led equity teams, youth participatory action research (YPAR), community circles, affinity groups, and student panels, school counselors can create spaces for students to not only share their experiences but also provide input on policies that affect their lives (Spellman, 2024). School counselors can intervene in internalized oppression through direct services such as classroom lessons and individual and group counseling by utilizing asset-based and culturally affirming counseling

Unpack

Mindset: Implicit Bias

Advocate

Data: Low enrollment rates for Black & Latinx students

Policy: Schoolwide AP/Honors signature

Interrupting the Cycle

Lopez Perry, 2021

Audit

Individual Barrier: Students confidence & motivation

Practice: Strictly enforce 3signature rule

Relearn

Support

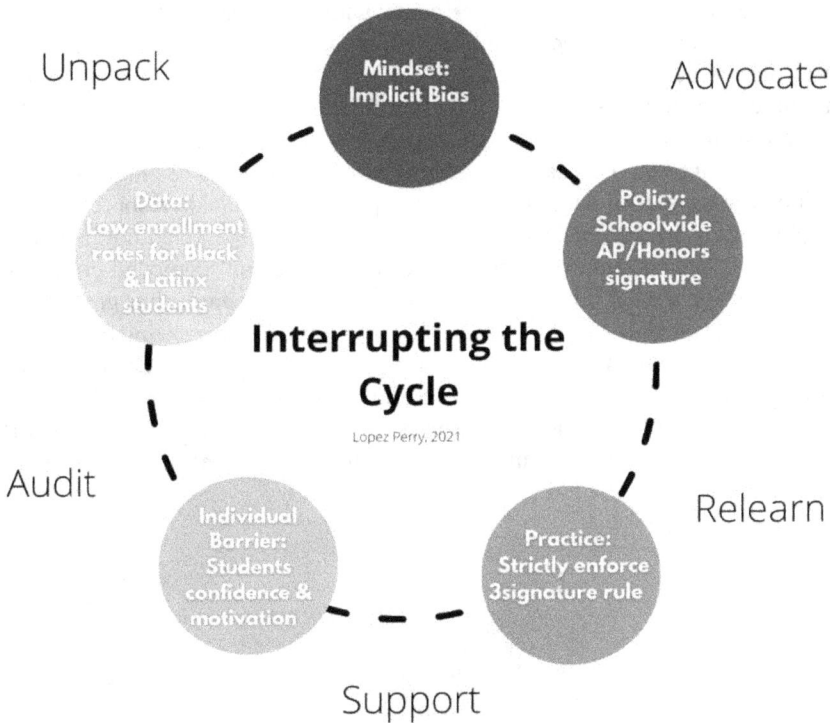

Figure 4.2 Interrupting the Cycle of Oppression

approaches (Fox et al., 2020; Steen et al., 2022). School counselors can conduct equity audits to uncover disparities and guide policy change (Skrla et al., 2009). They can disrupt ideological oppression by unpacking beliefs and biases and challenging the ingrained ways of being (Atkins & Oglesby, 2018). Finally, they can help others within the school community explore their beliefs via consultation and professional development workshops.

Healing Students and Reforming Systems

Ultimately, school counselors must identify the underlying barriers and determine when targeted supports are appropriate and when systems change is necessary. Data analysis often leads us to default to individual and group interventions, overlooking the systemic barriers and reinforcing deficit thinking, the belief that something is lacking in the student rather than the system. The focus becomes "fixing" students instead of addressing the oppressive systems contributing to their challenges (Katz, 1985). As authors, we suggest a justice-oriented approach that prioritizes anti-oppressive practices to address systemic issues.

It involves recognizing the broader context in which harm has occurred and is set up to continue to occur unless disrupted. It aligns with our philosophy of justice introduced in Chapter 1 and follows a two-pronged strategy focused on immediate student support and long-term systemic change (Figure 4.3). The first prong focuses on healing the harm caused to students through culturally responsive supports. This can include individual or group counseling, consulting with necessary school partners, or making referrals to outside resources. These supports build on students' strengths and agency rather than pathologizing their challenges. The second prong involves changing the environmental conditions that perpetuate the harm through systemic change. This approach is grounded in asset-based, equity-focused, and social justice principles, leveraging the strength of the school community while challenging institutional norms. Data is used as an audit tool to identify disparities and inequities within the school environment. Once identified, school counselors can engage in advocacy efforts with educators, administrators, families, and community partners to drive systemic improvements (Cheatham & Mason, 2021).

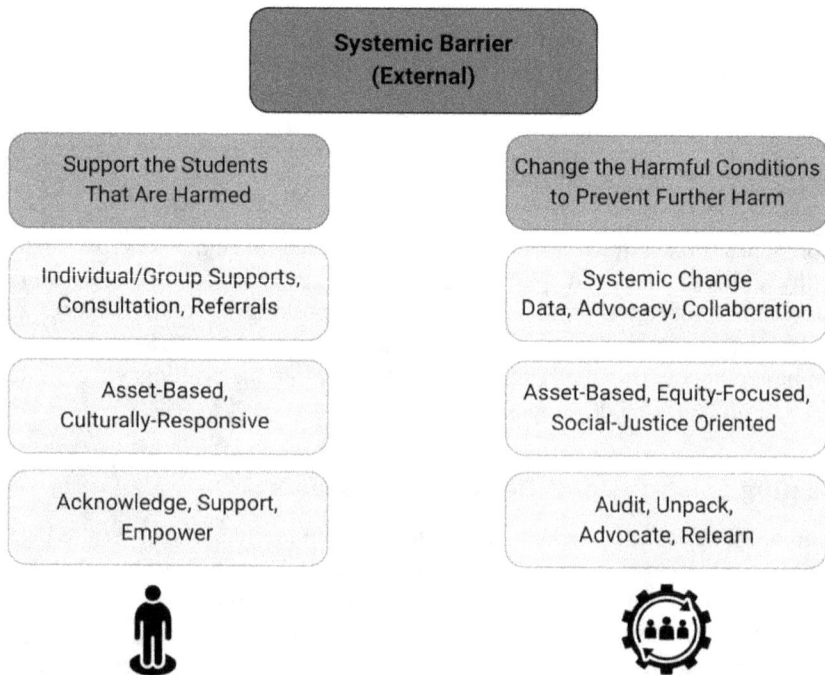

Figure 4.3 A Justice-Oriented Approach to Addressing Barriers

Through their leadership, school counselors help foster a culture of accountability, helping their community unpack personal and institutional biases that contribute to deficit thinking. They engage in difficult conversations with colleagues, facilitate professional development opportunities, and collaborate with school leadership to implement equitable practices. During this process, they embrace and model continuous professional growth and relearn new and more effective ways of practice that align with anti-oppressive practices. By focusing on healing individual harm and addressing the root of inequity, school counselors can drive meaningful change that transforms the educational experiences of current and future students.

Pay Attention to the Man behind the Curtain

A critical aspect of leadership is the ability to question the legitimacy of hidden power structures. A common framework for maintaining power in the United States is White Supremacy Culture (Okun, 1999). The 15 characteristics and behaviors of WSC explain how they manifest and how organizational cultures impose these standards that are often invisible to many. Much of what appears as authority is often a carefully constructed facade designed to hoard power and maintain the status quo (Wickens & Gupta, 2022). The character Oz exemplifies the illusion of power in L. Frank Baum's original book, but it is in the 1939 film adaptation, *The Wizard of Oz,* directed by Victor Fleming where this theme is visually amplified. Frank Morgan, the actor who played Oz, actually appeared in five different roles- Professor Marvel, the squeaky-voiced doorman at the entrance of the Emerald City, the carriage driver with the Horse of a Different Color, the guard at the Wizard's chamber, and the Wizard himself. Like this casting choice, systems of oppression can mask their true nature by presenting multiple facades. While it may appear that decisions are collaborative, control remains in the hands of a select few. Our first introduction to Frank Morgan is as Professor Marvel, a con man fortune teller preying on Dorothy's naivete, offering her a vision of the future. By the same token, Oz used the people's fear, gullibility, and ignorance against them. He allowed them to believe he was a powerful Wizard, and they built the city for him. Over time, the mystique around him built to the point where his supposed acts were considered legendary, and he became known as Oz the Great and Powerful. When Oz would have to deal with anybody firsthand, he would use elaborate costuming, special effects, and his talent for ventriloquism to make them believe that he was much more than he was. Similar to Oz, institutions use a lack of transparency and fancy window dressing to keep up the allure to their constituencies.

This illusion, which we refer to as the Oz Effect captures the façade of authority that conceals the underlying power structure. Within this construct, individuals and systems operate in the shadows to maintain control and suppress challenges to their dominance. As a result, these structures reinforce this centralized power and go unexamined, much like top-down leadership styles that prioritize control over collaboration. Several studies have criticized the limitations of top-down leadership for creating change, including lack of cognitive complexity in developing solutions, lack of buy-in, and risk of becoming leader-dependent (Kezar, 2012). In contrast, shared leadership decentralizes power, fostering more complex solutions and ideas, greater buy-in and consensus, and diverse expertise to draw from (Pearce & Conger, 2003). *Institutional power dynamics* are the rules and systems that determine who holds power within organizations and larger systems. This can include who can make decisions, how policy and funding are set, or how licenses and credentials are granted. *Interpersonal-level power dynamics*, on the other hand, refer to the everyday interactions like who gets heard, who leads conversations, or who feels safe to speak. Morgan (1997) points out that organizations can act in oppressive ways by normalizing domination and oppression, resisting change that challenges institutional norms, and favoring the interest of certain groups over others. Kezar (2011) examined the power dynamics between top-down authority figures and bottom-up grassroots leaders in education. She identified five types of power dynamics: oppression, silencing, controlling, resistance, and microaggressions. The most extreme form, oppression, involved threats to job security, while silencing was the most prevalent. Resistance and microaggressions were subtle but more pervasive, creating barriers by consuming people's time and placing obstacles in their path. She found, grassroots leaders were able to challenge these power dynamics in several ways by building alliances and coalitions, recognizing resistance as a form of power, and leveraging external networks to overcome resistance. As leaders and advocates within the educational system, school counselors must see beyond the curtain of false authority and use their collective power to confront and expose tactics that maintain the status quo. In Chapter 7, we will learn more about coalition building and how Dorothy and her friends utilized this approach to challenge Oz's authority and eventually expose him as a fraud.

The Spectacle of the Emerald City: Institutions in the Profession

A key detail in Baum's (1900) *The Wonderful Wizard of Oz* offers deeper insight into how the illusion of power can manipulate perception and compel conformity. In the book, the citizens of Emerald City are required to wear green-tinted spectacles at all times. These mandatory glasses serve as a device for misleading its people, making everything in the Emerald City appear green creating the illusion of a sparkling city.

In a similar vein, many institutions in education and counseling are upheld by "green-tinted spectacles," creating an illusion that they are in the best interest of students or the profession when, in reality, they often benefit those in power or maintain institutional norms. Forty years ago, Katz (1985) highlighted calls from practitioners to reexamine the theory and practice of counseling, a conversation that is just as relevant today. She argued that the major components of white culture, such as individualism, action orientation, rigid time schedules, the scientific method, and the "Protestant Work Ethic," were pervasive in counseling and called on the profession to make explicit the values from which our models, theories, practices, and research are based. This call remains urgent today. Now, as then, it is time for us to take off the glasses and see these systems for what they are.

Counseling is the Handmaiden of the Status Quo

The green-tinted spectacles metaphor becomes especially relevant when we look inward at how counseling has preserved ideologies under the guise of care. The school counseling profession is not immune to upholding oppressive systems that reinforce inequities and privilege dominant cultural norms. Despite the illusion of accountability, Arredondo and colleagues (2020) contend that the counseling profession has seen little progress over the past 50 years. Counseling accreditation standards, which are intended to ensure quality and accountability, have done little to disrupt the status quo. Even with the presence of diversity-related standards, counselor education programs remain predominantly composed of white counseling students and are still taught by majority white professors (Arredondo et al., 2020). Multicultural counseling remains limited to a single course, and core theories in counseling, career development, and human development remain outdated, Eurocentric, and are taught in a non-integrative way (Arredondo et al., 2020; Mason et al., 2022). Because counseling theory and practice developed out of the experiences of white therapists and researchers working almost exclusively with white client systems, it is vital to acknowledge that the profession reflects white cultural values. For instance, Eurocentric counseling approaches tend to focus on childhood experiences, developing self-concept, or attempting to modify behaviors, often disregarding environmental factors and cultural experiences (Katz, 1985). The stages that counseling theories have progressed through reflect the biases and prejudices of white theorists of the time, including the pathological view of minorities, the genetic deficiency model, the culturally deficient model, and the culturally different model (Sue, 1981). Many counselor education programs still rely on outdated, Eurocentric models and theories. While these approaches may be widely criticized today, at the time they were developed, they were regarded as best practices within the profession.

These issues extend into the everyday tools and frameworks currently used by school counselors. Given that school counseling and education have been shaped by white, Christian, and Eurocentric cultural perspectives, school counselors must be critical consumers of current research, theory, and practice in our field. While programs like SEL, Positive Behavior Intervention Supports (PBIS), and trauma-informed practices were developed with the intention of supporting students, they are often weaponized through carceral logic and deficit-centered approaches. Camangian & Cariaga (2021) critique hegemonic SEL pedagogies for focusing on controlling student behavior rather than fostering true emotional growth. Similarly, trauma-informed practices and Adverse Childhood Experiences (ACES) screenings have been misused to pathologize or stigmatize students, particularly those from racially minoritized communities (Goldin et al., 2021; Khasnabis & Goldin, 2020; Winninghoff, 2020). The school counseling profession must confront the realities of the inequities they perpetuate and critically examine the theories and practices that shape our field.

Capitalism and Commercialism in School Counseling

As school counseling has progressed as a profession, capitalism and commercialism have also taken hold in some ways. There are many frameworks and practices in education we adopt because they are the milieu of the time and because they are what sells well. Teachers Pay Teachers (TPT) is wildly popular, and many school counselors have been able to monetize their professional expertise to develop successful side hustles (Sabella & Lerner, 2019). Capitalism is a systemic structure of supply and demand maintained by certain people or groups. Commercialism is the resulting overemphasis on profit. Consider for a moment the ASCA National Model. First came the ASCA National Standards by Dr. Carol Dahir in 1997, which paved the way. The first edition of the ASCA Model (2003) was written by school counseling leaders at the time, Dr. Judy Bowers and Dr. Trish Hatch with support from Dr. Carol Dahir, Dr. Chari Campbell, Dr. Norm Gysbers, Drs. Curly and Sherri Johnson, Dr. Bob Myrick, and others. The model finally gave school counselors some basic bricks to stand on, pointed us toward an idea of a destination we could aim for, and gave us credibility we needed for so long (Church, 2025). All in one book was a framework, a guide, to be adapted based on students needs, program setting, and available resources for a school counselor or program to purchase. If you knew someone who had it, you could borrow it and consult with them about how they were applying the model in their school.

At the time of this writing, on the ASCA website the following items/services related to the Model and the Recognized ASCA Model Program (RAMP) were listed:

- ASCA Model book (4th edition), $44.95
- Two ASCA Model Implementation Guides, $44.95 each
- Three additional books aligned with the Model for $24.95 each
- ASCA Model one-day training for $3,750
- Two-year ASCA Model training for schools or districts (price not listed)
- ASCA Model portal at a per school per year rate ranging from $25 (five years) to $100 (one year)

- RAMP fee of $250 per year for ASCA member, $500 for non-members
- RAMP coaching packages for $3,375 per school
- ACSC or ASCA-Certified School Counselor, application costs of which are up to $400
- ASCA membership is $129 which provides a discount for many related materials and trainings

School counselor leaders must ask, what does it mean that there are so many of these products and services to purchase? Does a school counselor need them to better implement the model? To be a better school counselor? All or just some? What is the real return on investment when it comes to creating change for students? Much of the research on the impact of the ASCA Model and RAMP is mixed (Burnham et al., 2024; Goodman-Scott et al., 2020, 2022; Hilts et al., 2019; Mullen et al., 2019; Randick et al., 2018).

The criteria, rubrics, and training standards for the model, the RAMP award, and other recognitions awarded by ASCA are set by the same group that takes the money that school counselors and districts pay to earn them. Many graduate programs teach school counselors in training the elements of a comprehensive, school counseling program through a variety of frameworks. The ASCA Model is often included in these because it is so widely proliferated and is adopted as part of state certification or licensure standards. Some districts use ASCA model-related questions in the interview process for school counselor positions. The typical novice school counselor in this day and age is likely to have at least a basic understanding of the ASCA model. Consider then the idea of planned obsolescence (Kenton, 2022). Typically, this is a term that applies to products like technology, including cell phones, which are deliberately manufactured to go out of style within a certain period of time so consumers will buy the next version (Kenton, 2022). However, in the case of the ASCA Model, as school counselors stay in the profession and if they apply for RAMP, the criteria change as the editions of the model change. Multiple models and their accompanying products add ongoing layers to the overall commercialism. In the profession of school psychology, there is also a national model. It is available to all practitioners and maintained on the National Association of School Psychologists (NASP) website (nasponline.org), membership is not required, and no purchase is necessary. An accompanying implementation guide is also available for free online and the recognition program application fee is on a sliding scale. Just prior to the publication of our book, we were heartened to see a preview of the 5th version of the ASCA National Model, a pdf to be made available free for download.

Twenty plus years later, the zeitgeist within school counseling has shifted since the ASCA Model was introduced. As school counselor leaders, the courage to confront means stopping to question why we do things the way we do. While the framework filled a much-needed gap in our history, and it continues to provide value for many school counselors, is the continued commercialization of the model sustainable for the future? To what end? The result creates the potential for inequities among school counselors and school counseling programs. In the world of ASCA and RAMP, there are those school counselors and districts who can afford additional training and supports and those who cannot (Mullen et al., 2019). These inequities likely create pressure for school counselors to appease their principals who want to compete with the school down the street, and pressure for principals to appease district administration who want to compete with the neighboring district. The framework of the ASCA Model was not likely meant to create such discrepancies but rather be able to be useful to all school counselors in all settings with all students.

We imagine a different scenario and hope you do too. One in which the value of collective liberation replaces the values of capitalism and commercialism. Instead of a system driven by continual product development, we envision a professional ecosystem rooted in collective wisdom and mutual support. Those leading always credit those who make contributions, even in perpetuity, for the historical record. If collective liberation is the goal, then every school counselor is supported by their profession with the basic tools they need. The monetization of opportunities is matched by subsidizing the same opportunities for those who experience barriers to access.

Righting the Ratios

Collective liberation can prioritize the quality of school counselor training and the ongoing supports to meet students' needs. At the time of this publication, mental health issues in schools are at a crisis level (CDC, 2024). School counselors, like their community counseling counterparts, are trained mental health professionals (Purgason et al., 2022). What is the "right" ratio of school counselors to students may not be as pertinent a question as what do school counselors need to do their job well (more school counselors could be one answer)? While as authors we believe that all students should have access to a fully qualified, and fully functioning school counselor, this does not necessarily mean a ratio of 1:250. Due to the fact that every school setting is unique, we argue that generally a lower ratio is probably better but that the number 250 is arbitrary. Research done by Nicola (2024) provides a historical case study of the 1:250 number. In it, she traces this ratio back to a suggestion made by James Bryan Conant in a 1959 report titled *The American high school today: A first report to interested citizens*. Conant was a scientist and president of Harvard with an interest in education reform. The report he drafted was not an in-depth study but rather a summary of findings and suggestions after visiting approximately 100 U.S. high schools in 18 states.

Capitalism may have us thinking more is better as the default option. More school counselors does not equate to quality training at the graduate level or through professional development. It also does not guarantee more support from administration for doing the job school counselors are trained to do in all three domains. Community and context matter. As an example, for low-resourced or rural school counselors, more school counselors may seem like the ultimate fix but not necessarily so if additional community-based services could support some of their more high need cases (Bryan & Henry, 2012; Henry & Fears, 2025). The ratio issue is a symptom of a complex, deep-seated devaluation of children, mental health, and school counselors.

Policing in Schools

Much like the illusion of inclusive and equitable practices in counseling, districts increasingly rely on policing in schools to maintain order and control, all the while providing a false sense of security and ignoring the deeper issues that contribute to student behavior. Policing in schools, often presented as essential for safety, has grown significantly since the 1970s, when fewer than 100 officers worked in schools. Today, 20,000 to 30,000 officers patrol K-12 schools (Javdani, 2019; Nance, 2015). When incidents such as fights or disruptions occur, the default response from policymakers, administrators, and even some caregivers is to call law enforcement rather than address the root causes. Our educational system's increasing reliance on police mirrors society's broader dependence on law enforcement to handle complex social issues like mental health crises, homelessness, and substance use.

This reliance on policing in education is not a new phenomenon, but rather a continuation of a long history of punitive measures used to control marginalized groups. For generations, schools have used violent policing and disciplinary practices rooted in racism to control Black, Latinx, and Indigenous students. During slavery, white enslavers punished enslaved Black people for attempting to learn to read (Span & Anderson, 2005). This pattern continued into the late 1800s to the 1970s when Indigenous children were forcibly assimilated into white culture through boarding schools that stripped them of their identity (Parks, 2022). In 1956, Southern resistance to school integration led to violent actions, such as white mobs in Mansfield, Texas, blocking Black students from entering a whites-only high school (Ladino, 1996). During this same period, Latinx students in California, Texas, and Arizona were segregated and harshly disciplined for speaking Spanish (Garcia, 2016; Powers, 2008; Wollenberg, 1976). These are only a few historical examples of how schools have served as sites of control and marginalization, laying the groundwork for the modern-day use of policing to enforce power and control.

While these practices are no longer as blatant, they persist in subtler forms under the illusion of safety and order. In the 1980s and 1990s, zero-tolerance policies emerged alongside Reagan's "War on Drugs," normalizing locker searches, canine surveillance, and suspensions (Drug Policy Alliance, n.d.). The Gun-Free Schools Act of 1994 institutionalized these practices, tying federal funding to mandatory expulsions for students bringing firearms to school (Heitzeg, 2014). After Columbine, these policies expanded to include minor infractions, embedding punitive measures into school discipline. The 2001 No Child Left Behind Act required schools receiving federal funds to refer students with firearms to the criminal justice system (Cooper, 2002). Following the Sandy Hook shooting, federal grants under Obama incentivized the hiring of school resource officers. Despite the rhetoric on school policing, findings on its effectiveness are mixed or inconclusive (James & McCallion, 2013; Price & Khubchandani, 2019; Stern & Petrosino, 2018). The few studies demonstrating positive results of these policies focus on participant perceptions of effectiveness rather than objective data (Raymond, 2010). With each new initiative, educators and the broader public become increasingly reliant on punitive measures rather than addressing the root cause of issues related to school climate and engagement.

These policies lay the foundation for punitive approaches, and school culture is further shaped by how law enforcement officers (LEOs) and school resource officers (SROs) are presented to students from an early age. Whether it is McGruff the Crime Dog, dancing LEOs and SROs, Paw Patrol cartoons, or career days, several tactics have been utilized to legitimize LEOs as a necessary part of the school environment (Carson Baggett & Selman, 2024). These strategies build on the policies described earlier, masking the systemic harm caused by school policing under the guise of mentorship and safety. Images of friendly officers with K-9s, officer mentorship programs, and playful forms of surveillance hide efforts to humanize militarized equipment that are used to harass, maim, and even kill. The goal is to legitimize authority through mentorship and education, and normalize surveillance and compliance, particularly for marginalized communities (Carson Baggett & Selman, 2024).

Traditionally, teachers and administrators were the principal agents of socialization, and classrooms, hallways, and playgrounds are the primary sites where socialization occurs (Brint, 2017). However, with increased policing in schools, educators have steadily withdrawn from teaching school norms in favor of security personnel (Simon, 2009). LEOs and SROs are more often being called to deal with disruptive behavior in the classroom, and the hallways of secondary schools have become spaces for security personnel (Peele & Willis, 2024, June 6). Simon (2009) contends that "through the introduction of police, probation officers, prosecutors and a host of private security professionals into the schools, new forms of expertise now openly compete with pedagogic knowledge and authority for shaping routines and rituals of schools (p.209)."

This shift is even more disturbing when we consider the pro-police argument often used by educators and board members, that LEOs play a valuable role in mentoring students. The paradox that the person who has the potential to incarcerate a student, should also serve as their mentor is both counterintuitive and morally reprehensible. That officers who disproportionately incarcerate Black and Brown fathers who guide their children's lives, should then step in and fill the void themselves is disturbingly reminiscent of chattel slavery's family separation and control. Rather than responding to students' mental well-being and social-emotional development through social-emotional learning and mental wellness supports, funding that could be utilized to develop systems of care is diverted to systems of punishment and policing. For example, in 2019–2020, Inglewood Unified spent $1.3 million on school police, but only $66,400 in PBIS training (Gon Ochi et al., 2020).

Beyond the claims of safety and security, the harsh realities of school policing must be recognized. Numerous studies have highlighted its adverse effects, including the criminalization of student behavior, heightened surveillance, and the disproportionate impact on marginalized communities. While research on the benefits of school policing is scarce, the harmful effects are notable. These include excessive use of force against students with disabilities (Shaver & Decker, 2017), a federal grant for school police that led to a decrease in high school graduation by 2.5% and 4% decline in college enrollment (Weisburst, 2019), and an increased risk for justice system involvement (Devlin & Gottfredson, 2018; Inniss-Thompson, 2017). At the same time, research has shown that school connectedness and school climate serve as critical protective factors, buffering youth against emotional distress, suicidal ideation, and attempts (Areba et al., 2021; Marraccini & Brier, 2017). However, the presence of SROs can undermine these protective factors. Students with higher levels of SRO interactions experience lower school connectedness (Theriot, 2016), and their presence has been associated with more negative feelings about school climate (Kupchik, 2010). Gonzalez (2021) calls school policing a public health issue, sitting at the nexus of two social determinants of health: education and racism. Although the mechanisms of policing have evolved over time, the underlying function of social control persists in various forms. As Annamma (2018) notes, school policing is rooted in white supremacy and the goal is not to surveil all bodies equally but to socially and spatially monitor Black and Brown bodies. In response, school counselors must help shift schools from a pedagogy of punishment and control to one of empathy and care. This shift is a crucial step in honoring the humanity of Black and Brown students, affording them the same grace given to white students: the opportunity to be seen in the full spectrum of their growth and cognitive development, to think, explore, make mistakes, and learn without fear of retribution.

In this section, we challenged you to remove the "green-tinted spectacles" and consider how your perceptions have been shaped by narratives that portray these institutions as inclusive and equitable systems. If you are having strong reactions to this section, it may be helpful to pause and reflect on whether your reactions are rooted in a vertical or horizontal moral system of beliefs. Is your response shaped by hierarchical structures and dynamics rooted in power and control, or do they align with a more collective perspective that considers those most impacted? Consider how your reactions fit within the cycle of oppression described earlier.

The Poppy Fields of Passivity and the Traps that Undermine Advocacy

In this chapter, we discussed the school counselors' role in recognizing and dismantling structures of inequality. Consequently, it is worth mentioning that leaders cannot expect to challenge oppressive systems without encountering resistance (see Chapter 6). Those who benefit from the status quo are unlikely to relinquish their power without a fight. When challenging power structures, the opposition will likely attempt to reduce your effectiveness through various attacks and encourage passivity. During her journey to the Emerald City, Dorothy and her friends unknowingly walk through the poppy fields, unaware of the dangerous power it holds. Not long after, Dorothy, Toto, and the Lion are fast asleep. Similar to how systems of oppression surround us, exhaust us, hoping we'll give up, school counselors can risk falling into a deep sleep of passivity and complicity. The fragrance of comfort, privilege, and a false sense of security can lull us into complacency, tempting us to accept things as they are. However, once we are aware of oppositional tactics and the risk, we can more consciously navigate through these fields of resistance. Individuals engaging in advocacy work must be able to recognize the dangers of the poppy fields. Familiarizing yourself with the tactics used by power brokers and strategies for responding can help you avoid the traps designed to weaken your efforts.

The first step in responding to attacks is recognizing them. The following list, referred to as the "10 Ds of Opposition," highlights ten of the more common tactics used to undermine progress. *Deflection* is used in two primary ways: to shift the focus away from the core issue to unrelated concerns or to pass the responsibility to other individuals with little or no authority. *Delays* are another frequent response and are often disguised as the need for additional information in the form of committees or hearings. The purpose is to slow the momentum of advocates and diffuse urgency. It bears mentioning that the demands for research and deliberation are rarely applied to oppressive policies, which are often enacted swiftly and with little scrutiny. *Denial* is used to refute any truth to either the problem you say exists or the solution you propose. *Discounting* occurs when adversaries suggest that the problem you are working on is not important or by questioning the legitimacy of your group or its efforts. At its most extreme, it can take the form of lies, mudslinging, and accusations. *Deception* refers to intentionally misleading by omitting information or providing false information. It can be carried out in various ways, including creating the illusion of action, such as forming new initiatives or committees that give the impression of addressing an issue, while taking no meaningful steps to implement change. Deception can also include manipulating statistics, withholding information, framing policies with misleading language (e.g., "school choice" ensures equity), or token representation, where underrepresented voices are included in the decision-making without being granted real influence or power. *Dividing* is characterized by dividing a group of advocates to reduce their effectiveness. Examples include pitting groups against each other, using identity to fragment movements, or selectively including certain members in decision-making while including others. This is a common tactic used against union organizing and coalitions, particularly when they consist of diverse members. *Dulcifying* or appeasing is utilized when small concessions are offered to calm and soothe a situation. When identifying this tactic, one should discern between a compromise and allowances that turn out to be meaningless. *Discrediting* is used to discount an individual or organization to the community at large. The credibility of the individual or organization is questioned through personal attacks or challenging their expertise or qualifications.

Destroying focuses on destroying or undermining another person or group, often through attacks on their reputation or career. When an organization's power is threatened, it may respond through tactics such as legal threats, sabotaging funding sources, or pressuring groups or individuals to remove content that challenges them. *Dealing* involves offering a compromise or giving up something in exchange for something else. Depending on the offer, this can be a victory for the group as long as what they are giving is equal to what they are receiving. Each of these tactics is akin to stopping to smell the poppy fields, and school counselors must recognize the bait and counter these strategies.

Embracing Moral Courage and Defining Your Role in Social Justice

In the face of such opposition, school counselors must cultivate moral courage. Leaders seeking to challenge the "Great and Powerful" status quo must have the courage and fortitude to carve out their role and purpose without succumbing to external pressures. In the context of leadership, moral rebels play an important role in challenging systemic injustice. Moral rebels are "individuals who take a principled stand against the status quo, who refuse to comply, stay silent, or simply go along when this would require that they compromise their values" (Monin et al., 2008, p.77). These individuals aren't concerned about fitting in with the crowd. When they must choose between fitting in and doing the right thing, they will likely choose to do what is right. These leaders resist oppressive systems and align their actions with their core values and beliefs (Sanderson, 2020). Individuals with moral courage possess traits that include a deep concern for others, altruism, empathy, and social responsibility (Sanderson, 2020). These traits drive them to feel the compassion needed to act, even at great personal risk. Moral rebels embody the principles of horizontal morality, challenging oppressive structures that centralize power and perpetuate inequality.

Challenging Oz or any system can appear intimidating and overwhelming if school counselors do not know what their roles should be or how to play to their strengths. Deepa Iyer (2024) outlines ten unique roles in her ecological social change framework. Consider the COVID-19 pandemic, a natural disaster or political unrest that has impacted your region or a human loss that your school community has grieved. In any of these, you likely can think of someone who has played each of these roles (p.42):

- Frontline Responder: organizes resources and communication
- Visionaries: provides hope, direction, and dreams of possibility
- Builders: Implements ideas and the vision
- Disrupters: takes risks to challenge the status quo
- Caregivers: Nurtures those involved, creates a community of care
- Experimenters: Innovates, invents, and helps switch gears
- Weavers: Sees the through-lines that connect ideas and people
- Storytellers: Share and create the stories, provide creativity
- Healers: Tend to pain and trauma from oppression

- Guides: Teach, advise, and counsel from a place of wisdom

The next part of the book will focus on collective action. Before moving forward, take a moment to reflect on the role you will play in recognizing and challenging the various types of oppression. Everyone has a role to play, big or small. Consider your strengths and where your energy and abilities can be best utilized in contributing to the collective effort.

Stepping into Your Ruby Shoes: Use of School Counseling Skills

The counseling microskills you use every day are exactly what is needed to make an impact. These skills are the building blocks for effective communication between a counselor and their client. Challenging systems does not require you to learn from scratch. It is about applying what you already know in new and impactful ways. Listening, questioning, observing, and influencing skills can help school counseling leaders engage in tough conversations. For example, a school counselor's listening skills can help individuals feel heard and create a space for meaningful dialogue even when their actions or decisions are being challenged. Strategic, open-ended, and reflective questions can be used to understand people's underlying beliefs and help them examine the implications of their behaviors and decisions, while observation skills can help them gain deeper insights into emotions and reactions that may not be verbally expressed. Influencing skills such as supportive feedback and gentle confrontation can be applied to explore inconsistencies or mixed messages.

References

American School Counselor Association. (2003). *The ASCA national model: A framework for school counseling programs*. American School Counselor Association.

American School Counselor Association. (2021). *The school counselor and antiracist practices*. Author.

Annamma, S. A. (2018). *The pedagogy of pathologization: Dis/abled girls of color in the school-prison nexus*. Routledge.

Areba, E. M., Taliaferro, L. A., Forster, M., McMorris, B. J., Mathiason, M. A., & Eisenberg, M. E. (2021). Adverse childhood experiences and suicidality: School connectedness as a protective factor for ethnic minority adolescents. *Children and Youth Services Review, 120*, 105637. https://doi.org/10.1016/j.childyouth.2020.105637

Arredondo, P., D'Andrea, M., & Lee, C. (2020). Unmasking white supremacy and racism in the counseling profession. *Counseling Today, 63*(3), 40–42.

Atkins, R., & Oglesby, A. (2018). *Interrupting racism: Equity and social justice in school counseling*. Routledge.

Baum, L. (1900). *The wonderful wizard of Oz*. George M. Hill Company.

Bell, J. (2013). *The four "I's" of oppression*. YouthBuild USA.

Brint, S. (2017). *Schools and societies* (3rd ed.). Stanford University Press. https://doi.org/10.1515/9781503601031

Bryan, J., & Henry, L. (2012). A model for building school-family-community partnerships: Principles and process. Journal of Counseling & Development, 90(4), 408–420. https://doi.org/10.1002/j.1556-6676.2012.00052.x

Burnham, J. J., Fye, H., Jackson, C. M., Ocampo, M., & Clark, L. (2024). A 20-year review of school counselor roles: Discrepancies between actual practice and existing models. Journal of Counselor Preparation and Supervision, 18(2), 1–19.

Camangian, P., & Cariaga, S. (2021). Social and emotional learning is hegemonic miseducation: Students deserve humanization instead. Race Ethnicity and Education, 25(7), 901–921. https://doi.org/10.1080/13613324.2020.1798374

Carson Baggett, H., & Selman, K. (2024). School copaganda in the U.S. South: Tinsel, twinkle, and police-youth programming. Crime, Media, Culture: An International Journal, 21(1), 46–68. https://doi.org/10.1177/17416590241259662

Centers for Disease Control and Prevention. (2024). Youth Risk Behavior Survey data summary & trends report: 2013–2023. U.S. Department of Health and Human Services.

Cheatham, C. B., & Mason, E. C. M. (2021). Using the ACA advocacy competencies as a guide to group work for supporting the career development of school-aged African American males. The Journal for Specialists in Group Work, 46(1), 62–74. https://doi.org/10.1080/01933922.2020.1856253

Chinook Fund. (n.d.). Supplemental information for funding guidelines. https://chinookfund.org/wp-content/uploads/2015/10/Supplemental-Information-for-Funding-Guidelines.pdf

Church, A. (2025, January 3). 20th anniversary celebration of the ASCA National Model at ASCA Conference — Hatching Results - School counselor training. Hatching Results - School Counselor Training. https://www.hatchingresults.com/blog/20th-anniversary-celebration-of-the-asca-national-model-at-asca-conference

Combahee River Collective. (1982). The Combahee River Collective statement. In G. T. Hull, P. Bell-Scott, & B. Smith (Eds.), All the women are white, all the Blacks are men, but some of us are brave (pp. 13–22). Feminist Press.

Cooper, E. F. (2002). The Safe and Drug-Free Schools and Communities Act: Reauthorization and appropriations. In R. V. Nata (Ed.), Progress in Education (Vol. 35, pp. 161–166). Nova Science Publishers.

Devlin, D. N., & Gottfredson, D. C. (2018). The roles of police officers in schools: Effects on the recording and reporting of crime. Youth Violence and Juvenile Justice, 16(2), 208–223. https://doi.org/10.1177/1541204016680405

Drug Policy Alliance. (n.d.). Uprooting the drug war: Education. https://uprootingthedrugwar.org/education/

First Books. (2023). Educators' insights on the conversation around banned books. First Books. https://firstbook.org/wp-content/uploads/2023/10/2023-Banned-Books-Survey-Results.pdf

Foxx, S. P., Saunders, R., & Lewis, C. W. (2020). Race, gender, class and achievement: A culturally responsive approach to urban school counseling. Professional School Counseling, 23(1, Part 2). https://doi.org/10.1177/2156759x19899184

García, O. (2016). Racializing the language practices of U.S. Latinos: Impact on their education. In J. A. Cobas et al. (Eds.), How the United States racializes Latinos: White hegemony and its consequences (pp. 101–115). Routledge.

Gill, B. V. (2022, October 14). E-waste: Five billion phones to be thrown away in 2022. BBC News.

Goldin, S., Duane, A., & Khasnabis, D. (2021). Interrupting the weaponization of trauma-informed practice: "… Who were you really doing the 'saving' for?" The Educational Forum, 86(1), 5–25. https://doi.org/10.1080/00131725.2022.1997308

Gon Ochi, N., Leung, V., Rodriguez, A., & Cobb, J. (2020). *Our rights to resources: School districts are cheating high-need students by funding law enforcement.* American Civil Liberties Union. https://www.aclusocal.org/sites/default/files/aclu_socal_right-to-resources.pdf

González, T. (2021). Race, school policing, and public health. *Stanford Law Review Online, 73*, 180. https://repository.uclawsf.edu/faculty_scholarship/1925

Goodman-Scott, E., Taylor, J. V., Kalkbrenner, M. T., Darsie, J., Barbosa, R., Walsh, K., & Worth, A. (2020). A multivariate analysis of variance investigation of school-level RAMP status across two states. *Counseling Outcome Research and Evaluation, 11*(1), 31–44. https://doi.org/10.1080/21501378.2019.1575696

Heitzeg, N. A. (2014). Criminalizing education: Zero tolerance policies, police in the hallways, and the school-to-prison pipeline. In A. J. Nocella II, P. Parmar, & D. Stovall (Eds.), *From education to incarceration: Dismantling the school-to-prison pipeline* (pp. 17–42). Peter Lang.

Henry, S. M., & Fears, A. (2025). A Rural School-Family-Community Partnership Model With Strategies for Social Justice Leadership. *Professional School Counseling, 29*(1a). https://doi.org/10.1177/2156759X251335950 (Original work published 2025)

Hilts, D., Kratsa, K., Joseph, M., Kolbert, J. B., Crothers, L. M., & Nice, M. L. (2019). School counselors' perceptions of barriers to implementing a RAMP-designated school counseling program. *Professional School Counseling, 23*(1). https://doi.org/10.1177/2156759X19882646

Inniss-Thompson, M. N. (2017). *Summary of discipline data for girls in U.S. public schools: An analysis from the 2013–2014 U.S. Department of Education Office for Civil Rights data collection.* National Black Women's Justice Institute.

Iyer, D. (2024). *Social Change Now: A Guide for Reflection and Connection.* Skinner House Books.

James, N., & McCallion, G. (2013, June). School resource officers: Law enforcement officers in schools. *American Journal of Community Psychology, 63*(3–4), 253–269. https://www.fas.org/sgp/crs/misc/R43126.pdf

Javdani, S. (2019). Policing education: An empirical review of the challenges and impact of the work of school police officers. *American Journal of Community Psychology, 63*(3–4), 253–269. https://doi.org/10.1002/ajcp.12306

Katz, J. H. (1985). The sociopolitical nature of counseling. *The Counseling Psychologist, 13*(4), 615–624. https://doi.org/10.1177/0011000085134005

Kenton, W. (2022). *What is planned obsolescence? How strategy works and examples.* Investopedia. https://www.investopedia.com/terms/p/planned_obsolescence.asp

Kezar, A. (2011). Grassroots leadership: Encounters with power dynamics and oppression. *International Journal of Qualitative Studies in Education, 24*(4), 471–500. https://doi.org/10.1080/09518398.2010.529848

Kezar, A. (2012). Bottom-up/top-down leadership: Contradiction or hidden phenomenon? *The Journal of Higher Education, 83*(5), 725–760. https://doi.org/10.1353/jhe.2012.0030

Khasnabis, D., & Goldin, S. (2020). Don't be fooled, trauma is a systemic problem: Trauma as a case of weaponized educational innovation. *Occasional Paper Series, 2020*(43), 5. https://doi.org/10.58295/2375-3668.1353

Kupchik, A. (2010). *Homeroom security: School discipline in an age of fear* (Vol. 6). NYU Press.

Ladino, R. D. (1996). *Desegregating Texas schools: Eisenhower, shivers, and the crisis at Mansfield high.* University of Texas Press.

Lorde, A. (1983). There is no hierarchy of oppressions. *Bulletin: Homophobia and Education, 14*(3/4), 9.

Marraccini, M. E., & Brier, Z. M. F. (2017). School connectedness and suicidal thoughts and behaviors: A systematic meta-analysis. *School Psychology Quarterly, 32*(1), 5–21. https://doi.org/10.1037/spq0000192

Mason, E. C. M., Dosal-Terminel, D., Kwag, D., Chang, M. K., & Carter, H. (2022). *Radically revising the delivery of the foundational counseling curriculum*. Southern Association of Counselor Educators and Supervisors.

Mason, E., Robertson, A., Gay, J., Clarke, N., & Holcomb-McCoy, C. (2021). Antiracist school counselor preparation: Expanding on the five tenets of the transforming school counseling initiative. *Teaching and Supervision in Counseling, 3*(2), 2. https://doi.org/10.7290/tsc030202

McClure, D. (2022). Book censorship and its threat to critical inquiry in social studies education. *Northwest Journal of Teacher Education, 17*(3), Article 9. https://doi.org/10.15760/nwjte.2022.17.3.9

Merriam-Webster. (n.d.). Oppression. *Merriam-Webster.com dictionary*. https://www.merriam-webster.com/dictionary/oppression

Monin, B., Sawyer, P. J., & Marquez, M. J. (2008). The rejection of moral rebels: Resenting those who do the right thing. *Journal of Personality and Social Psychology, 95*(1), 76.

Morgan, G. (1997). *Images of organization*. Sage Publications.

Mullen, P. R., Stevens, H., & Chae, N. (2019). School counselors' attitudes toward evidence-based practices. *Professional School Counseling, 22*(1), 2156759X18823690.

Nance, J. P. (2015). Students, police, and the school-to-prison pipeline. *Washington University Law Review, 93*, 919. https://openscholarship.wustl.edu/law_lawreview/vol93/iss4/6

Nicola, T. P. (2024). Understanding the recommended student-to-counselor ratio's persistence: An institutional theory perspective. *Journal of Education, 204*(3), 634–648. https://doi.org/10.1177/00220574231182328

Okun, T. (1999). White supremacy culture. https://www.whitesupremacyculture.info/uploads/4/3/5/7/43579015/okun_-_white_sup_culture_2020.pdf

Parks, K. I. (2022). Indigenous boarding schools in the United States and Canada: Potential issues and opportunities for redress as the United States government initiates formal investigation. *American Indian Law Review, 47*(1), 37–70. https://www.jstor.org/stable/27221515

Pearce, C. L., & Conger, J. A. (2003). All those years ago: The historical underpinnings of shared leadership. In C. L. Pearce & J. A. Conger (Eds.), *Shared leadership: Reframing the hows and whys of leadership* (pp. 1–18). SAGE Publications. https://doi.org/10.4135/9781452229539.n1

Peele, T., & Willis, D. J. (2024, June 6). *When California schools summon police*. EdSource.

Powers, J. M. (2008). Forgotten history: Mexican American school segregation in Arizona from 1900–1951. *Equity & Excellence in Education, 41*(4), 467–481. https://doi.org/10.1080/10665680802400253

Price, J. H., & Khubchandani, J. (2019). School firearm violence prevention practices and policies: Functional or folly? *Violence and Gender, 6*(3), 154–167. https://doi.org/10.1089/vio.2018.0044

Purgason, L. L.; Chan, C. D.; & McKibben, B. (2022) "Introduction to the Special Section: Suicide Risk Assessment and Intervention in School Counselor Training," *Teaching and Supervision in Counseling*: Vol. 4 : Iss. 2 , Article 5. https://doi.org/10.7290/tsc04n072

Randick, N. M., Dermer, S., & Michel, R. E. (2018). Exploring the job duties that impact school counselor wellness: The role of RAMP, supervision, and support. *Professional School Counseling, 22*(1). https://doi.org/10.1177/2156759X18820331

Raymond, B. (2010). *Assigning police officers to schools* (Vol. 10). Department of Justice, Office of Community Oriented Policing Services. https://perma.cc/6WPR-LT8Y

Sabella, R. A., & Lerner, S. M. (2019). *School counselor side hustle: How school counselors and educators can monetize their time and talents beyond the classroom.* Sabella & Associates, Inc.

Sanderson, C. A. (2020). *Why we act: Turning bystanders into moral rebels.* Harvard University Press.

Shaver, E. A., & Decker, J. R. (2017). Handcuffing a third grader: Interactions between school resource officers and students with disabilities. *Utah Law Review,* 2017(1), 229.

Simon, J. (2009). *Governing through crime: How the war on crime transformed American democracy and created a culture of fear.* Oxford University Press.

Skrla, L., McKenzie, K. B., & Scheurich, J. J. (Eds.). (2009). *Using equity audits to create equitable and excellent schools.* Corwin Press.

Smith, A. (2015). Heteropatriarchy and the three pillars of White supremacy: Rethinking women of color organizing. In T. D. Dickinson & R. K. Schaeffer (Eds.), Transformations: Feminist pathways to global change (pp. 264–272). Routledge.

Span, C. M., & Anderson, J. D. (2005). The quest for "book learning": African American education in slavery and freedom. In A. L. Cook, & I. Levy (Eds.), *A companion to African American history* (pp. 295–311). Wiley-Blackwell.

Spellman, Q. (2024). Representation and empowerment through school culture and curriculum shifts. In A. L. Cook, & I. Levy (Eds.), *Activating youth as change agents: Integrating youth participatory action research in school counseling* (pp. 142–161). Oxford University Press.

Steen, S., Vannatta, R., & Ieva, K. (2022). *Introduction to group counseling: A culturally sustaining and inclusive framework.* Springer Publishing Company.

Stern, A., & Petrosino, A. (2018). *What do we know about the effects of school-based law enforcement on school safety?* WestEd.

Sue, D. W. (1981). *Counseling the culturally different: Theory and practice.* John Wiley & Sons.

Sue, D. W., & Sue, D. (1977). Barriers to effective cross-cultural counseling. *Journal of Counseling Psychology, 24*(5), 420. https://doi.org/10.1037/0022-0167.24.5.420

Theriot, M. T. (2016). The impact of school resource officer interaction on students' feelings about school and school police. *Crime & Delinquency, 62*(4), 446–469.

Weisburst, E. K. (2019). Patrolling public schools: The impact of funding for school police on student discipline and long-term education outcomes. *Journal of Policy Analysis and Management, 38*(2), 338–365.

Wickens, J. D., & Gupta, A. (2022). Leadership: The act of making way for others. *Studies in Conservation, 67*(sup1), 319–325.

Williams, M. J. (2014). Serving the self from the seat of power: Goals and threats predict leaders' self-interested behavior. *Journal of Management, 40*(5), 1365–1395. https://doi.org/10.1177/0149206314525203

Winninghoff, A. (2020). Trauma by numbers: Warnings against the use of ACE scores in trauma-informed schools. *Occasional Paper Series, 2020*(43), 4. https://doi.org/10.58295/2375-3668.1343

Wisse, B., & Rus, D. (2012). Leader self-concept and self-interested behavior. *Journal of Personnel Psychology 11*(1), 40–48. https://doi.org/10.1027/1866-5888/a000054

Wollenberg, C. (1976). *All deliberate speed: Segregation and exclusion in California schools, 1855–1975.* University of California Press.

Young, I. M. (2008). Five faces of oppression. In G. L. Henderson & M. Waterstone (Eds.), *Geographic thought: A praxis perspective* (pp. 55–71). Routledge.

Part 2

Facing Oz

Chapter 5

Power, Politics, and Influence, Oh My!

In Part 1, we introduced the premise of the book, why it is needed at this time, and reacquainted readers to concepts of leadership. Highlighting emotional intelligence and related concepts, we reminded readers that school counselors are primed for leadership even if what is needed on the path ahead is new and different. Finally, Part 1 closes with a big picture view of systemic oppression, and challenges school counselors to pull back the curtain.

Education, especially public education, is a political matter; therefore, school counseling is also political. The word "political" simply means "of or relating to government," according to Merriam-Webster. The government can be within the school itself, or it can be local, state, or federal. Funding, policy, regulations, and legislation that impact schools all come from a form of government, be it the PTA or the U.S. Congress. The idea that school counselors should or can remain neutral amid a political climate is not only a false narrative, but it is also a dangerous narrative for the marginalized groups school counselors serve— neutrality positions school counselors to be complicit with the white supremacist, oppressive, patriarchal norms of schools.

As authors, we delayed the publication of this book so that we could contextualize it within the timing of the 2024 U.S. Presidential election. Educators across our nation are overwhelmingly challenged and stressed by the political state. In one study, more than half (52%) would not recommend the profession to young adults. (Beshay & Beshay, 2024; *Teaching in Polarized Times,* 2024). We fully recognize that some of our readers and their school communities experience very real censorship and grueling impacts of the current federal, state, and local dictates and policies in their work settings. Likewise, so do many of the counselor educators, supervisors, and coordinators who work to provide training, conduct research, and support practicing and emerging school counselors.

One reason school counselors may struggle to gain traction in their advocacy efforts is their inability to recognize and engage in the political aspect of the work, as they often believe they are supposed to remain neutral. Neutrality messaging exists, and in cases where school counselors serve as mediators, this may be appropriate. However, in the case of advocacy, neutrality is not only

DOI: 10.4324/9781032679174-7

impossible, but it can also be harmful. We explain to readers the importance of getting involved in education politics. School counselors may think they don't have time to advocate or hesitate to dip into political waters. Some may think they are avoiding getting involved in politics; however, it is important to remember that the policies and practices that impact our daily work and students' lives are political. While politics can involve political parties, party labels can be a distraction. School counselors must focus on critical thinking and acting on issues and policies that impact their students. With increasing demands and limited resources, being politically savvy is imperative.

This chapter teaches school counselors how to focus their advocacy efforts within their circle of influence and the pitfalls of focusing on their circle of concern. School counselor leaders benefit from developing working relationships with key stakeholders who can advance their cause. Developing organizational awareness is crucial for navigating the political process in advocacy work. This includes (1) understanding the structural framework of the system they are working in, (2) understanding the interpersonal dynamics within their school or district, and (3) identifying the key decision-makers and influencers. When school counselors have organizational awareness, they can better use their understanding of relationships, hierarchies, and decision-making processes to communicate more effectively. This chapter also introduces the reader to exercises such as a SWOT (strengths, weaknesses, opportunities, and threats) analysis that can enable individuals to assess the internal and external factors that may hinder or facilitate your group's advocacy strategy to refine your goals, objectives, and activities. Additionally, we guide the reader through a "power mapping" analysis to help them identify the levers and relationships within their school or district that they can leverage to gain access to and influence. Readers will also benefit from the advocacy story of Kristy Brooks, a school counselor in Chicago Public Schools. We conclude this chapter by providing examples of how school counselors can work together to understand their circle of influence and develop a sharper sense of organizational awareness.

Pause and Reflect

1 How do you assess the power dynamics in your school or any new organizational system that you enter?
2 How do you shift your own approach once you know where the power lies?
3 What unique skills or knowledge do you have that others do not in your building?
4 In what ways are you most persuasive? (one-on-one, in a presentation, in a small group, etc.)
5 Who are likely partners or allies in your school?

Understanding Power

There are multiple types of power that school counselors should understand. French and Raven (1959) are well known for a framework of six types of power that include:

1 Coercive: Power comes from having the ability to punish others
2 Expert: Power comes from having highly desired knowledge or skills
3 Informational (added later by Raven): Power comes from being able to control information
4 Legitimate: Power comes from a perceived formal role
5 Referent: Power comes from perceived likability or worth
6 Reward: Power comes from having the ability to reward others

District and school administrators, board members, police officers, and elected officials are ones we tend to think of as having legitimate power. These people may have the added advantage of some of the other forms of power but not always. For example, a publicly well-liked board member who is a university researcher, may also have referent and expert power. Whereas a principal who is very close with the superintendent, knows what positions are on the chopping block, and is feared by staff, has coercive and informational power.

Using Political Skills across a Cast of Characters

Leadership often involves encounters with a host of characters who will either help or hinder your efforts at systemic change. Developing political skills will help you navigate the various personalities and their personal agendas. Ferris et al. (2005) defined political skill as the "ability to understand others at work effectively and to use such knowledge to influence others to act in ways that enhance one's personal and organizational objectives" (p.127). Political skills include social astuteness, interpersonal influence, networking ability, and apparent sincerity. Politically skilled school counselors understand social interactions and accurately interpret people's behaviors and motives. Social astuteness is helpful when working with both individuals and navigating the large school context. This skill helps leaders adapt and tailor their language, tone, and approach to their audience, making them more effective in influencing others. When attempting to influence an audience, try to get a picture of who is in the room. Who do they represent? Is it students, families, or a particular community? Pay attention to what their needs are. What challenges do they face, what are their goals, and what pressures are they under? From there, consider what will move them to take action or support our position. Sometimes, this means aligning our message with their values, priorities, or interests. For example, if a school counselor is working with a teacher who is resistant to changing their curriculum but recognizes that the same teacher values engagement, the school counselor might emphasize how these changes will improve student interest and participation. Politically skilled individuals adjust their behavior to fit different situations, helping them get the responses they want from others. They also make effective use of a diverse network of people. We discuss the importance of networking for coalition building in Chapter 7. Lastly, politically skilled leaders are sincere; they come across to others as authentic and trustworthy.

Political skill has been moderately associated with job satisfaction, organizational commitment, burnout, task performance, and overall career success (Chen et al., 2022; Munyon et al., 2015; Summers et al., 2020). Studies found that when roles require high social interaction and relationship management, individuals with political skills tend to perform better in both tasks and in their overall jobs (Bing et al., 2011; Chen et al., 2022). On the other hand, individuals with low political skills may struggle to recognize which influential figures to build social networks with or may have difficulty fostering trust and respect within these networks due to a lack of social awareness (Jaugan & Genuba, 2021). School counselors can develop social astuteness by practicing observing others; this is an easy extension of school counselor training. Be mindful of who dominates conversations and who influences others, just as we would when using our group skills. To improve your networking abilities, engage with people outside of your usual circles, such as school board meetings, committees, teacher groups, and parent groups. Building connections across various groups can help broaden your influence.

Knowing the Land of Oz: Organizational Awareness and Power

Leaders understand the context in which they work. In the words of our colleague, Dr. Renae Mayes, "You can't dismantle what you don't know." Successful leaders observe the culture of their organization and the broader community context to learn both the written and unwritten rules, as well as the power dynamics. Knowing your school's or district's organizational hierarchy is key to effecting change. For example, does your district have assistant or associate superintendents or directors? What are their positions and roles within the organizational hierarchy? At what level in your school or district are decisions being made, and through which decision-making process? Are they centralized at the district level, or do sites have local control? If you are part of a union, knowing how they function within your district, the strength of collective bargaining agreements, and how to engage with union representatives can help you influence organizational processes and structures. Understanding the cogs in the wheel can help you navigate the levers of change effectively.

School districts and P-12 schools are hierarchical, with higher-paid administrators overseeing lesser-paid educators and daily operations. Policymaking is made by elected officials serving on school boards or in the state legislature; this is where the politics are. Those who are least likely to be represented or have their voices heard the least are those for whom the system has made it harder to access administrative and policymaking positions. Commonly, these groups include low-income populations, undereducated persons, undocumented or non-voting individuals, non-native English speakers, minoritized groups relevant to the demographic (e.g., Black or African American, Hispanic or Latino, Indigenous or Native American, LGBTQIA+), and young students. If you are a school counselor who does not live in the community where you work, you have ways to influence policy through the relationships you make and nurture. If you are a school counselor who lives in the community where you work, you have additional and even greater power to influence policy through your vote and relationship building.

School counselors, as leaders, must consider *how, where, and when* to use their power. It is not uncommon for school counselors to feel powerless in the school system because they manage outrageous caseloads, deal with heavy mental health crises, vicarious trauma, and compassion fatigue, and are frequently misunderstood and misused in their professional roles. For these reasons, some school counselor leaders may channel their leadership energy into professional advocacy efforts, whereas advocating for the role also benefits students and communities. Still, when it comes to the students and communities they represent, school counselors do hold power by virtue of their position in the school, their education, and the potential social, political, or economic capital they can leverage to create change.

In Chapter 2, we discussed the complementary relationship between leadership and advocacy, as displayed in earlier versions of the ASCA National Model diamond. It is natural for conversations with school counselors and those in training to include advocacy with leadership. What thrust me (Erin) into my first leadership position at the state school counseling association level was an intense desire to advocate based on my work with students with disabilities. In 2000, any Georgia student receiving special education, gifted, or ESOL services was not counted in the Georgia state funding formula for school counselors. Ultimately, with the work of a core group from our school counseling association, we garnered support from legislators through lobbyists. It took about ten years for the funding formula to be changed and another ten years for the actual funding to be included in the state budget. The entire process was political and involved a staunch group of leaders and advocates who never gave up. Other states have stories like this. A critical point is that I knew nothing about state politics at the beginning, and I didn't consider myself a political person, but I learned what I needed to. I also didn't think I had the time, but again, the issue was important enough that I made the time wherever I could. Others did the same thing alongside me, and we learned together. Still others have helped me update my skills since about how advocacy work changes. I've met many school counselors who have been down a similar path.

If you can imagine the brick road as a roller coaster, then it's easy to also imagine how the ups and downs, twists and turns of power plays and political games can make one nauseous. Nash (2010) writes about several different types of advocates, based primarily on emotional states, which are relatable to school counselors. Nash outlines these five: the radvocate, madvocate, sadvocate, fadvocate, and gladvocate (pp.13–14). The radvocate is an extremist in thought (as in radical), yet always after the root cause analysis. As authors, educators, and researchers, we experience and witness these radical moments in ourselves and in school counselors-in-training when there is an issue we just can't let go of. The madvocate is fueled to action by anger (likely the stage I started at in 2000). The sadvocate uses their vulnerability for persuasion. The fadvocate may appear as a performative ally, seemingly supportive of any and every cause. The gladvocate is welcoming and committed to its own cause, but is open to other perspectives. Nash makes a case for the benefits and challenges of each type of advocate but also states that each advocacy approach may have its unique time, place, and audience.

SWOT Analysis and Power Mapping

Discussions of power and politics in the school arena can be highly charged but there are some strategies for bringing everyone to the table and hearing all perspectives. School counselors can lead their colleagues and coworkers through these conversations by facilitating cooperative conversations with specific strategies. Two of these strategies are the SWOT Analysis and Power Mapping. You may be familiar with either of these but together they can be complementary tools to help you see where to direct your brick road next.

Let's say you have been a long-standing member of a school-level committee and have recently been asked to serve as a new co-chair. You and the co-chair note that some significant district changes (e.g., demographics have shifted, district lines have been redrawn, a new principal and board member have come into play) have happened as the two of you take on your new roles. The committee has been cohesive, but they haven't had to work in the context of this many changes at once. During your annual summer meeting, the two of you decide to include a SWOT analysis as part of the agenda. The SWOT Analysis includes reviewing as a group the school or team's SWOT. This review process aims to aid the group in getting a clear picture of what is working well and where resources (i.e., time, budget, effort) need to go. Dorothy and company would have benefitted from stopping for a SWOT analysis, but it probably wouldn't have added to the storyline. SWOT analyses can help reshape visions, missions, strategic plans, school improvement goals, and school counseling program goals. Makos (2024) suggests going beyond just listing items in each category and also discussing the strength or expansiveness of each item. School staff may need to recognize that some items may be a significant issue for external partners or that a weakness could be turned into an opportunity (Figure 5.1).

SWOT ANALYSIS OF A SCHOOL

SWOT analysis is strategic planning and strategic management technique used to help a person or organization identify Strengths, Weaknesses, Opportunities, and Threats.

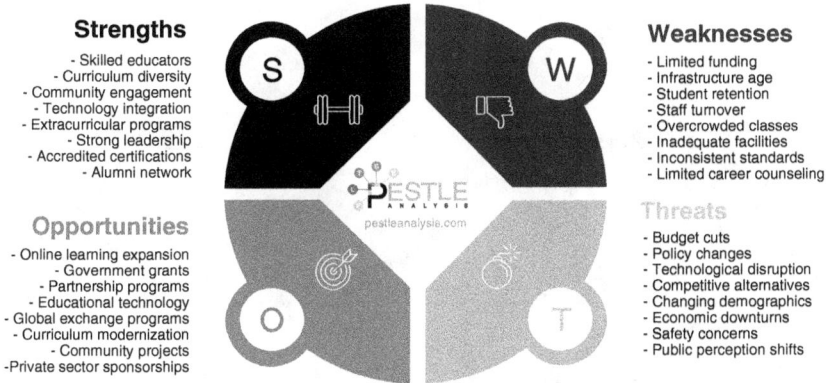

Strengths

- Skilled educators
- Curriculum diversity
- Community engagement
- Technology integration
- Extracurricular programs
- Strong leadership
- Accredited certifications
- Alumni network

Weaknesses

- Limited funding
- Infrastructure age
- Student retention
- Staff turnover
- Overcrowded classes
- Inadequate facilities
- Inconsistent standards
- Limited career counseling

Opportunities

- Online learning expansion
- Government grants
- Partnership programs
- Educational technology
- Global exchange programs
- Curriculum modernization
- Community projects
-Private sector sponsorships

Threats

- Budget cuts
- Policy changes
- Technological disruption
- Competitive alternatives
- Changing demographics
- Economic downturns
- Safety concerns
- Public perception shifts

PESTLE ANALYSIS
pestleanalysis.com

Figure 5.1 SWOT Analysis of a School in 4 Steps from J. Makos

Imagine you are trying to get a new initiative in your school. You recognize that the principal ultimately has the final say, but who else influences that decision? Is it their trusted Assistant Principal, a veteran teacher at the site, or a particular parent group? Who can help, who might resist, and who is on the fence are important factors to consider when strategizing. Power mapping is a simple visual exercise that helps you identify the key decision-makers and influencers in your political environment. It can help you identify the levers and relationships that you can take advantage of to gain access and influence. This includes those who may oppose your plan and who is in the middle and could be brought over to your side. When mapping the key players, you want to determine how much influence they have over the decision (power) and whether or not they support your goal (position). The aim is to identify three primary groups: the individuals who can give you what you want (target), those who will try to stop that from happening (opponents), and those who might help you (allies). Power mapping can help you see the landscape so that you can strategize effectively. An example of a power map can be seen in Figure 5.2.

Influence, Concern, and Control

With large caseloads and numerous responsibilities, some school counselors may wonder how they will find the time and energy to influence change. Other school counselors may recognize the need for changes at their site but are unclear on where to begin. During my (Caroline) first year as a school counselor, I was hired at a new school that was heading into its second year. With no school counseling program in place and the school culture still in its infancy, I wondered,

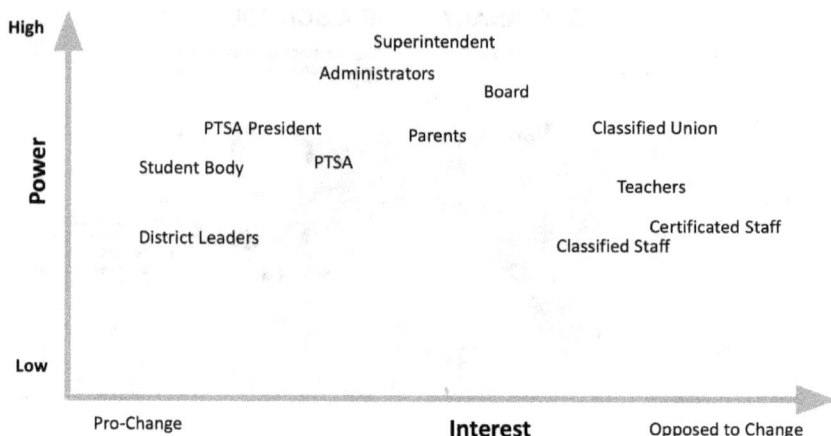

Figure 5.2 Sample Power Map from R. Pianta

"Where do I begin?" Thankfully, my principal sent her entire team of teachers and me to a training in Stephen Covey's *"The Seven Habits of Highly Effective People."* It was there I learned about the Circle of Influence, which transformed how I approached my work and continues to remain relevant today, particularly with regard to systems change and advocacy. The Circle of Influence is a useful framework for understanding where a school counselor can effect change and consists of two Circles. The first inner circle is called your Circle of Influence and consists of things we care about and can impact. The second outer circle is called the Circle of Concern, things we care about but can't control. The energy we put into our Circle of Concern is negative. If you focus on the Circle of Concern (things you can't change) and neglect the Circle of Influence (things you can change), people will see you as ineffective, and over time, your Circle of Influence will get smaller. This can add to feelings of stress, helplessness, and exhaustion because you cannot change anything in the Circle of Concern.

The key is to focus your energy on those things that you can influence, which will enable you to make effective changes. Because you can effect change, others will see you as an effective person, and your influence will grow into areas that were once out of your control. One way to utilize this concept is by identifying key players who have the power to influence opinion or policy and leveraging that influence to help you achieve your desired goal. I would often consider which colleagues had influence at my school and leverage that relationship to help move some of our more resistant colleagues. It helped me think strategically about the relationships that I needed to nurture. The Circle of Influence can also help you focus your energy and resources in areas where you can make the most impact. There will always be a wide range of concerns to deal with as an equity leader, the idea is to focus on those issues at your school, district, or organization that are within your realm of control. By doing so, you will gradually extend your influence into larger areas. As others begin to see you as an effective leader, your influence and impact will grow.

Setting up for The Long Haul

In the next section, readers will explore an example of a school counselor utilizing their leadership and advocacy to impact change. This example highlights how leadership is an evolving set of skills that builds on itself and often takes you to places you might not have imagined, how leadership happens in community, and how authentic leadership is a commitment of effort over time. For this example, it is helpful to have a basic knowledge of the difference between union and right-to-work states, as these designations mean different things for employees, including educators. In the United States, there is about a 50/50 split in unionized and right-to-work states. California, where Caroline works, is a unionized state, but Georgia, where Erin works, is a right-to-work state. In unionized states, educators typically are required to pay a union fee as part of their employment contract. This fee goes toward collective bargaining (i.e., negotiation) and other services that support laborers in the district (*Labor Law & Amp; Unions Overview,* 2024). In right-to-work states, there may be no union, or educators may not be required to pay a union fee as part of their contract. In the case where there is no union, educators may join professional associations. Still, no party or group is doing collective bargaining on behalf of laborers in the school district. There are a variety of opinions about the pros and cons of unions vs. right-to-work. Some educators will tell you unions are helpful, but they don't always negotiate for what school counselors or other educators need, or they become scapegoats in the community. On the other hand, school counselors in right-to-work states may be glad not to be required to pay union dues but have a more challenging time getting their voices heard because no one legally represents them as a group. Union and professional association membership vary greatly from state to state. School counselors are encouraged to be active in advocacy efforts that champion justice for students and with organizations that serve members and protect their rights.

Moving mountains:

Leveraging collective union power to provide all students access to school counselors by Kristy Brooks (personal communication, January 15, 2024) Professional School Counselor, Leader, and Advocate, Founder of the Chicago Teachers' Union Counselors' Committee.

"Have you heard of the old socialist slogan, 'educate, agitate, organize?" It's the blueprint we followed to fight the misuse of school counselors in Chicago Public Schools (CPSs) and win monumental shifts in contract language, giving us the right to do the work we're trained for. When I first started this fight, I didn't have a blueprint. I had a lot of love for my students on the South and West sides of Chicago and a great deal of anger that I, as the sole school counselor in the building, was not accessible to them unless they were in crisis. That love plus anger would eventually turn me into an outspoken advocate. Still, first, I had to learn to channel my frustrations, find a platform to amplify my message, and, most importantly, find a team so I was not fighting alone.

My master's program at the University of Colorado in Colorado Springs trained me in the American School Counselor Association (ASCA) model and prepared me well to understand the intricacies of advocating for my students. Dr. Rhonda Williams, one of my professors, taught lessons that had a lasting impact on how I viewed my role as a school counselor. One lesson I recall involved working with a small group of people, holding onto part of one long rope, and being asked to make different shapes with the rope while blindfolded. It's an activity I still use with my student counseling groups today. One of the meanings I took away from this activity was that to change the shape of things, you often need more than one person. It takes multiple people, who all might control a small piece, to focus on a shared vision to be successful in creating lasting change. This activity also taught me that lasting change isn't quick and easy, which kept me going throughout the decade of work ahead of me.

Fresh out of grad school in 2006, I was ready to tackle my first job as a school counselor on the South side of Chicago. Only after I was hired did I learn that I was also the case manager in charge of Individualized Education Plans (IEPs) and 504 plans, which are legal special education and medical documents. I was scheduling, planning, and running these legal meetings and writing and signing off on legal paperwork. This case manager role, also known as a director of special education, was assigned to about 75% of elementary and middle school counselors in CPS when I entered the district. Many of my school counseling colleagues and I were also assigned other non-counseling duties of test coordinator, lunch and recess monitor, substitute teacher, disciplinarian, records manager, and many more. Some of these duties, like being a case manager who helps families of students with disabilities understand their legal rights, were really important jobs but not what I was trained in or hired to do. Most counselors in my district were school counselors in title only, not in the work we performed. I was discouraged that the school counseling role was nothing like the ASCA model I had prepared for and that this was considered normal in my district. I changed schools a few times in hopes of finding an administrator who would let me do more school counseling, but despite promises to the contrary, faced the same problem at each Chicago public school.

I watched my students struggle with so many traumas: family substance abuse problems, gang issues, violence, assault, grief and loss, not returning to school after they graduated 8th grade, and many more, all while I was stuck doing non-counseling duties each day. No matter how many hours I worked after school or how many lunch breaks I skipped, there was never time to implement any kind of comprehensive counseling program. I responded to crises when they arose but did little to prevent problems by teaching classes, running small groups, or giving much 1-1 short-term counseling support other than to those students in crisis. I coached sports after school without pay to find time to bond with and support some students, but it wasn't a replacement for all students having access to a school counseling program. It was agonizing to have students with significant needs, know I was trained and ready to support them, and not be allowed to because of the mountain of duties assigned that have nothing to do with school counseling. I called and emailed school counseling and special education department heads in my district to voice my concerns but was continuously told that's how it's done in CPSs. Counseling colleagues told me our district lost many good counselors when they left to do school counseling work elsewhere. I didn't want to leave; I wanted to change things. Young people in Chicago deserved access to school counselors, and I decided I wouldn't leave without a fight.

I remember one week in 2010 when I was at work until 7:00 pm each night, sharpening pencils and packing boxes with state testing materials. I decided I needed to educate others on what school counselors should be doing. I wrote an email to a new district school counseling department leader I'd met recently and poured out my disappointment and anger about how misused school counselors were in Chicago. She responded with an idea: form a school counselors' committee with the Chicago Teachers Union (CTU) to bring together other school counselors in the district to advocate for change. I met with our newly elected union leaders and began discussing the contrast between appropriate school counseling duties and what we were doing in Chicago's public schools. The "educate" piece of the blueprint had to start at the beginning, within our union, our schools, our district, and our communities.

Our first CTU Counselors' Committee event was a Chicago school counselors' social promoted by our union and local universities with school counseling programs. The union provided food, and we lined up speakers from state counseling associations and CTU leadership. I spoke at this event and appealed to my colleagues to join our new union Counselors' Committee to change how Chicago misused its counselors. Those who worked in CPS schools understood the urgency with which I spoke because they faced the same frustrations. It's not difficult to agitate a crowd of colleagues who face the same problem day in and day out. At that fired-up social, I met the first few members of our committee and my team, who fought with me each step of the way for the next ten years.

Our CTU Counselors' Committee met with the CPSs' district negotiating team in 2012 to voice our concern over counselors being misused in Chicago. They listened and told us we were doing great work but that the district didn't have the money to hire more counselors. Although CTU went on strike in 2012 and won important things for our students and our union, we didn't win any contract language to make school counselors more accessible to CPS students. It turns out that educating the district people in charge about the misuse of school counselors and asking them nicely to correct the problem didn't get us anywhere. We spent

Figure 5.3 Chicago public school students and community members on the strike line

the next four years upping our "educate" and "agitate" game by writing op-eds that were printed in newspapers, speaking at board of education meetings, meeting monthly with heads of district counseling and special education departments, surveying counselors and collecting data on time spent in non-counseling duties, making and sharing flyers with infographics of our data, and speaking at community events sponsored by our union. We also had to educate ourselves on how the contract negotiating process worked and how early we had to prepare to put us in a better position next time. In addition to very long workdays, the added stress of data collecting and multiple monthly meetings was taking its toll on our small team of CTU Counselors' Committee members. When the next contract was up for negotiation in 2016, we needed a win ... and we got one (Figure 5.3).

A few members of our CTU Counselors' Committee joined the CTU bargaining team for the 2016 contract negotiations. We spoke with CTU members about our proposals for a student-to-counselor ratio and job duty protections in the next contract. When it came time to bargain about our proposals with the district bargaining team, we wrote and shared a proposal defense that included a data overview of what struggles our youth in Chicago were facing, what school counselors were spending their time on in CPSs (it was mostly non-counseling duties), and what the data showed about how school counselors can help. The district responded with loose contract language about administrators trying to assign appropriate school counseling duties to counselors, but we knew it wasn't enough. Only after a vote of 25,000 CTU members to move forward with a strike did the district offer us better contract language. In the new offer, *school counselors were allowed to refuse the added role of case manager, director of special education,* starting the following school year. This was a massive win for the majority of elementary and middle school counselors in Chicago who were forced to take on this added job. Our union did not go on strike in 2016, but the

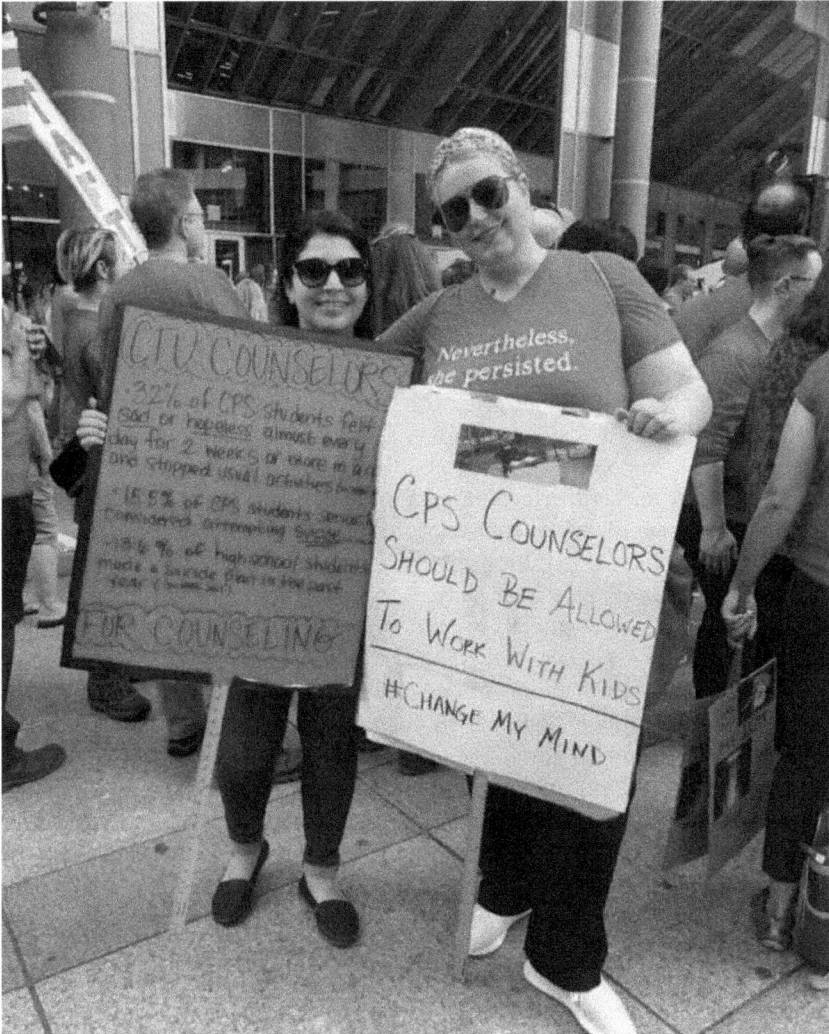

Figure 5.4 Chicago public school counselors on strike with the Chicago Teachers Union

threat of the powerful CTU organizing and voting to give our bargaining team that power to call one forced the district's bargaining team to agree to partially protect our school counseling duties (Figure 5.4).

Our CTU Counselors' Committee continued to educate, agitate, and organize for the next three years. We spoke out against our crushing caseloads, sometimes more than 1,000 students to one school counselor, and still being assigned various non-counseling duties. We did interviews with local and national newspapers and TV shows, spoke at more board of education meetings, marched at rallies, made t-shirts, and handed out more infographics flyers. Some of our counseling colleagues hesitated to refuse the case management role as that was all they knew while working as a Chicago school counselor. Supporting one another as we moved forward and enforced the new contract language was key. We created online spaces to connect with CTU counseling colleagues across our district. We pushed the district to allow counselors to meet up in geographical groups periodically during the school day as Counselor Professional Learning Communities to learn from each other's best practices and discuss common concerns. A district school counseling department leader collected meaningful city-wide data that showed how widespread the misuse of school counselors was and highlighted the meaningful work counselors did when we were allowed to do counseling in Chicago schools. All of this work paved the way for our next round of contract demands.

When the next contract negotiations began in 2019, we again submitted proposals in line with ASCA-recommended ratios and appropriate duties for school counselors. We wrote another 50-page data-driven proposal defense and presented it to the district's bargaining team. This time, we added videos showing the impact of school counselors in our schools. We passed around Talk Tickets, a student self-referral for school counseling support, to the district bargaining team made up mostly of lawyers. After no concessions on our contract proposals and little movement on most of our unions' proposals overall, our expertly organized CTU once again voted to give our bargaining team the ability to call for a strike. This time around, we had to use it. The CTU and Service Employees International Union put 36,000 teachers, support staff, and teaching assistants on strike for 14 days—the long days of marching, picketing, bargaining, and rallying paid off. In addition to getting nurses and social workers in all of our schools, we finally won stronger language that a principal must assign school counselors responsibilities in line with the ASCA Model; no more prep teaching, recess and lunch duty, subbing, records, and test coordination. We also won small concessions on adding additional counselors at some schools. After this new contract language was fought and won in 2019, my school counseling job duties in Chicago were finally what they should be (Figure 5.5).

As with any monumental shift in a large system, turning around the role of a school counselor within a district was not quick or easy. Personally, I was never comfortable in the spotlight, but I had to speak out to utilize the media to help spread our message. The risk of speaking out against the district I worked for was real; I lost my counseling position twice before being tenured and was threatened by administrators with disciplinary action for advocating for students' rights. In counseling sessions, I teach my students to be brave to facilitate growth, and I had to summon my courage to continue the cause no matter the cost. My least favorite counseling class was about statistics and using data, but I learned to collect and package it to add evidence to our narratives. There is no way I could have educated so many, agitated so thoroughly, or organized so efficiently without the backing of the mighty Caucus of Rank and File Educators (CORE) CTU

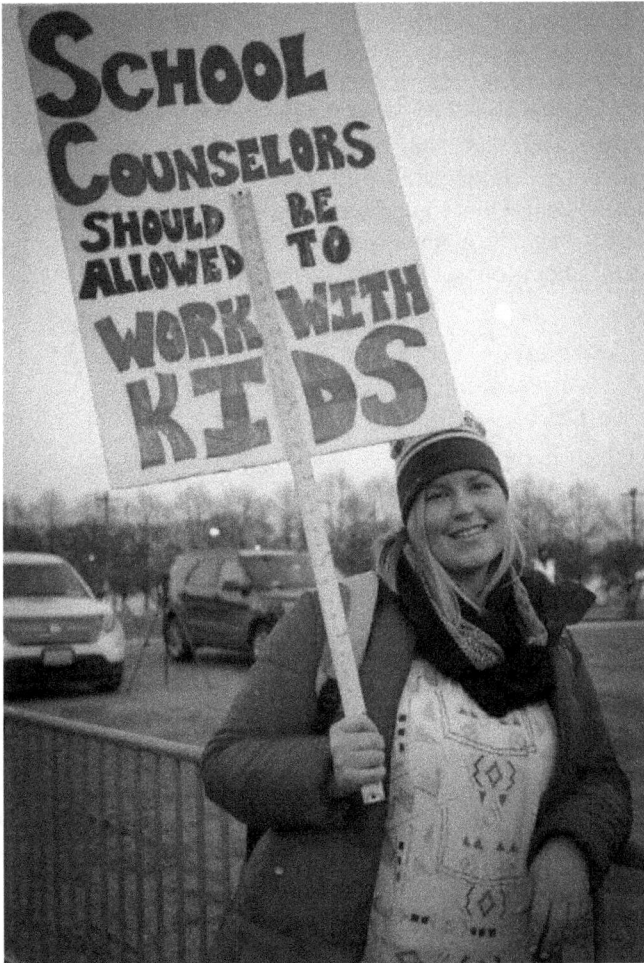

Figure 5.5 Kristy Brooks of the counseling committee of the Chicago Teachers Union.

and four of my Chicago counseling colleagues: John Casey, Amanda Szaraz, Katie Shoemaker, and Lissette Flores. We are the fighting five who worked tirelessly for a decade to change things for the Chicago youth we work with daily and believe in steadfastly. The work will continue; our contract needs a 1:250 student-to-counselor ratio and clearly listed appropriate and inappropriate job duties. We need to support counselors who want to enforce the contract language but might not feel comfortable doing so. More dedicated CTU Counselors have joined committee meetings and taken on leadership positions to bring this fight into the future.

When I think back to the start of my career, with those 12-hour workdays spent in constant frustration and buried in non-counseling duties, I recall how alone I felt. A few years later, a small group of counselors was dedicated to attending meetings and making plans for change. A few years ago, I remember marching with tens of thousands of educators in downtown Chicago, on strike and giving up pay indefinitely, to fight for the schools Chicago students deserve. I wish all school counselors could find solidarity in their colleagues, unions, and communities to move the mountains necessary to clear a path for all students to have access to school counselors.

Types of Advocacy

Committee Level

Committee work is a logical and realistic step for many school counselors to enact leadership and increase their organizational awareness. At a minimum, school counselors should be on their local school leadership team, providing feedback and insight to administrators based on their unique training and perspective. Committee work can be done at various levels and in various spaces, including at the local school, the school district, within the school counselor association or union, or in the community. In today's world, we encourage counselors to be strategic about the committees they agree to be on; aiming for how to do the most good for students while also holding boundaries to protect themselves from burnout.

Volunteer Level

The volunteer level is ideal for (a) those who have limited time or experience, and (b) for starting out with a type of advocacy that is brand new. Not everyone can make a weekly or monthly commitment or has the skills or knowledge needed for extended advocacy work. The volunteer level can allow you to shadow someone in an advocacy activity that you would like to learn more about or ease your way into. Examples of this might be serving as a panelist or speaker at a school board meeting on behalf of your district area community or school counselors, or taking a two-hour block of time one weekend to make calls or find research on an issue your local union or association needs support for.

Legislative Level

Legislative advocacy is an intimidating type of advocacy for many school counselors. However, it is necessary to know the sociopolitical landscape in which students, families, communities, and schools exist now more than ever. Legislative advocacy benefits from some of the natural leadership skills that school counselors already possess (e.g., relationship building, active listening) and often requires learning new ones (e.g., how to track bills, understanding legislative terms). Knowledge alone is step number one. Consider what you do or do not know from this list:

- Your polling locating
- Names of your state legislators and how to contact them
- Names of your congressional legislators and how to contact them
- The legislative cycle or session, when bills are drafted, read, and voted on
- Which legislators sit on education, youth, or mental health-related committees
- If your state association has legislative priorities, a day at the capitol, or a lobbyist
- Which legislators have successfully passed education, youth, or mental-health-related bills?

Stepping into Your Ruby Shoes: Use of School Counseling Skills

Most school counselors have dispositions and skills that provide a foundation for navigating power, politics, and generating influence. Although graduate training programs may not explicitly state this, it is indeed true. Power, politics, and influence are, at their core, about closely observing and understanding human behavior and strategically managing relationships. The skills used in observing, active listening, reflecting, and building rapport with students or their families to provide counseling services can be equally, though differently, useful in creating systemic change.

References

Beshay, & Beshay. (2024, April 14). *What's it like to be a teacher in America today?* Pew Research Center. https://www.pewresearch.org/social-trends/2024/04/04/whats-it-like-to-be-a-teacher-in-america-today/

Bing, M. N., Davidson, H. K., Minor, I., Novicevic, M. M., & Frink, D. D. (2011). The prediction of task and contextual performance by political skill: A meta-analysis and moderator test. *Journal of Vocational Behavior, 79*, 563–577.

Chen, H., Jiang, S., & Wu, M. (2022). How important are political skills for career success? A systematic review and meta-analysis. *The International Journal of Human Resource Management, 33*(19), 3942–3968. https://doi.org/10.1080/09585192.2021.1949626.

Ferris, G. R., Treadway, D. C., Kolodinsky, R. W., Hochwarter, W. A., Kacmar, C. J., Douglas, C., & Frink, D. D. (2005). Development and validation of the political skill inventory. *Journal of Management, 31*, 126–152.

French, J. R. P., Jr., & Raven, B. (1959). The bases of social power. In D. Cartwright (Ed.), *Studies in social power* (pp. 150–167). Univer. Michigan.

Jaugan, J. C. S., & Genuba, R. L. (2021). *A causal model on political skills of public secondary school teachers. Multidisciplinary International Journal of Research and Development, 2*(3), 1–29. https://www.mijrd.com/papers/v2/i3/MIJRDV2I30001.pdf

Labor Law & Unions Overview. (2024, July 10). LawInfo.com. https://www.lawinfo.com/resources/labor-law/labor-law-unions-overview.html

Makos, J. (2024, June 24). *A SWOT analysis of a school in 4 steps.* PESTLE Analysis. https://pestleanalysis.com/how-to-do-swot-analysis-of-your-school/

Munyon, T. P., Summers, J. K., Thompson, K. M., & Ferris, G. R. (2015). Political skill and work outcomes: A theoretical extension, meta-analytic investigation, and agenda for the future. *Personnel Psychology, 68*, 143–184.

Nash, R. J. (2010). "What is the bnest Way to be a social Justice advocate?": Communication strategies for effective social justice advocacy. *About Campus, 15*(2), 11–18. https://doi.org/10.1002/abc.20017

Summers, J. K., Munyon, T. P., Brouer, R. L., Pahng, P., & Ferris, G. R. (2020). Political skill in the stressor-strain relationship: A meta-analytic update and extension. *Journal of Vocational Behavior, 118*, 103372.

Teaching in polarized times. (2024, July 11). American Federation of Teachers. https://www.aft.org/ae/summer2024/krueger

Chapter 6

The Wickedness of Resistance

This chapter represents a pivotal point in the leadership journey. Although in Chapters 4 and 5 we presented many obstacles to systemic change, here we present perhaps the main obstacle to leadership, resistance. Resistance is to be expected. We also suggest that sometimes, we ourselves, as school counselor leaders, present the greatest resistance. Others get in our way, but we also get in our own way. While resistance may often be wicked, it can sometimes be a helpful teacher.

In *Leadership & Liberation*, Dr. Seán Ruth highlights that influence comes down to leadership that is "being strategic, being intentional, and being persistent" (p.239). Throughout the book, Ruth emphasizes that leadership is rooted in relationships, noting many skills counselors possess that have already been mentioned, such as active listening, use of minimal encouragers, paraphrasing, and reflecting. Further, he realistically outlines four steps in managing resistance to change:

1 surfacing the resistance
2 respecting the resistance
3 exploring the resistance
4 staying close and listening

Ruth advocates for understanding that resistance to change is an expected and natural part of relationship-building that leaders should learn to handle, rather than be afraid of.

Knowing why some advocacy efforts provoke opposition can help school counselors lead organizational change. School counselors are naturally collaborative, so resistance may not be a comfortable energy to navigate. However, to be an effective leader, one must understand the nature and function of resistance. First, individual, group, and organizational resistance are defined and differentiated. Next, four types of resistance are explained, categorized as intentional or unintentional and covert or overt. Understanding the predictable motivations and behaviors of resistance allows school counselors to plan and strategize accordingly.

DOI: 10.4324/9781032679174-8

Recognizing how one responds to conflict is essential to facing resistance. To understand conflict, we revisit emotional intelligence from Chapter 3 and prompt readers to examine their emotional responses to resistance and conflict. Our responses can escalate or de-escalate a conflict, depending on how we manage emotions. To de-personalize resistance and conflict, school counselors must understand that many factors beyond the current situation influence people's behaviors. Individuals can avoid taking resistance personally by understanding underlying factors such as learned and cultural responses. Learned responses to conflict are the behaviors and strategies individuals develop through personal experiences and observations of how others handle conflict. These responses are what have worked for the individual in the past, and they can be positive or negative. Cultural responses to conflict refer to how conflict is handled within a particular culture or society. Different cultures have varying norms, beliefs, and expectations around conflict resolution; some value directness while others value harmony. Cultural messages shape our understanding of relationships and influence how we name, frame, assign blame, and make efforts to resolve conflict. Ill-prepared leaders may see conflict as an obstacle or a negative response to change and become conflict-avoidant. However, leaders hoping to enact change in schools must lean into conflict and see it as an opportunity to work toward change for the sake of students. Conflict can become an opportunity for engaging in conversation with the goal of achieving mutual understanding. Anticipating and de-personalizing the resistance is half the battle. From there, school counselors must use techniques to navigate the resistance without getting sidetracked from their goal.

We explore various methods for dealing with resistance to change, including education and communication, participation and involvement, facilitation and support, negotiation and agreement, manipulation and co-optation, as well as explicit and implicit coercion. This chapter covers how to choose the most suitable approach for a given situation, the relative benefits of each approach, and how school counselors can effectively apply their counseling skills.

Pause and Reflect

1 What is your first thought when faced with resistance?
2 What is your first emotion when faced with resistance?
3 What happens in your body?
4 Do you have a typical course of action?
5 How might you respond differently based on who the person is?
6 How comfortable are you in general, with resistance or conflict?
7 What family influences exist in your ways of dealing with resistance?
8 What does healthy conflict look like to you?

Sources of Resistance: Individual, Group, and Organizational Resistance

O'Connor (1993) says, "when everyone within an organization responds to change easily, then this is as fortunate as the situation is unusual" (p.30). Likewise, in his book *Leadership & Liberation: A Psychological Approach*, Seán Ruth notes that leaders should expect attacks as part of their role. Ruth explains that attacks on leaders are not always about the individual factors of the leaders themselves, but more often a result of the systemic factors in which the leaders operate. Identifying the source of resistance is a critical first step; sometimes, this is obvious, but not always. When there are multiple sources of resistance (e.g., different staff or parent groups) or they are not easy to identify (i.e., you receive feedback through a survey, but it is anonymous), school counselors are wise not to act without identifying all the correct sources.

Janis (1982) suggests there are three types of resistance: individual, group, and organizational, and each is influenced by a combination of personal and systemic factors. Individual resistance occurs when employees resist change based on their unique perceptions, personalities, and needs. The context of resistance must be understood before the resistance itself can be understood. Consider how the Scarecrow, the Tin Woodman, and the Lion each initially resisted the idea of approaching Oz based on their perceptions of themselves; it took others to persuade them that they were worthy and capable. It might be worth considering that when facing resistance from those in your group, it could be because they don't know if they are capable or worthy of something you are asking them to do, rather than simply think they are being hard-headed. This could be a psychological factor of resistance. If members of your group have concerns about the time and energy commitment (economic) being asked or if they will need to spend time away from family (social), then these are other potential factors of resistance. Again, we refer you to Ruth's steps earlier and suggest that school counselors are well-suited for all of them, especially steps 3 and 4—exploring the resistance and staying close and listening.

As a school counselor leader, despite our skills, it may still be challenging to deal with resistant individuals. However, it is not that unlike dealing with resistant students if we keep in mind something underlies the resistance and that we can usually address it. The following three levels from Maurer (n.d.) present three levels individuals typically have for resisting change.

Level 1: *"I don't get it."* This cognitive response comes from a lack of understanding the need for change or information related to the change.
Level 2: "I don't like it." This emotional response comes from fearing the outcome or consequences of change.
Level 3: *"I don't like you."* This interpersonal response may indicate a lack of trust or confidence in the leader.

Multiple people's resistance can create group resistance, sometimes resembling a phenomenon known as groupthink. Most school counselors or P-12 educators have witnessed numerous examples of student groupthink in school settings; these instances often occur in classrooms, on playgrounds, in cafeterias, during sporting events, and also online. When it comes to educators in a system, there may be certain groups (e.g., administrators, educators, school counselors, other staff, parents, community partners) that carry more status or set the norms. Such groups may drive resistance throughout the system. It's helpful to pay attention to who these groups are, how they interact, and the state of their cohesiveness. Job security, habit, and economic factors greatly influence individual resistance. Shared experiences and common goals or values can create group resistance.

Organizational resistance is an organization's tendency to resist change and desire to maintain the status quo. Companies that suffer from organizational resistance become inflexible and are unable to adapt to environmental or internal demands for change. Some signs of organizational resistance include internal power struggles, poor decision-making processes, and bureaucratic organizational structures (Janis, 1982).

Remembering Toto in the Basket

Throughout *The Wonderful Wizard of Oz*, Dorothy holds fast to Toto in a basket, which can represent our values as leaders. Dorothy and Toto have a symbiotic and faithful relationship, but there are times when Toto is in danger, and the Wicked Witch wants to separate him from Dorothy. Leaders repeatedly face forms of resistance that work to challenge their values, so the most important practice is first recognizing when this is happening. Resistance can come from outside your organization or from within, so it's also important not to be surprised if it comes from an unexpected source, such as your boss or a close coworker.

Ryan Holiday, author of several books related to Stoic philosophy, wrote *The Obstacle is the Way: The Timeless Art of Turning Trials into Triumph*. In the introduction, he writes, "The obstacle in the path becomes the path. Never forget, within every obstacle is an opportunity to improve our condition" (p.7). Holiday also frequently quotes Marcus Aurelius, who said, "What stands in the way, becomes the way. The impediment to action advances action." Obstacles or resistance can be instrumental in reconnecting us to our values, identifying our true allies, or pointing us to the work most worth doing. Countless times, we, as authors of this book, can point to obstacles (e.g., events, circumstances, people) in our paths that made it possible to write it.

Which Witch: Types of Resistance

It's important to remember, as school counselors, that when taking on leadership positions, others may see you becoming part of "the system." Resistance,

Types of Resistance to Change		
	Covert	
Unconscious	Survivor	Saboteur	Conscious
	Zombie	Protester	
	Overt	
based on the work of Carol A O'Connor 1993 © 2014 SkillsYouNeed.com		

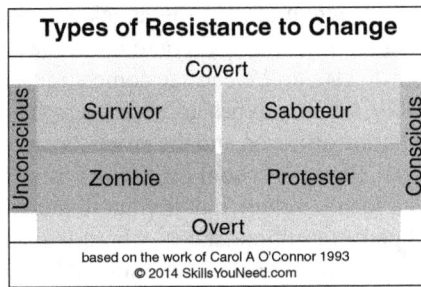

Figure 6.1 O'Connor Types of Resistance to Change

therefore, should be anticipated, not as a response to us personally but as a response to the system. When considering the types of personalities in a school, district, or community, school counselors know there is a range. That said, there are also types of resistance to look for. O'Connor (1993) divides resistance into four types based on behavior: covert or overt, unconscious or conscious. Covert resistance is harder to detect and happens behind the scenes, whereas overt resistance is obvious and out in the open. Conscious resistance is pointedly motivated, whereas unconscious resistance may be known to the leader but not to the resistor. As Figure 6.1 shows, at each intersection is a specific profile: the survivor, the saboteur, the zombie, or the protestor. The survivor goes completely undetected to themselves or anyone else, contributing nothing to change, but often fully believing they are helping out. The saboteur knowingly works in the shadows to prevent change or intentionally ignores it. The zombie may "talk the talk," but they cannot "walk the walk" and will just continue to do what they've always done. The protester is the open and obvious resistor who may be annoying, but is usually the easiest to identify.

O'Connor further suggests using the following five questions (p.34) to understand where resistance may come from. They suggest that if the answer is "no" to any of these questions, that is the area to explore for varied perspectives.

1 Do those asked to implement the change realize it is based on a serious need?
2 Do those involved describe or understand the need in the same way?
3 Is there a common end-goal for change to which everyone agrees?
4 Does everyone believe the goal is attainable and helps the company?
5 Is there unanimous confidence in the person selected to manage the change?

When the Resistance Is Extra Wicked

Resistance of an aggressive kind is in another category and may be an attack. Ruth (2006) breaks down attacks on leaders into five basic types and provides suggestions for each: (1) the leader is attacked for making a mistake; (2) the attacker wants the leader's attention; (3) the attacker is testing the leader; (4) the attacker is intentionally projecting pain onto the leader; and (5) the leader is attacked as a threat to the system. We can see some similarities between Ruth's types of attacks and O'Connor's types of resistance to change, particularly between the attacker wanting attention and the protestor, and the attacker project- ing pain and the saboteur. Because school counselors often represent something larger (e.g., a system, an idea, a value), that is what is sometimes being attacked. We have seen this happen in multiple states, where legislation has challenged school counseling through attacks on social-emotional learning (Abrams, 2023), threatened to replace school counseling positions with chaplains in several states (Reinbold, 2024) and in some, did, or targeted them in state wars on gender and sexuality (Voght, 2022). These situations may perpetuate a Toxic Triangle, which we discussed in Chapter 2. It goes without saying that in all these battles, the students have the most to lose.

When We Are the Resistance

Most of the time, we'd like to think that others are the resistance we are up against, but we can be the wicked ones, and the resistance can come from within. It may not be easy to see or acknowledge, but our own resistance can manifest as complicity, apathy, passivity, or even aggression. When those closest to us express concern or notice changes, we need to let them step in. In Baum's *The Wonderful Wizard of Oz*, the poppy fields distract and put Dorothy and the Lion to sleep, costing precious time on their journey to the Wizard. It took Scarecrow, the Tin Woodman, and thousands of mice to move them from the fields so they could wake up.

After the results of the 2024 election, white school counselors or scholars like me (Erin) should expect our BIPOC colleagues, and those who are multiply marginalized, to be more than tired of us; they are exasperated. Coalition building will require greater effort on our part because we haven't done our part as a group in the past. As "Glindas," our version of "good" is equivalent to white feminism that amounts to sugar-coated, performative, standing-on-the-sidelines niceness instead of authentic, action-oriented solidarity. Western and white peoples' his- tory is rife with colonization and religious persecution, and few universally cel- ebrated examples of community building. White feminist culture is still built on the characteristics of white supremacy, like perfectionism and power hoarding (Okun, 1999). We may laugh at pop culture expressions of this in movies like *Mean Girls,* but we should be keenly aware of its reality in the widespread use of relational aggression in many settings.

White school counselors would do well to reacquaint themselves with Helms' model of white racial identity development (Helms, 1990) and accept that we are not as multi-culturally competent as we want to be (Placeres et al., 2022).

White school counselors and those with other privileges must keep tendencies for saviorism in check (Jackson & Rao, 2022). We refer readers to discussions of cultural and intellectual humility in Chapter 3. Social justice work does not make room for recognition; it demands room for restitution and reparations (see A Justice Philosophy for School Counseling in Chapter 1).

Furthermore, we see a sort of resistance in the way of conformity to executive orders and messaging from the federal administration. Numerous people and organizations engage in a phenomenon called "anticipatory obedience," in which they comply ahead of any real threat (Snyder, 2017, p.18). It is as if they actively choose to lie down in the poppy fields, expecting to be overcome, or with a preference for docility. This poses risks to school counselors and students if administrators or others are unaware of the consequences of what they are complying with.

Strategies for Dealing with Resistance

Similar to Maurer's three levels, Kotter and Schlesinger (2008) identify four reasons that people resist change: low tolerance for change, fear of losing something of personal value ("I don't like it."), misunderstanding the reason for change ("I don't get it."), or disbelief in the need for change in the organization ("I don't like you."). The authors then present six common strategies for dealing with resistance based on their analyses of many organizational changes. Starting with education and ending with coercion, these strategies range from least intensive to most intensive. For school counselor leaders, all approaches from education and communication to negotiation and agreement are reasonable and familiar in most situations because we have valuable skills to use. When it comes to manipulation and coercion, however, these may be less familiar from a counselor's perspective, more challenging, and possibly unethical, so they should be avoided (Figure 6.2).

The Push-Pull influencing styles (Folkman, 2022) allow school counselors to adapt their style based on who they are influencing and what they hope to gain. If you are the leader, a push style emphasizes your agenda, is ordered around a set of rules or standards, and is likely to be more prescriptive in how work gets done. The pull style is more about others' agendas, emphasizes motivation, and provides more room for flexibility in how work is done. Depending on the people you are leading, one style may work better than the other. However, Folkman (2022) and his research colleague discovered that in many corporate settings, a combination of push and pull was preferred by most employees. A complementary practice that is well documented in the counseling literature, is that of broaching race, ethnicity, and culture (Day-Vines, et al., 2007). Young, Day-Vines and additional scholars tie broaching to leadership, noting that school counselors must broach with high degrees

Methods for dealing with resistance to change

Approach	Commonly used in situations	Advantages	Drawbacks
Education + communication	Where there is a lack of information or inaccurate information and analysis.	Once persuaded, people will often help with the implementation of the change	Can be very time consuming if lots of people are involved
Participation + involvement	Where the initiators do not have all the information they need to design the change, and where others have considerable power to resist.	People who participate will be committed to implementing change, and any relevant information they have will be integrated into the change plan.	Can be very time consuming if participators design an inappropriate change
Facilitation + support	Where people are resisting because of adjustment problems.	No other approach works as well with adjustment problems.	Can be time consuming, expensive, and still fail
Negotiation + agreement	Where someone or some group will clearly lose out in a change, and where that group has considerable power to resist.	Sometimes it is a relatively easy way to avoid major resistance.	Can be too expensive in many cases if it alerts others to negotiate for compliance
Manipulation + co-optation	Where other tactics will not work or are too expensive	It can be a relatively quick and inexpensive solution to resistance problems.	Can lead to future problems if people feel manipulated.
Explicit + implicit coercion	Where speed is essential, and the change initiators possess considerable power	It is speedy and can overcome any kind of resistance	Can be risky if it leaves people mad at the initiators

Methods for dealing with resistance to change | Source: Kotter and Schlesinger's 2008 article "Choosing Strategies for Change"

Figure 6.2 Kotter & Schlesinger Methods for Dealing with Resistance to Change

of frequency and intentionality to create change for students and in systems (Young, et al., 2025).

Negotiation and conflict resolution are other strategies for dealing with resistance. Barsky (2017) emphasizes the importance of being prepared for negotiation and approaching conflict resolution. Preparation can allow school counselor leaders to assess their heart-brain balance, EI functioning, consider multi-cultural contexts and differences, identify preferred outcomes, and plan ahead.

Consider these Questions for Preparing to Negotiate a Conflict

"What is the nature of the difference underlying the conflict?" (p.138)
    "How should cultural diversity be taken into account?" (p.139)
    "How is the social context of the conflict affecting the parties and their choices for resolution?" (p.139)

In school communities, relationships can be easy and casual. Negotiation is a process of attempting to reach an agreement and thus may benefit from more formality, including setting (i.e., scheduled time in an office vs. impromptu in the hallway), written agendas, goals, notes, and finalized commitments

(Barsky, 2017). It may also be helpful to have a mediator or third party for facilitation. Furthermore, in the bargaining process, it is essential to be clear about your goals but also to be flexible in your approach to resolution, as it is possible to learn new information or change your perspective on the problem (Barsky, 2017).

Energy and Time for Dealing with Resistance

Facing resistance is a time and energy drain, especially if you are fighting it on a consistent basis. Similarly, leadership and advocacy are not easy. Nash (2010) says, "The first rule of transformational leadership is this: Things will most likely go wrong before they go right." Taking breaks at every stage is necessary. I (Erin) have a Banksy-inspired sign next to my desk that reads, "If you get tired, learn to rest, not to quit." Such is the case with resistance; expect it to always be there and keep working through it.

School counselors, especially those who hold marginalized identities, need to consider the amount of energy and time they invest in dealing with resistance. In fact, school counselors of marginalized identities may wish to engage in their own campaigns of resistance using Tricia Hersey's model of *Rest is Resistance*. Rest in all its forms can demonstrate that systems grounded in imperialism, capitalism, and oppressive characteristics of white supremacy culture, like schools, will not perpetuate the narrative that educators and students are not enough simply by being who they are. This includes setting very clear and firm boundaries about when they arrive at and leave campus, who is informally directed to them, when they check email or respond to phone calls, and how many and which committees they serve on (i.e., not being tokenized). We encourage readers to soak up Chapter 8.

Stepping into Your Ruby Shoes: Use of School Counseling Skills

To be a leader is to deal with resistance. Even to be a counselor is to deal with resistance. Resistance is all around us in many forms. As counselors, we have been trained to meet our students where they are, which means helping them at their current stage of development. The same rings true for those resistant to change. Our nature, dispositions, training, and, hopefully, our values, set us up better than some others for understanding and managing resistance. Reframe resistance not as something that can get in your way, but as something you have the skills to work through.

References

Abrams, Z. (2023). *Teaching social-emotional learning is under attack*. American Psychological Association. https://www.apa.org/monitor/2023/09/social-emotional-learning-under-fire.

Barsky, A. E. (2017). *Conflict resolution for the helping professions* (3rd ed.). New York, NY: Oxford University Press.

Folkman, J. (2022). To get results, the best leaders both push and pull their teams. *Harvard Business Review Digital Articles*, 1–6.

Helms, J. (1990). *Black and white racial identity: Theory, research, and practice*. Praetor Publishers.

Hersey, T. (2022). *Rest is resistance*. Little Brown Spark.

Holiday, R. (2014). *The obstacle is the way*. Portfolio.

Jackson, R., & Rao, S. (2022). *White women: Everything you already know about your own racism and how to do better*. Penguin Books.

Janis, I. (1982). *Groupthink: Psychological studies of policy decision and fiascoes.* (Revised and enlarged edition of Victims of Groupthink (1972)). Houghton Mifflin.

Kotter, J. P., & Schlesinger, L. A. (2008). Choosing strategies for change. *Harvard Business Review, 86,* 7/8, 130–39.

Maurer, R. (n. d.). https://rickmaurer.com/articles/resistance-to-change-why-it-matters/

Nash, R. J. (2010). "What is the best way to be a social justice advocate?": Communication strategies for effective social justice advocacy. *About Campus, 15*(2), 11–18. https://doi.org/10.1002/abc.20017

O Connor, C. A. (1993). Resistance: The repercussions of change. *Leadership & Organization Development, 14*(6), 30–36. https://doi.org/10.1108/01437739310145615.

Okun, T. (1999). White supremacy culture. https://www.whitesupremacyculture.info/uploads/4/3/5/7/43579015/okun_-_white_sup_culture_2020.pdf

Placeres, V., Davis, D. E., Williams, N., shodiya-zeumault, shola, Aiello, M., Petion, G., & Mason, E. (2022). School counselors and multicultural counseling competencies: Are we as competent as we think we are? *Professional School Counseling, 26*(1a). https://doi.org/10.1177/2156759X221086751

Reinbold, D. (2024). *A disturbing trend: Pushing religious chaplains on public schools.* The Humanist. https://thehumanist.com/commentary/a-disturbing-trend-pushing-religious-chaplains-on-public-schools/

Ruth, S (2006). *Leadership & liberation: A psychological approach*. London: Routledge.

Snyder, T. (2017). *On tyranny: Twenty lessons from the twentieth century.* (1st ed.). Tim Duggan Books.

Voght, K. (2022, April 24). *'Really scary and sad': How school counselors got caught in the GOP's culture-war dragnet.* Rolling Stone. https://www.rollingstone.com/politics/politics-features/dont-say-gay-school-counselors-students-mental-health-1342328/

Young, A., Day-Vines, N. L., Xiong, Y., & Miller, J. (2025). A socially just framework: School counselor leadership and broaching practices. Professional School Counseling, 29(1a). https://doi.org/10.1177/2156759X251350053

Chapter 7

Somewhere Over the Rainbow

The Power of Collaboration and Coalition Building

In *The Wonderful Wizard of Oz,* Dorothy Gale is swept away from a dull, gray prairie in Kansas, into a vibrant and unfamiliar land. Upon her arrival in Oz she is introduced to a rich spectrum of colors, characters, and possibilities. Dorothy's journey of growth unfolds in full color, much like a rainbow which often symbolizes hope, awareness, and transformation. In other instances, it can signify a bridge to something better, including a more authentic self or a more just world. In the context of school counselor leadership, envisioning better systems for students can be akin to reaching for the end of the rainbow. As school counselors, we tend to be natural dreamers with big visions of the types of learning environments and supports that would help our students thrive. So, how do we begin to make these dreams a reality? How do we create a bridge to a world of our own making? It can seem impossible, particularly when, like Dorothy, the world around us is so gray and stormy. We believe the answer is not to abandon the pursuit of the dream; rather, it is essential to remember that our dreams fuel our souls and our day-to-day efforts for children. Instead, school counselors must remind themselves that collective liberation does not come from the work of a single leader but from the shared aspirations, work, and commitment of a united group. Like Dorothy, our path toward liberation is not solitary. Instead, we must forge alliances with kindred spirits who share our vision of justice and equity.

School counselors are natural collaborators working with educators, families, and communities to create optimal learning environments for students. In a counseling session, school counselors develop collaborative relationships with students to support them in achieving their goals. This collaboration often extends to consultation with parents, staff, teachers, and administrators on how to best support students. As leaders, school counselors also establish collaborative partnerships with community organizations to secure much-needed resources for their schools. At the core of each of these interactions is the cultivation of relationships, the establishment of shared goals, and a charge to improve students' lives. School counselors are bridge builders by the very nature of their training and work. They build collaborative relationships with school partners at every level and apply these collaborative skills daily. However, when undertaking social justice work,

DOI: 10.4324/9781032679174-9

school counselors, like Dorothy, seeing the entire rainbow of possibilities, must expand their view of collaboration to recognize the fullness of collaborative relationships and when to apply each type to achieve their goals.

Pause and Reflect

1 How do you identify potential allies and determine whom to approach?
2 What strategies have you used in the past to foster successful collaborations?
3 How would colleagues describe your collaboration style?

School Counselors Collaborating across the Spectrum

Whether school counselors are engaging in advocacy work at the microlevel or macrolevel, addressing inequalities in education is too complex a task for one person to tackle alone and often requires a multifaceted approach to address effectively. The major systems of oppression (i.e., racism, sexism, heterosexism, ableism, classism, ageism) that impact students and families are deeply intertwined. To achieve collective liberation, all forms of oppression must be dismantled. That means our advocacy efforts must also be interconnected. However, addressing these complex issues requires significant time and attention. It requires planning and coordination and a range of strategies to be effective. School counselors looking to create meaningful change benefit from extending their collaborative skills and forming partnerships, coalitions, and alliances with those with common interests. These relationships provide the infrastructure for collective liberation. Coalitions allow groups of individuals to come together for a common goal, pooling their resources and expertise, amplifying their voice and influence, and consistently holding decision-makers accountable through ongoing advocacy efforts. This sustained pressure can increase the likelihood of decision-makers addressing the concerns and demands of the coalition and potentially lead to meaningful policy change. Coalitions enable people to influence systemic change and drive advocacy initiatives at a larger scale, and building these relationships requires distinct skills, which we explore in detail in this chapter. Before we begin, let's take a moment to understand some of the historical roots of coalition building.

The History of Coalition Building

Most school counselors enter the profession to support children and help shape a learning environment that allows students to thrive. For many of us, our "whys" come from noble and sincere intentions to do right by students. Yet education is currently facing attacks that do not make our work any easier. Whether it is anti-LGBTQ policies, backlash against ethnic studies, anti-SEL movements, or attacks on the very purpose of school counselors themselves, it can all feel overwhelming and, at times, hopeless. However, in these difficult moments, we challenge you to look beyond the storm to that place beyond the rain and thunder, somewhere over the rainbow where dreams take root. The future of education lies within the vibrant spectrum of hopes, dreams, and shared aspirations that unite individuals to improve the lives of children. School counselors are the builders of rainbow bridges, and your power lies in finding and bringing these individuals and their common interests together.

The Rainbow Coalition

One powerful source of inspiration comes from the social movements of late 1960s Chicago, where a diverse group of communities united to pursue anti-capitalist, anti-racist, and anti-classist goals. In this unexpected collaboration, Black radicals, confederate flag-waving white Southerners, and street-gang-turned-activist Puerto Ricans discovered common ground, uniting to establish the renowned Rainbow Coalition. Fostering coalitions across racial, class, and gender lines, the Rainbow Coalition, particularly the "Original" Rainbow Coalition, stands out as a testament to the convergence of shared interests. The formation of the original Rainbow Coalition in late 1960s Chicago was initially conceived by Bob Lee and Fred Hampton of the Illinois Black Panther Party (ILBPP) in direct response to the shared struggles and systemic challenges faced by African Americans, Puerto Ricans, and poor whites (Sonnie & Tracy, 2011; Williams, 2013).

During this period in Chicago, these communities were experiencing similar struggles, including poverty, unemployment, police violence, substandard housing, inadequate schools, and limited access to social services. The close physical proximity of these segregated but interconnected neighborhoods created opportunities for interaction and collaboration, turning their isolated hardships into shared challenges. The Black Panther Party (BPP) was mobilizing their communities on Chicago's west side, while on the north side, the Young Lords, a group composed of predominantly Puerto Rican migrants began their own organizing. Jose "Cha Cha" Jimenez, inspired by political activism after being incarcerated for drug possession, led the Young Lords. Witnessing Puerto Rican residents being displaced due to redevelopment and drawing inspiration from successful civil rights movements like the Black Panther Party, Cha Cha made a pivotal decision. He steered the Young Lords away from being a street gang. He redirected their focus toward providing critical services like childcare and free food to their neighborhood, modeling their approach after the Black Panthers in addressing the needs of their community. Simultaneously, poor white migrants from Appalachia formed the Young Patriot Organization (YPO) in response to police harassment and discrimination they were experiencing in uptown Chicago.

The intersectionality of their struggles played a crucial role in bringing together these diverse communities with a common goal of challenging systemic injustices. The initial meeting between representatives of BPP and YPOs occurred during a fortunate scheduling mix-up. Both Bob Lee and the Young Patriots were scheduled to speak at the same event attended by predominantly middle-class whites. At this event, Bob Lee, the BPP chapter's Field Marshall, critically observed common purpose and identity. Although the Young Patriots were scheduled to discuss police brutality, middle-class whites in the audience dismissed the issue, noting it was not a priority. During this engagement, Lee expressed his shock, stating,

> Coming from the South, it was a culture shock for me; I had never seen that before because in the South, whites were united around race... I had never seen whites attack poor whites before. I had never seen poor whites having to explain themselves to other whites before.
>
> (Williams, 2013, p.133)

At that moment, recognizing that their interests were aligned with a shared identity rooted in class and purpose (organizing for their respective community), Bob Lee initiated the steps for forming a coalition. He connected with the leaders of YPO and worked to foster an understanding of their unified struggles and goals, which marked the birth of the Rainbow Coalition. Bob Lee effectively connected the grievances expressed by white Appalachian migrants centered around police brutality, poverty, and joblessness to those of the African American community. The Young Lords soon joined under the coalition's umbrella, combining resources and sharing strategies for providing services and aid that the government and private sector would not. As a leader, Bob Lee was gifted at listening closely to the challenges of those around him and breaking through isolation. Through effective coalition building, Bob Lee and Fred Hampton brought together seemingly polar opposite organizations to develop a shared identity, pool their resources, and provide essential services such as health clinics, clothing drives, daycare programs, and legal advice modeled on those of the Black Panthers. The Rainbow Coalition transformed Chicago's political landscape, inspiring others to adopt similar approaches in their community.

The East LA Walkouts and Student Activism

At the same time, a parallel wave of resistance was emerging in East Los Angeles led by students determined to reclaim their education. Students have long been at the forefront of organizing to advocate for various causes and drive social change. One of the largest student movements occurred in 1968 amidst the Civil Rights Movement and the Vietnam War. During this period, Mexican-American students in the Los Angeles Unified School District (LAUSD) were growing increasingly frustrated with the systems of inequality in education (García & Castro, 2011). At the time, Mexican-American students were experiencing a 60% dropout rate from high school, and those who did graduate averaged an eighth-grade reading level. In some schools, students who only spoke Spanish were segregated from their peers, and in others, school staff recommended Mexican-American students educational curricula meant to help students with disabilities (Library of Congress, n.d.). The few students who went on to higher education were funneled into vocational programs and discouraged from attending college (Library of Congress, n.d.). In response, students, teachers, parents, college students, and activists began to organize (Figure 7.1). Their goals included bilingual education, representative teacher hiring practices, more school counselors, smaller class sizes, and better facilities (Radio Caracol, 2020, January 7). When their needs were unmet, the students threatened to walk out of homerooms before attendance could be taken, targeting the schools financially.

Over 15,000 Mexican-American students and teachers from seven different high schools in LAUSD organized the largest student-led walkout in American history, known as the East LA walkouts or "Blowouts" (Library of Congress, n.d.; Figure 7.2). While their demands were not immediately met, the walkouts drew national attention to the schools' disparities. Their efforts set in motion the

Figure 7.1 Students demand the removal of John Hogan, a teacher at Roosevelt High School who made racist remarks toward students, at a Los Angeles Unified School District Board of Education meeting, 1968. Photo by Devra Weber, UCLA Chicano Studies Research Center's La Raza Photograph Collection

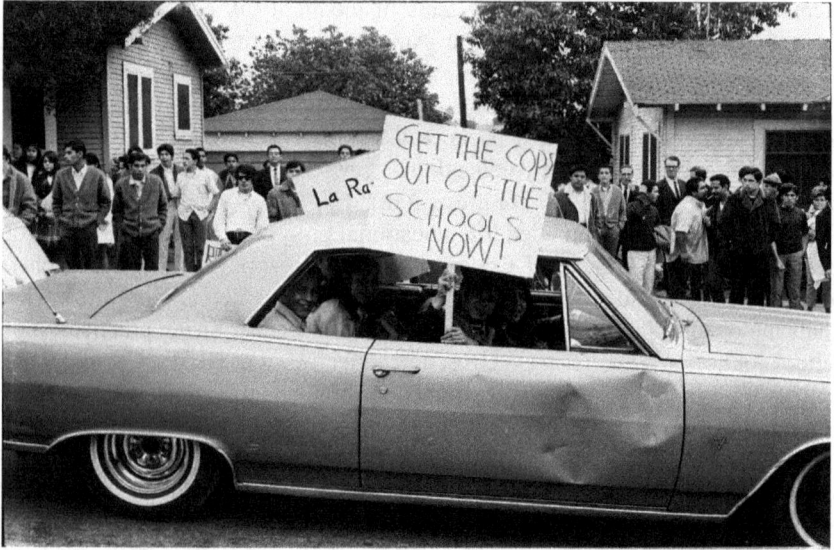

Figure 7.2 Protesters in a car drive by with a sign that reads "Get the Cops Out of the Schools Now!", 1968. Photo by Devra Weber, UCLA Chicano Studies Research Center's La Raza Photograph Collection

formation of bilingual education and ethnic studies in California P-12 schools, the recruitment of more Latinx teachers and administrators, and the establishment of Chicana/o studies classes, programs, and departments across the United States. Keep in mind that while a coalition may not meet all its immediate demands, it often sparks a movement, creating a chain reaction that moves the needle toward progress. Steadfast leaders can see the big picture and understand that organizing may not result in immediate wins but are willing to stay the course for long-term gains.

The Collaboration Continuum

Building on this historical context, let us explore how school counselors can expand their capacity for collaboration. The Collaboration Continuum describes the spectrum of collaborative relationships that vary in depth, interaction, and cooperation. School counselors frequently collaborate with others via networking, consultation, and the coordination of student support services. As leaders for social justice and equity, school counselors can use the Collaboration Continuum (Figure 7.3) to deepen their collaborative skills. By moving beyond initial relationships to more formal collaborative processes, school counselors can create a rainbow of opportunities for change. The Collaboration Continuum emphasizes collective impact and the role of school counselors in influencing policies, procedures, practices, and broader systemic improvements.

	Networking	Consultation	Coordination	Partnership	Coalition	Alliance
PURPOSE	Build connections, make new relationships, build on existing relationships / Create a basis for support / Expand influence or visibility within professional or social circles	Cooperative relationship with others / Seek information from diverse groups of people to develop a better understanding of an issue or to advance a solution to a problem / Plan together, and make joint decisions and strategies based on shared information and perspectives	Align efforts and resources towards a common goal. / Ensure that tasks or services are organized efficiently, minimizing duplication of efforts and optimizing resources	Establish deeper relationships and commitment / Short-term relationship with specific objectives in mind / Formed when two parties agree to work together to achieve a common purpose or undertake a specific task	Generally involve shorter-term relationships among members and are focused on a specific objective / Being limited in time and goal, alliances tend to be less demanding on members	Primary focus is on creating policy or systemic change to address the root issue.Joint advocacy and/or shared resources / Usually involves long-term relationships among members / Permanence can give clout and leverage in pursuing shared goals
LEADERSHIP SKILLS	Communication and Relationship-building	Active Listening and Problem Solving	Organization and Project Management	Trust Building and Vision Alignment	Strategic Leadership and Flexibility	Diplomacy and Conflict Resolution
FOCUS	Common Interest	Collaborative Problem Solving	Common Plan	Mutual Support	Common Identity	Common Strategy
PROCESSES	Low-key involvement / Minimal decision making / Share ideas and exchange information / Primarily work within existing structures / Informal communications	Shared effort in reaching agreement on a joint goal or activity / Collaborative problem-solving and decision-making / Work with both existing structures and advocate for change / Communicate as needed	Clear definition of goals and objectives / Individuals working and contributing independently to various parts of a goal / Maintain self-interest while advancing mutual interest / Focus on alignment within existing structures / Communicate as needed, with an emphasis on coordinating efforts	Shared commitment in establishing mission and vision / Collaborative efforts in reaching agreement on a joint need. / Formalize roles and responsibilities.Sharing rewards and risks collectively / Regular communication and shared decision-making / Merging individual interests with the interests of others	Shared efforts in cultivating a vision for group success / Agreed upon shared means to achieve goals / Joint strategic planning / Formal structures for decision making / Collective decision-making / Efforts involved in developing and executing a shared plan of action / Shared resource allocation	Shared commitment to mission and vision / Formalized structures and decision-making processes / Collective identification of members / Development of a communication plan / Clear accountability with shared efforts / Formal sharing of resources, risks, costs, benefits, and responsibilities

COLLECTIVE IMPACT

Lopez-Perry, 2024

Figure 7.3 The Collaboration Continuum.

The next section describes the purpose and processes for each type of collaborative relationship, identifies which kind of relationship is most suitable for a given situation, outlines the leadership skills necessary for each level, and provides guidance on progressing across the continuum to. It is important to note that the leadership skills build upon each other as individuals move across the continuum.

Networking involves interacting with others to establish connections, strengthen existing relationships, and exchange information. The relationships are sparked by common professional or personal interests. A strong network provides a foundation for support and allows leaders to expand their influence or visibility within their professional or social circles. Networking is not primarily focused on decision-making; it revolves around exchanging ideas and information. Instead of challenging or changing established norms, networking leverages existing systems to open communication channels and create opportunities for collaboration. In such contexts, effective communication and relationship building are essential leadership skills. School counseling leaders who are skilled communicators utilize networking to establish trust, facilitate mutual understanding, build credibility, and influence others. This can facilitate lasting connections within the network that set the stage for other types of collaborative relationships across the continuum. Therefore, effective leaders carefully construct their networks to meet their specific needs. According to Ibarra and Hunter (2007), three types of networks include personal, operational, and strategic networks.

- *Personal networking* consists of kindred spirits outside your organization who can help you learn and find opportunities for personal advancement and development. Examples include joining a professional association, participating in online communities, participating in social events or mixers, or attending conferences.
- *Operational networking* involves connecting with individuals who can help you do your work efficiently. All leaders benefit from creating relationships with individuals who can help them do their job effectively. Examples include participating in school and district committees or task forces to improve policies and programs, collaborating with your school's data specialist to improve your counseling program's data collection and usage, or building relationships with local community organizations to provide resources to students and families.
- *Strategic networking* focuses on building connections with people outside your control or influence who can help you achieve your goals. This may include establishing relationships with board members, introducing yourself to your school's parent-teacher association or school site council, or connecting with district administrators or directors who may have political influence.

Consultation is the process of exchanging information and opinions from diverse groups to enhance understanding of an issue or advance a solution to a problem. In education, the emphasis is typically on shared understanding and collaborative problem-solving. Collaborative consultation focuses on joint problem-solving, decision-making, shared responsibility, and goal agreement (Idol et al., 1995). Leadership skills such as active listening and effective problem-solving are key in guiding the consultation process toward meaningful outcomes. School counselors who can engage in active listening with their collaborators can understand different perspectives, identify underlying concerns, and pinpoint key issues. They utilize their problem-solving skills to guide consultation toward meaningful outcomes by addressing conflicts, facilitating consensus among members, and directing solutions that move the group to their shared goals. Individuals involved in consultation communicate as needed to ensure an exchange of ideas that address the issue. This process may involve working within existing structures or advocating for change. Consequently, the reach of consultation is often targeted and may involve a limited number of school partners. School counseling leaders regularly consult with administrators, teachers, or school partners to advocate for the needs of individual students, promote policies that foster equity and inclusion, or raise awareness or sensitivity about an issue affecting a student or student population.

Coordination involves organizing individuals, groups, or services to contribute to a common plan. The purpose is to align resources and energy to ensure efficiency, minimize duplication, and optimize resources. Individuals or groups contribute independently toward a common goal ensuring their efforts align with existing structures. Communication occurs only as needed with an emphasis on coordination. In this collaborative process, leaders utilize organization and project management skills to identify roles, align resources, streamline workflows, and establish a framework for accountability. School counselors often engage in coordinating efforts when they facilitate the appropriate delivery of instructional and support services. They work with partners in and outside of the school to identify and share academic, behavioral, and social-emotional support and services. They also develop systems to ensure consistent practices across providers and that students and families have equitable access to these services.

Partnerships are a cooperative relationship where two or more people or groups work together toward mutual goals or objectives. They can be short-term or long-term, focusing on providing each other with mutual support or sharing resources. Because rewards and risks are shared, this type of collaborative relationship requires leaders to work toward establishing deeper relationships and more formal commitments. When bringing people together, leaders must work with their potential partners to develop a shared commitment to establishing the mission and vision of their partnership. Essential leadership skills include trust building and vision setting. Given this, partners should formalize roles and responsibilities and maintain regular communication and shared decision-making. Leaders addressing smaller, more localized issues may benefit from strategic partnerships. In schools, counselors may build partnerships with outside organizations to bring students resources or support each other's advocacy efforts for change within their schools or districts. For example, a school counselor who partners with a local non-profit organization would want to meet to establish mutual goals and objectives, formalize each other's role in working toward these goals, and establish a schedule and method for communicating to discuss progress, challenges, and make joint decisions related to adjustments.

Coalitions are more formal and strategic collaboration between organizations or groups who unite through a shared identity and purpose. These diverse groups typically come together for short-term relationships to collectively address a particular challenge, advocate for a common cause, or achieve a specific goal. Given their limited time and scope, coalitions tend to be less demanding than alliances, allowing for synergy, sustainability, and focused efforts. Once goals are met, a coalition may disband or reconfigure based on emerging challenges or new objectives. Members collaborate to develop a unified vision for success, agree on strategies to accomplish goals, engage in joint planning, and allocate resources collectively. The formality of these structures helps mitigate risk and improve efficiency. In navigating the dynamic and complex environments, collective decision-making becomes critical and allows coalitions to extend their influence to macrolevel issues. Consequently, strategic leadership and flexibility are crucial in this process. Coalition building amplifies the voices and needs of marginalized and oppressed populations, challenges power structures, and promotes systemic change. This strategic approach to collaboration helps people come together and overcome feelings of isolation, inadequacy, and powerlessness.

Alliances, like coalitions, involve multiple actors from different sectors who come together for mutual benefit. Their distinction lies in their scope, objective, and duration. In essence, alliances involve more enduring, strategic partnerships built on long-term commitments to shared goals. This deeper collaboration requires a more significant sharing of resources, risks, costs, benefits, and responsibilities. This depth allows alliances to effectively address complex and interrelated issues by leveraging collective expertise and influence. Building alliances is a dynamic and active approach that addresses deep-rooted issues and actively challenges and reshapes existing structures. Leadership skills such as diplomacy and conflict resolution are most prominent in this collaborative process. Leaders must articulate their position clearly and be open to listening to others' viewpoints while calmly dealing with the range of attitudes and behavior within the collaborative framework. These diplomatic skills empower leaders to study and think critically about situations, recognizing when circumstances are evolving and need adapting.

Collaborating for Collective Impact

Having described the various collaborative relationships, let us now focus on leveraging partnerships, coalitions, and alliances for collective impact. Kania and Kramer (2011) point out that no single person or organization is responsible for any significant social problem, nor can any individual or organization cure it alone. Instead, individuals must move toward a Collective Impact approach in which multiple organizations or entities abandon individual agendas in favor of a common agenda. Unlike other types of collaborative efforts on the Collaboration Continuum, such as networking, consulting, and coordinating, Collective Impact initiatives involve a centralized infrastructure, a dedicated team, and a structured process that leads to a common agenda, shared measurement, continuous communication, and mutually reinforcing activities among all participants (Kania & Kramer, 2011). Consequently, the more formal structures and processes of partnerships, coalitions, and alliances aligns well with this model.

School counseling leaders who move across the Collaboration Continuum toward Collective Impact mobilize people to address adaptive challenges. Kania and Kramer (2011) distinguish between technical and adaptive problem-solving, particularly in education (Table 7.1). *Technical challenges* have clearly defined problems with known solutions that individuals or organizations can implement. For instance, peer conflicts in school could be solved by implementing a peer mediation program. This is considered a technical issue because there are established models and protocols for training mediators and evidence-based strategies for resolving conflicts among peers effectively. Technical challenges can often be solved with managerial skills and available resources.

On the other hand, *adaptive problems* in education are more complex, harder to identify, and tied to deeper systemic patterns. For example, addressing the achievement gap between students from different socioeconomic backgrounds is an adaptive challenge because the factors contributing to this gap are multifaceted. Even if there was a clear solution, no single entity or organization has the resources or authority to address these underlying issues and fully bring about lasting change. Instead, adaptive problems often require a multifaceted and coordinated approach that can be addressed through the collective impact of partnerships, coalitions, and alliances. Systems of oppression exist at various levels (classroom, school, district, county, state) and across

Table 7.1 Technical Challenges and Adaptive Problems

Technical Challenges	Adaptive Problems
The problem and solution are clear	The problem and solutions are complex
Concrete, clear solution	Requires changes in values, beliefs, roles, relationships, & approaches to work
Can be solved by an authority or expert	People with the problem do the work of solving it often through experimentation
Requires small changes in just one or a few places	Requires change in numerous places

structures (education, health, economy, housing, transportation, food access) that interconnect to impact our students and their families. The biggest mistake when exercising leadership is treating an adaptive challenge as a technical problem (Heifetz et al., 2009). While it would be nice to believe that problems in education can be solved quickly and easily, the reality is that lasting change often requires a mixture of technical and adaptive strategies. Understanding the difference between the two types of challenges helps leaders respond more effectively. School counselors working to create meaningful change understand that adaptive problems require thoughtful analysis, deep engagement, and multifaceted solutions that necessitate a collective approach and work toward building a community of like-minded people to support the work of one another.

Principles of Collaborating for Collective Impact

When school counselors expand their collaborative relationships to include partnerships, alliances, and coalitions, liberatory principles rooted in equity, social justice, and transformative leadership become fundamental. Traditional models of leadership and collaboration often employ a top-down approach, which is antithetical to liberatory practices. The following guiding principles, which are drawn from Wolff et al. (2017), provide clarity on collaborative leadership, including focus, accountability in decision-making, consistency in behavior and communication, and alignment with ethical values of equity and social justice. Applying these principles ensures that leaders are co-conspiring rather than co-opting movements.

Principle 1: Prioritize the voice of those most affected by injustice and inequity.

Our collaborative relationships are not exempt from societal issues like systemic racism, sexism, homophobia, transphobia, and ableism. Leaders must actively recognize the underlying power dynamics at play, as they can perpetuate or exacerbate inequalities and marginalization. Creating psychological safety, and opportunities for shared leadership is critical. Individuals should feel free to express themselves, share their stories, and voice their concerns without fear of judgment or repercussion.

Principle 2: Acknowledge and address structural inequalities

Effective leaders recognize that surface-level changes are not enough to address the pervasive inequalities entrenched within our systems and structures. Treating the symptoms will only provide short-term relief. They recognize that neglecting to address the root cause allows the rot to spread, resulting in profound consequences for marginalized students and their families.

Principle 3: Catalyze leadership and power at every level

Coalition building is multifaceted and requires multiple leadership roles and responsibilities to operate effectively. The history of coalition building has shown us that movements are most effective when marginalized communities lead initiatives and serve as the driving voice shaping policies. Leaders encourage members to take on different roles within the coalition and identify opportunities for individuals at every level to develop their leadership skills through mentorship, training, or coaching.

Building Processes for Collective Impact

As mentioned earlier, partnerships, coalitions, and alliances are a great way to pool resources, plan, and address urgent problems in your school or community to create change. While each has slightly different meanings and functions, the steps to establishing and developing these relationships are pretty similar. Given this, in the next section, we will use "coalition" for consistency when describing the establishment processes.

Define the Issue

Coalitions often form around a shared purpose or need. A common cause, perspective, or social position can foster solidarity and collective action (Obach, 2010). During her quest, Dorothy was particularly skilled at explaining her problems, listening to the concerns of others, and identifying a mutual need and common goal, which allowed her to form a partnership with the Tin Woodman, Scarecrow, and Cowardly Lion. Before forming the core leaders for your coalition, consider the perspective and position that drives its establishment. First, define the problem you are trying to address and consider why it is important. This will be helpful as you begin connecting with others who share similar concerns. Then, ask yourself, what factors contribute to the problem? When grappling with issues related to educational equity, there are often various factors at play. Therefore, it is vital to look at the problem from all angles. Figuring out why the problem has developed will help as you formulate your goals and objectives, ensuring you get to the root cause. Next, determine the nature of the problem. This will guide your approach to addressing it. Is the problem technical, adaptive, or both? Adaptive challenges address deeper issues and often require confronting the status quo, which in turn requires changing people's values, beliefs, and behaviors (Heifitz & Linsky, 2009). If the problem is an adaptive challenge, consider if there are mindsets and behaviors your coalition will need to change to move your cause forward. Sometimes, you will be faced with competing values or priorities or long-standing customs and practices that need to evolve. In other instances, people may simply not be aware of the habits, mindsets, or cultural norms that are maintaining the problems. This lack of awareness can make the problem difficult to resolve. Lastly, examine how the problem is impacting students or other key partners (families, colleagues, and the larger community). Taking a moment to understand and articulate the fundamental problem and your perspective on the issue will guide your recruitment efforts toward individuals who align with and can contribute to your objectives. Remember, adaptive challenges are complex, and you do not need to have all of the solutions to the problem. You simply need to be able to articulate the issue in order to seek out individuals with a shared purpose in addressing the issue.

Exercise: The "But Why?" Technique for Uncovering Root Causes

The "But why?" technique is one method used to identify the underlying causes of a school or community issue.

1 Identify an Issue: Start by selecting an issue or challenge you would like to explore.
2 Start by asking, "Why does this issue exist?"
3 Each time an answer is given, a follow-up "But why?" is asked.

Finding Your Core Leaders and Groups

Now that you have defined the problem, identify potential allies who not only understand the issue at hand but can also advance the cause you have identified. Skilled leaders spend a great deal of time and effort creating and nurturing a network of people they can call on, learn from, and collaborate with. Likewise, successful coalitions rely on a group of core leaders who can bring together cross-sector groups and stakeholders and take decisive action (Mizrahi & Rosenthal, 2001). Without these individuals, initiatives risk stagnation, becoming mere forums for information exchange rather than catalysts for change. Considering this, your core leaders should share one or more of the following qualities: a commitment to the coalition's objectives, credibility within their community, strong connections to both the community and key decision-makers, political acumen, and specialized expertise (Lopez-Perry & Whitson, 2022). Seek out individuals who not only exhibit innovative thinking and a willingness to take risks but also demonstrate a strong commitment to addressing the challenge. Mizrahi and Rosenthal (2001) found that a leader's commitment to the cause and a leader's competence were the top contributing factors to a coalition's success. Additional factors that help leaders mobilize resources and rally support include a commitment to building coalition unity, equitable decision-making structures, and mutual respect.

Strong recruitment begins with clearly defining leaders' roles. Core leaders play a pivotal role in establishing goals, inspiring unity, and developing strategic plans that consider the broader context. They should assist in identifying potential challenges and opportunities for collaboration while remaining flexible in adjusting strategies as needed. Bear in mind adaptive challenges require learning to understand what is going on and making adjustments as new information is presented. These leaders can zoom in to analyze the fine details while also zooming out to understand the broader context and larger goals of an issue. Therefore, it's imperative to avoid selecting individuals who can't see the forest through the trees. Those who become too absorbed in the minutiae risk losing sight of the overarching goals and prioritize trivial matters, hindering the group's progress.

Core leaders help identify and engage key policymakers and decision-makers who are aligned with coalition goals. As "bridge builders" and "coalition brokers" (Obach, 2010), they act as connectors, facilitating communication, building trust, and bridging gaps between stakeholders with differing backgrounds. Their dual identities and cross-sector knowledge help provide a rich understanding of the differing perspectives of two or more distinct groups.

Recognizing the unique contributions of each individual or group is not only beneficial but necessary for the success of your coalition. Creating a diverse range of perspectives and expertise is akin to the alliance created by Dorothy with the Tin Woodman, Scarecrow, and the Lion. She surrounded herself with the right people to support her in times of crisis. Once formed, each one contributed uniquely to the group, making them more resilient, dynamic, and capable as they encountered challenges along their journey. Similarly, your members should empower the coalition to navigate political forces and propel initiatives forward. As you consider which groups to integrate into your coalition, look across various sectors such as student groups, parents and families, community opinion leaders, nonprofits or advocacy organizations, community organizers and activists, educators and school staff, academic researchers or research institutions, and government officials and policymakers.

When it comes to advocacy work, students and their caregivers should serve as a compass directing your efforts. Remember, our guiding principles of collective impact urge us to prioritize the voice of those most affected by injustice and inequity. Students must help drive the decision-making. The leadership of the Pomona Student Union in Pomona Unified School District (Keller, 2019) illustrates how youth can organize for meaningful change (see Beyond the Rainbow: Building Student and Community Coalitions for Equity and Access). Similarly, the transformative advocacy efforts led by Students Deserve, made up predominantly of students of color and led by Black students played a central role in the removal of police presence on campus in LAUSD (Kim, 2024). In 2019, Students Deserve ended random searches on students, and in 2020, it eliminated police use of pepper spray on all district campuses. Their most successful efforts to date have been the $25 million divestment from the police budget and its reinvestment into student programming. Students better than anyone can envision what schools should be and have the fortitude and energy to keep moving down the yellow brick road.

Beyond the Rainbow: Building Student and Community Coalitions for Equity and Access

In 2016, the activist group Gente Organizada (Organized People) began organizing in Pomona, California after a 16-year-old experienced police violence at the Los Angeles County Fair. By 2019, youth leaders from Gente Organizada discovered that the Pomona Unified School District (PUSD) had illegally diverted district funds intended for foster youth, English learners, and low-income students to law enforcement and security. Outraged, students, led by the Pomona Student Union and Gente Organizada, launched a campaign demanding the district redirect the funds. With support from Public Advocates Inc. and the ACLU of Southern California, their advocacy succeeded, leading PUSD to restore over $2 million to programs supporting high-need students and reinvest in additional school counselors.

Keller, A. (2019, September 12)

As you incorporate different groups into your coalition, remember that community opinion leaders can also play a critical role. They have an audience or following that trust them as a source of information for their interests (Parau et al., 2017). Because of this, they often have the influence to mobilize a large number of people and can help garner community support for your initiative. These community leaders can serve as "coalition brokers." They can help your coalition build credibility within the community and support communication between the coalition and community (Valente & Pumpuang, 2007). Lastly, they may be the lasting support left behind if the coalition or leaders leave, helping to carry on the goals of the initiative.

In addition to community opinion leaders, a wide range of partners such as local nonprofits, advocacy organizations, and community-based organizations can bring expertise and resources to the table. Community organizers and activists are skilled at mobilizing communities, raising awareness, and advocating for change. For instance, organizations such as Public Advocates and Gente Unidos played a critical role in helping students in Pomona Unified School District (PUSD) mobilize the community. Academic researchers can offer evidence-based insights and assist with data collection through survey development, focus groups, and the analysis of existing data. The California Association of School Counselors included counselor educators in their coalition, who could offer insights into the latest research and provide evidence-based solutions for legislators and journalists. Lastly, government officials and policymakers are powerful collaborators when advocating for policy changes and securing necessary resources. Whether you are looking to create systemic change at the district level or state level, government officials (mayors, city council members, state senators, and representatives) and policymakers (school board members, policy advisors, teachers' unions, and professional associations) can leverage their expertise, influence, and resources to address complex social issues. Once you have assembled your partners, ensuring they are aligned around a shared vision and purpose is critical.

Establish a Shared Vision and Purpose

At the heart of any coalition is a commitment to a common vision or purpose. Studies identify collective vision as vital for effective collaboration (Kammer et al., 2021; Robertson, 2007). A collective vision defines who you are, where you are going, and how you will get there. It outlines the group's aspirations and long-term goals. Remember that rainbow way up high? The land that you heard of once in a lullaby? Creating a vision for where you are headed can inspire others and serve as a call to action, ensuring everyone is working toward the same goal. For coalitions, the vision typically starts with something bigger than themselves. When partners have a clear purpose and a shared vision, it creates a sense of ownership and a foundation on which your partnership can weather any storm (e.g., tornado). This shared vision is a freedom dream. Scholar R.D.G. Kelly (2003) explains the power of freedom dreaming. Multiple social and political movements including the Civil Rights Movements, the Women's Movement, the Labor Movement, and the LGBTQ+ Movement all utilized freedom dreaming. Rather than activists focusing the energy of the movements on the forces against them, they focused on the dream they created of how they wanted the world to be; this was the freedom dream. In this way, all their efforts were directed at constructing a new vision rather than being mired down in the old systems that oppressed them and those they fought for.

When individuals understand who they are and what they are striving for, they can unite around a common purpose, fostering a shared sense of belonging to something bigger than themselves. This shared identity forms the foundation for collaboration toward shared outcomes (Bavel & Packer, 2021). Within a shared identity, group behaviors are built on a sense of connection created by shared values, beliefs, and goals, allowing coalitions and alliances to endure challenges and persist over time. Research has demonstrated that leaders capable of fostering a shared identity impact group members' efforts and performance (Stevens et al., 2019). It also extends beyond performance and influences key factors such as intentional mobilization and self-efficacy (Miller et al., 2021). Creating a shared identity starts with an understanding of the group's purpose.

A great question to answer is, "Who is served by the work we do?" For many of us, the answer will be students. The next step is to identify the group's core values. These principles will shape decision-making and the culture of your coalition. Finally, the coalition should set concrete, actionable goals that align with these values and their overarching purpose. These goals will provide the group direction, serve as a benchmark to measure progress and sustain momentum in collective efforts. Ultimately, having a clearly defined vision and purpose helps minimize confusion and competing interests regarding the purpose of the group.

Beyond the Rainbow: A Historic and Powerful Alliance of the Big Three

There was a time when the California Association of School Counselors (CASC) operated in isolation, unaware of the collective strength we could wield through collaboration. That changed in a pivotal moment—one that reshaped our approach to advocacy.

While presenting a CASC-sponsored bill to the California Senate Education Committee, we were blindsided. A lobbyist for school psychologists, whom we had never engaged with publicly opposed our legislation. We lacked both awareness and the influence to counter his stance. In that moment, it became clear: working alone left us vulnerable. If we wanted to drive meaningful change, we needed strategic allies.

This realization set in motion a transformational shift. We reached out to key stakeholders—the associations representing school psychologists and school social workers—and formed what is now known as the "Big Three." Together, we aligned around shared goals and a fundamental commitment: we would never publicly oppose one another's initiatives. Instead, we would amplify each other's efforts, presenting a unified front for student support services.

From this partnership, the Pupil Services Coalition was born. Grounded in trust and transparency, it evolved into a powerful force in education advocacy. We expanded our influence beyond legislative hearings, publishing joint statements, shaping policy positions, and engaging directly with legislators and the Governor's office.

Over time, our coalition grew to include school nurses and teachers' unions, further solidifying our impact. Today, those seeking to shape California education policy recognize the necessity of working with us—not just for support, but to avoid opposition.

What began as a moment of weakness became the foundation of a movement. Our journey proves a simple truth: when we stand together, our voices cannot be ignored.

Loretta Whitson, Ed.D., CASC Executive Director

Create Structures for Communication and Decision-Making

With a shared vision in place, the next step is to develop clear structures for communication to maintain alignment. Communication is key to developing and maintaining relationships between coalition members, community members, and policymakers. Coalitions often consist of various organizations or individuals with their own culture, work style, and preferred way of communicating. To help bridge differences between groups and ensure meaningful collaboration, leaders should create shared methods for internal communication and public engagement. These structures not only help build trust but ensure that no one feels left out of the loop and that everyone has access to relevant information and opportunities to share their perspectives. Additionally, clear communication with the media and the community will increase your chances for publicity and support when you need them.

One way to facilitate communication and decision-making is through meetings. School counselor leaders are often in positions where they supervise others because they are heads of departments, chairs of committees, or in roles that afford them opportunities to coordinate the work of others. While formal meetings are sometimes necessary, they are not always productive. In Kim Scott's book *Radical Candor* (2019), she presents a series of meeting types (including non-meetings) that vary in their approach, goal, and format to optimize the gifts of those working with you and the time you have with them. While Scott's audience is likely business leaders, multiple suggestions can apply to schools as long as an anti-racist and anti-oppressive approach is the focus. The whole chapter is worth reading (pp.199–225), but here are a few key points adapted for school counselor leaders:

1 Separate meetings for debating issues and making decisions. This can divide time into sharing perspectives and concerns from deciding next steps. Time in between debating and deciding meetings may help resolve conflicts or interpersonal issues over rushing to make a move in the midst of an emotional process.
2 Get around. Schedule time for impromptu visits to places like the mailroom, cafeteria, lounge, classrooms, or other spaces where you will run into those you work with. Create opportunities to check in on them personally or discuss an issue in a low-stakes environment. It can go a long way with transparency for those working with you to have their own time to express themselves, experience you as a human being, and know they are valuable.

Communication is more than just exchanging information, coalition members need to feel valued and free to authentically contribute to the group. Building psychological safety is foundational in coalition building. It influences how groups of people interact, share ideas, and navigate challenges. Psychological safety is a shared belief held by members of a group that the group is safe for interpersonal risk-taking and a sense of confidence that the group will not embarrass, reject, or punish someone for speaking up (Edmondson, 1999). Identified as the number one characteristic of successful high-performing teams, psychological safety encourages behaviors such as open communication, voicing concerns, and seeking feedback (Bergmann & Schaeppi, 2016; Pearsall & Ellis, 2011). Schein and Bennis (1965) identified psychological safety as a critical component of organizational learning and change. While psychological safety encourages honest and open dialogue within your group, coalitions must also consider how they communicate their cause to the broader public.

Develop a Well-Defined Narrative

Developing a political narrative around an advocacy issue is a necessary step in shaping the way people feel, think, and respond to an issue. The political narrative isn't just a theoretical concept; it is a tool shapes perspectives and alters relationships between social groups and individuals (Graef et al., 2018). Narratives can be wielded for positive change or harm. We have witnessed the effects of narratives that have emerged in education that have framed public schools as sites of "indoctrination," which have fueled efforts to ban books, restrict discussions about race and gender, and censor curricula. A common mistake we as authors have seen school counselors make is not staying ahead of the narrative on advocacy issues. Rather, their advocacy often starts after a narrative has already been formed, making the work much more difficult. It requires challenging entrenched beliefs and misconceptions that have already gained traction. Bolman and Deal (2017) assert that good political leaders clarify what they want and what they can get. Coalitions must stay informed about current trends and shifts in public opinion and drive the narratives accordingly.

One way to look at forming a political narrative is to think about it as "storytelling." What is the story about the overall issue that relates to the well-being of children? What professional associations and groups draw a line from children's well-being to their work? How are the di-erent players situated within that narrative? The framing of one's narrative can be a strategic influencing tool for communicating a problem, cause, and potential solution (De Bruycker, 2017). When advocates proactively create the narrative, they shape the discourse from the outset. It allows them to frame the issue in a way that positions themselves as leaders in the conversation.

Exercise: Narrative Development

1 Who are the people you need to reach to move your narrative?
2 What is the big idea you want to move? Think one level up from your tactic or policy.
3 Why should decision-makers care about this issue? Tie it to values.
4 How can the messengers and storytellers most effectively deliver and move this narrative?

Educate and Engage the Public

Building and maintaining engagement in a cause may be one of the more challenging aspects of advocacy work. How do you bring attention to an issue while simultaneously motivating individuals to take action toward addressing it? The American Counseling Association (ACA) Advocacy Competencies emphasize that counselors play a critical role in advocating for systemic change through collective action by engaging in public awareness campaigns and communicating information in ways appropriate for the target population (Toporek & Daniels, 2018). However, the scope of view on an advocacy issue and the solutions can vary significantly. Because of this, individuals are often willing to commit in different ways to a cause. Engaging supporters requires a strategic and nuanced approach.

Gideon Rosenblatt (2010) offers the Engagement Pyramid Framework as a method for dividing supporters into segments based on their level of engagement. This framework has been used in grassroots community activism (Case & Zeglen, 2018). It refines the ACA Advocacy Competencies and extends the idea of creating public awareness to creating opportunities for public engagement. The pyramid contains six levels that range from lower-level to medium- or high-level commitment activities. *Observing* is the first level of engagement and begins with individuals showing interest in the cause and awareness of the organization or campaign, often learning more through social media, friends, or media outlets. The second level, *Following*, involves being open to receiving information and engaging with the organization by reading or watching content. *Endorsing* is the next level, which consists of simple, low-risk actions such as signing a petition, making a small donation, or sharing content. The fourth level, *Contributing,* involves more significant action, such as joining a group, attending events, or making larger donations. At the higher end of the pyramid is *Owning*, where individuals make a more significant investment of their time, money, and social capital. At this point, they are more involved in advocating for the campaign, creating content, engaging in public speaking, or becoming deeply involved in volunteer work. Finally, at the very top of the pyramid is *Leading*, where individuals take on leadership roles within the campaign helping to organize and motivate others.

School counselors can use this structure to plan the range of engagement strategies and tactics at their disposal. It provides an avenue for matching these strategies with those most likely to succeed in carrying them out. People move up the Pyramid of Engagement by first becoming aware of an issue, then coming to understand its importance and relevance to their lives, then deciding to participate in a campaign and, only over time, developing leadership status within that movement. This process may or may not be linear, and not everyone continues to move up the pyramid. Some people will find a spot that is comfortable for them and stay there. That is fine—the pyramid is not meant to imply that one level of engagement is better than another. Remember, a strong base needs individuals at all levels of the pyramid.

Stepping into Your Ruby Shoes: Use of School Counseling Skills

You may not realize it, but your group facilitation skills are powerful tools in this work. School counselors are trained to understand the stages of group development, including forming, norming, storming, working, and terminating. This knowledge, combined with your group facilitation skills, will be invaluable as you bring groups of people together for a cause. By understanding these phases, you can anticipate challenges as members assert their ideas, work through disagreements, and attempt to define their roles within the group. Basic group counseling skills such as reflecting content and feeling, summarizing, linking members, drawing members in, and attending to the here and now can help foster effective communication and create an inclusive environment where all members feel heard (Steen et al., 2022). Leadership in coalition building involves more than simply bringing people together. It includes managing group dynamics, clarifying goals, assessing progress, identifying solutions, and being accountable to one another. Tapping into your group counseling expertise will enable you to strengthen connections and navigate the complexities of collective action.

References

Bavel, J. J. L., & Packer, D. J. (2021). *Creating a shared identity and the psychology of collaboration. Journal of Applied Social Psychology, 51*(2), 101–113

Bergmann, B., & Schaeppi, J. (2016). A data-driven approach to group creativity. *Harvard Business Review, 12*, 43–62.

Bolman, L. G., & Deal, T. E. (2017). *Reframing organizations: Artistry, choice, and leadership.* John Wiley & Sons.

Case, R. A., & Zeglen, L. (2018). Exploring the ebbs and flows of community engagement: The pyramid of engagement and water activism in two Canadian communities. *Journal of Community Practice, 26*(2), 184–203.

De Bruycker, I. (2017). Framing and advocacy: A research agenda for interest group studies. *Journal of European Public Policy, 24*(5), 775–787. https://doi.org/10.1080/13501763.2016.1149208

Edmondson, A. C. (1999). Psychological safety and learning behavior in work teams. *Administrative Science Quarterly, 44*, 350–383.

García, M. T., & Castro, S. (2011). *Blowout! : Sal castro and the Chicano struggle for educational justice.* University of North Carolina Press.

Graef, J., da Silva, R., & Lemay-Hebert, N. (2018). Narrative, political violence, and social change. *Studies in Conflict & Terrorism, 43*(6), 431–443. https://doi.org/10.1080/10576 10X.2018.1452701

Heifetz, R. A., Linsky, M., & Grashow, A. (2009). *The practice of adaptive leadership: Tools and tactics for changing your organization and the world.* Harvard Business Press.

Ibarra, H., & Hunter, M. (2007). How leaders build and use networks. *Harvard Business Review, 85*(1), 40–47.

Idol, L., Paolucci-Whitcomb, P., & Nevin, A. I. (1995). *Collaborative consultation: A comprehensive approach.* In L. Idol, P. Paolucci-Whitcomb, & A. I. Nevin (Eds.), *Consultation and collaboration in school and community settings* (pp. 5–24). Longman.

Kammer, J., King, M., Donahay, A., & Koeberl, H. (2021). *Strategies for successful school librarian and teacher collaboration.* School Library Research, 24.

Kania, J., & Kramer, M. (2011). Collective impact. *Stanford Social Innovation Review, 9*(1), 36–41.

Keller, A. (2019, September 12). *Pomona Unified reallocates $2 million to programs for high-needs students.* San Gabriel Valley Tribune. https://www.sgvtribune.com/2019/09/12/pomona-unified-reallocates-2-million-to-programs-for-high-need-students/

Kelley, R. D. (2022). *Freedom dreams: The black radical imagination.* Beacon Press.

Kim, I. (2024, March 11). *How students led a historic $25M divestment from LA school police.* NBCU Academy. https://nbcuacademy.com/school-police-defunding/

Library of Congress. (n.d.). East Los Angeles walkouts.

Lopez-Perry, C., & Whitson, L. (2022). Engaging in political leadership and macrolevel advocacy: School counselors leading for student mental wellness. *Journal of Counselor Leadership and Advocacy, 9*(2), 87–98. doi:10.1080/2326716X.2022.2085214

Miller, A. J., Slater, M. J., & Turner, M. J. (2021). Shared identity content between leader and follower influences intentional mobilization and challenge and threat states. *Psychology of Sport and Exercise, 54*, 101914.

Mizrahi, T., & Rosenthal, B. B. (2001). Complexities of coalition building: Leaders' successes, strategies, struggles, and solutions. *Social Work, 46*(1), 63–78.

Obach, B. (2010). Political opportunity and social movement coalitions: The role of policy segmentation and nonprofit tax law. In N. Van Dyke & H. J. McCammon (Eds.), *Strategic Alliances: Coalition Building and Social Movements*, 197–218.

Parau, P., Lemnaru, C., Dinsoreanu, M., & Potolea, R. (2017). Opinion leader detection. In F. A. Pozzi, E. Fersini, E. Messina, & B. Liu (Eds.), *Sentiment analysis in social networks* (pp. 157–170). Morgan Kaufmann.

Pearsall, M. J., & Ellis, A. P. J. (2011). Thick as thieves: The effects of ethical orientation and psychological safety on unethical team behaviour. *Journal of Applied Psychology, 96*, 401–411.

Radio Caracol. (2020, January 7). Episode 1: East LA walkouts [Audio podcast episode]. In *East LA Walkouts Podcast.* SoundCloud. https://soundcloud.com/radiocaracol/episode-1-east-la-walkouts-podcast

Robertson, A. (2007). Development of shared vision: Lessons from a science education community collaborative. *Journal of Research in Science Teaching, 44*(5), 681–705. https://doi.org/10.1002/tea.20162

Rosenblatt, G. (2010). The engagement pyramid: Six levels of connecting people and social change. https://www.the-vital-edge.com/engagement-pyramid/

Sage.Sonnie, A., & Tracy, J. (2011). *Hillbilly nationalists, urban race rebels, and Black power: Community organizing in radical times.* Melville House Publishing.

Schein, E. H., & Bennis, W. (1965). *Personal and organizational change through group methods.* Wiley.

Scott, K. (2019). *Radical candor: Be a kick-ass boss without losing your humanity.* St. Martin's Press.

Steen, S., Vannatta, R., & Ieva, K. (2022). *Introduction to group counseling: A culturally sustaining and inclusive framework.* Springer Publishing Company.

Stevens, M., Rees, T., Steffens, N. K., Haslam, S. A., Coffee, P., & Polman, R. (2019). Leaders' creation of shared identity impacts group members' effort and performance: Evidence from an exercise task. *PLOS ONE, 14*(7), e0218984. https://doi.org/10.1371/journal.pone.0218984

Toporek, R. L., & Daniels, J. (2018). 2018 update and expansion of the 2003 ACA Advocacy Competencies: Honoring the work of the past and contextualizing the present. https://bit.ly/3nOIPmJ

Valente, T. W., & Pumpuang, P. (2007). Identifying opinion leaders to promote behavior change. *Health Education & Behavior, 34*(6), 881–896.

Williams, J. (2013). *From the bullet to the ballot: The Illinois chapter of the Black panther party and racial coalition politics in Chicago.* University of North Carolina Press.

Wolff, T., Minkler, M., Wolfe, S. M., Berkowitz, B., Bowen, L., Butterfoss, F. D., & Lee, K. S. (2017). Collaborating for equity and justice: Moving beyond collective impact. *Nonprofit Quarterly, 9*, 42–53.

Chapter 8

There's No Place Like Home
Finding Rest in Community

Let's be clear: leadership and advocacy work can be exhausting. Constantly challenging the status quo and addressing deeply ingrained systemic injustices requires a great deal of energy. Managing one's emotions, recognizing and naming injustices, navigating power dynamics, addressing resistance, and coalition building are all important aspects of leading for liberation that have been explored throughout this book. However, it is important to acknowledge that these tasks require our time and active effort. If you are leading this work in your school, district, community, or professional organization while simultaneously belonging to a marginalized social group, feelings of dehumanization, exploitation, and erasure are likely not foreign to you. Social justice leaders, particularly those of the global majority, often carry the emotional labor of supporting and advocating for and with marginalized students and their families. Our fight is often tied to our identities and love for our communities; the political is personal.

Yet social media is making the world smaller, and the constant barrage of news updates can become overwhelming. The endless stream of videos, articles, and social media posts documenting the physical, psychological, and emotional attacks on marginalized communities can be overwhelming. The weight of bearing witness to trauma and suffering, especially of those in your community to systemic injustices can take a toll on one's mental and emotional well-being. Add to this that, like other counseling professionals, school counselors deal with a wide range of student academic, career, and social-emotional needs which can lead to a greater risk for burnout (Mullen & Crowe, 2017). Studies have shown that early career school counselors and school counselors who face role ambiguity or role incongruity are more likely to experience higher levels of burnout (Fye et al., 2020; Kim & Lambie, 2018; Mullen et al., 2018). In an effort to provide the essential care our students need during these turbulent times, school counselors must develop a practice of rest and care for themselves and their community. As we discussed in Chapter 7, freedom dreaming allows us to visualize the future that we want to live in, and rest is a necessary part of the dreaming process.

DOI: 10.4324/9781032679174-10

In this country, the struggle for racial justice, equity, and liberation is centuries-long. It cannot be achieved passively or overnight. Leaders must commit to active engagement. They must commit to the long haul. To do so, school counselors must care for themselves and others in ways that ensure the work is sustainable while simultaneously recognizing our shared humanity. Systems of oppression and those who seek to maintain power will engage in oppositional tactics with the intent to exhaust you, to remove your space for rest and peace in order to deter you from continuing the work. The most powerful way to fight back is to lead with gentleness, love, and care for yourself and those around you. However, it is important to recognize that white supremacy culture trains us all to internalize attitudes and behaviors that do not serve us (Okun, 1999). Concepts such as individualism, grind culture, and sense of urgency are all rooted in capitalism, classism, patriarchy, and white supremacy culture (Berg & Seeber, 2016; Hersey, 2022). When school counselors internalize these principles, it can often lead to feelings of isolation and burnout.

In response to these challenges, self-care has been widely promoted in the counseling literature (Aibing & Xinying, 2020; Jones & Pijanowski, 2023; O'Halloran, & Linton, 2000; Skovholt & Trotter-Mathison, 2014) and many of us likely came from school counselor training programs that emphasized the importance of self-care (CACREP, 2024). Our professional associations contend that self-care is an ethical imperative that ensures optimal professional effectiveness (ACA, 2014; ASCA, 2022). However, the problem with common self-care guidance is that it shifts the blame and responsibility to the individual and obscures the need for systemic change and collective responsibility. This narrow focus on the individual lacks consideration of factors that may affect one's ability to engage in self-care, including organizational culture, racism and discrimination, gender inequality, environmental inequality, and healthcare access (Johnson et al., 2023).

In *The Wonderful Wizard of Oz* Dorothy, the Tin Woodman, the Scarecrow, and the Cowardly Lion all at various points engage in behaviors that embrace community care over toxic individualism. We are well aware that Dorothy's singular goal is to get back home to her loved ones, yet throughout her journey, she consistently stops to help others, be it oiling the Tin Woodman to free him from his rusted state, helping the Scarecrow down from the pole or comforting the Cowardly Lion. In each instance, her values and yearning for connection and community call on her to lead with love and care for those around her. Each one has their own individual interest, be it the Tin Woodman's desire for a heart, the Scarecrow's wish for a brain, or the Lion's longing for courage, yet they put their faith in the group and ultimately come together to provide care and support for one another along the way. At various points, they encounter obstacles deliberately designed to test their resolve and compel them to either abandon their quest or strengthen their solidarity. In the same spirit, transformative and liberatory leadership recognizes that we are inextricably linked to each other, and our wellness and wholeness are also connected.

In Chapters 1 and 2, we asked you to look at leadership from a liberatory perspective involving both individual and collective liberation. As we conclude this final chapter and our journey down the yellow brick road, we ask you to liberate yourself from the ideas of toxic individualism and grind culture. These concepts prioritize productivity over humanity and are harmful to the leadership and advocacy work of school counselors. To move us toward a practice of a deeper and more sustainable form of holistic care, we offer an alternative to the trappings of isolation and burnout. The current systems meant to support and protect the common good, including healthcare, education, social safety nets, housing and economic policies, and environmental protections, have, in the course of time, been stripped from beneath our feet, leaving very little left to help us gather our bearings. To counteract this, we call on you to challenge practices that prioritize healing in isolation and move toward a practice of collective care and relational healing by finding rest in the embrace of your community. With that in mind, the Circles of Care framework is introduced as a means for co-regulation, mutual support, and systems change. Close your eyes and remember, "there is no place like home."

Pause and Reflect

1 In what ways do your personal experiences and upbringing influence your approach to self-care and community care?
2 How does your cultural background affect how you view, receive, and offer care?
3 Are there any cultural taboos or stigmas related to care and rest that affect your willingness to seek or provide support?

The Importance of Social Connectedness and Support

Several theories have been proposed to explain the association between social connectedness, support, and overall wellness. One of the most well-known theories is John Bowlby's attachment theory (1973), which suggests that infants are biologically wired to form attachments as a survival strategy. This theory emphasizes the central role of caregivers in providing safety and security, which can influence attachments later in life. Social support and buffering theory assert that social support protects individuals from the negative effects of stress (Cohen & Willis, 1985). Social belonging theory suggests that individuals have a basic need to form and maintain positive social relationships, contributing to their sense of identity and mental well-being (Baumeister, 2012). A recent meta-analysis of social connectedness research confirmed that social connection is a basic human need that is essential to our overall health and well-being (Wickramaratne et al., 2022). The effects of strong support and connectedness are not limited to infants and youth. Among older adults (50 years and older), feelings of connectedness and social support are associated with better self-rated physical and mental health (Asante & Castillo, 2018). In fact, social support was more important than a sense of group membership for their physical and mental health, suggesting that among older adults, the quality of relationships is prioritized over simply belonging to a group. The benefits of social support also extend into the workplace, where support from a workplace leader can reduce psychological distress following a traumatic event (Birkeland et al., 2017).

Conversely, studies have demonstrated the harmful effects of disconnectedness on emotion, behavior, and brain structure. Disruption in social interaction during critical developmental periods can negatively impact cognitive, social, and verbal performance, increasing vulnerability to mental health issues (Kennedy et al., 2016; Sonuga-Barke et al., 2017; Zeanah et al., 2009). School closures during COVID-19 have been associated with mental health problems among students due to a prolonged physical isolation from their peers, teachers, extended family, and community network (Loades et al., 2020). Among adults, COVID "social distancing" was associated with reversible brain changes commonly associated with stress and anxiety (Xiong et al., 2023). Prolonged social isolation in adults, including prisoners under solitary confinement, empty nesters, and those experiencing social distancing, can lead to changes in their social homeostatic set-point, their internal need for social interaction, which in turn may lead to depression, aggression, or social anxiety (Xiong et al., 2023). The effects are far-reaching; feelings of loneliness can actually reduce our immune system response (Pressman et al., 2005). Remarkably, feelings of loneliness become our internal red flag signaling to us that we are deficient in social relationships (Masi et al., 2011).

Individualism vs. Collectivism (Me vs. We)

The value of social connectedness and support has long been recognized by BIPOC communities through the practice of community care. This approach relies heavily on the collectivistic beliefs of these communities and recognizes that the well-being of the individual is inherently tied to the well-being of others. Scholars have debated the relationship between individualism and collectivism. Some researchers suggest that individualism and collectivism are at opposite ends of a continuous spectrum (Oyserman et al., 2002; Taras et al., 2014), while others propose two independent constructs (Markus & Kitayama, 1991; Oyserman, 1993; Singelis, 1994). Nevertheless, one thing that scholars can agree on is that individualism and collectivism make up a portion of a culture's core set of values. In light of this, examining how these values influence how we view, provide, and receive care is essential. Oyserman and colleagues (2002)

Table 8.1 Individualistic vs. Collectivistic Cultures

Individualistic Cultures	Collectivistic Cultures
• "Me" Culture	• "We" Culture
• Independence	• Community
• Think in terms of "I"	• Think in terms of "we"
• Self-reliance	• Selflessness
• Everyone grows up to look after him/herself and his/her immediate family only	• People are born into extended families or in other groups that continue protecting them in exchange for loyalty
• Individual decision-making is best	• Group decision-making is best
• Tasks prevail over relationships	• Relationship prevails over task
• Personal Achievements	• Group achievements

define individualism "as a worldview that centralizes the personal- personal goals, personal uniqueness, and personal control- and peripheralizes the social" (p.5). Hofstede (1980) defines individualism as prioritizing personal rights over obligations, focusing on oneself and immediate family, emphasizing personal autonomy and self-fulfillment, and basing one's identity on one's personal accomplishments. Alternatively, collectivism is defined as a worldview based on "the assumption that groups bind and mutually obligate individuals," where "the personal is simply a component of the social (Oyserman et al., 2002, p.5)." Understanding the differences between these worldviews can help you become more conscious of how your cultural lens shapes your approach to health, well-being, and relational care. Table 8.1 outlines key differences between these worldviews.

Embracing Heart Work through Circles of Care

Building on our exploration of individual and collective approaches, as well as the benefits of social care and support, the Circle of Care framework conceptualizes care as a series of concentric and interrelated circles, each focusing on a different aspect of care (Figure 8.1). The center circle represents *self-care*, which is our personal awareness of mind, body, and soul. It includes your identity, beliefs, values, and your perception of how care is offered and received. The knowledge and experience gained from these core elements build our capacity to engage in the next circle of care, community care. *Community care* , as defined by Mehreen and Gray-Donald (2018), is "seeing members' well-being— particularly their emotional health—as a shared responsibility of the group rather than the lone task of an individual." When we engage in community care, we move beyond individual privilege, recognize how systems harm others' safety and well-being, and take shared responsibility for the safety and well-being

Figure 8.1 Circles of Care

of those in our community. The awareness and experience gained from these interactions enhance our ability to engage in the next circle of care, *collective action*. This final circle focuses on dismantling the systems that impede caring and nurturing environments while simultaneously building new systems that embrace humanity, love, and care. Collective action is a radical expression of care. It is rooted in liberation and stands firmly against all forms of oppression.

Remember we said these circles of care are interrelated? Moving from the inner circle (self-care) outward also necessitates movement from the outer circle (collective action) inward. Think of these Circles of Care like a beating heart radiating in and out, reminding us of our humanity. As the world around us changes, systems constantly evolve as those in power seek to maintain dominance. These oppressive systems are not new, but rather how they manifest shifts. As we respond to these changes through collective action, it is important for us to turn our attention inward, pause, and recalibrate. Leaders should take time to reflect on how these new practices or systems impact relationships within community care and the adjustments that need to be made to ensure the needs of those who are most impacted are addressed. We must ask ourselves, how do we adjust the way we show up for each other? Oppressive systems have a tendency to rebrand themselves over time. This means that while the fundamental structures of oppression may persist, they often adapt their appearance or methods to maintain influence and control in changing social contexts. These subtle or not so subtle rebrands disguise themselves in ways that appear either less harmful or more socially acceptable, making it challenging to notice its impact on our beliefs and actions. Therefore, leaders must take one more step back and re-engage in self-care. The constant pressure to work and grind robs us of our time to pause, reflect, and critique systems. When we rest, we give ourselves the time and clarity to question how these new faces of oppression influence our beliefs, values, and ability to engage in caring and loving ways. Rest allows us to recalibrate and reorient as we lead through these circles of care. As we move through each circle of care, we challenge you to move beyond shallow wellness work and engage in deeper, more sustainable practices of care that address the root causes of exhaustion rather than just the symptoms.

Self-Care

Self-care originally began as a medical concept used by doctors to encourage mentally ill and elderly patients needing long-term care to treat themselves and develop healthy exercise habits. During the women's movement and civil rights movement of the 1960s and 1970s, self-care became a political act, a way for marginalized groups to take charge of their health in response to the failures of a white, patriarchal medical system (Nelson, 2015). For instance, the Black Panther Party created Community Survival Programs based on the immediate needs of the community, which included programs such as general education diploma (GED) classes, free breakfast programs, free health programs, and Women, Infants, and Children (WIC, Carpini, 2000). Each program, inspired by collective care, became a tool for self-care and survival for groups whose humanity and care had historically been ignored. Unfortunately, when creations or concepts originating from marginalized communities (e.g., meditation) gain popularity, they can become mainstream, diluted, and commercialized. This was the case for self-care; in the late 1970's and early 1980s self-care and wellness became synonymous with fitness and wellness lifestyles of white and wealthier communities (Surmitis et al., 2018). Self-care became co-opted, appropriated, and whitewashed to cliché spa days, wellness retreats, and yoga classes. While we enjoy a good spa day, there is so much more to self-care, particularly for those leading for equity. This commercialized view of self-care ignores the structural barriers to care faced by marginalized groups. Their failure to thrive is blamed on a lack of initiative or motivation.

Missing from the current school counseling discourse on self-care is the importance of school counselors of color not only surviving but thriving in oppressive spaces and systems that harm their sense of self and community. Historically, for marginalized groups, self-care has symbolized an act of resistance against systemic oppression and discrimination. Audre Lorde, a Black civil rights activist, writer, lesbian, and feminist who was especially prominent between the 1960s and 1980s, invoked in her book *Burst of Light* (1992), "Caring for myself is not self-indulgence, it is self-preservation, and that is an act of political warfare." Lorde reflected on how she had given much of her life and self to civil rights activism—and how acts of self-care were essential not only for her survival but as a form of political resistance. The significance of self-care transcends individual action; our ability to understand and care for ourselves serves as the basis for our ability to build structures of care. As such, we suggest an approach to self-care that nurtures holistic health and well-being. In the next section, we examine self-care through the concept of deep holistic wellness, using the Wellness Wheel as a framework.

The Wellness Wheel

The Wellness Wheel outlines six interconnected dimensions of personal wellness, which include physical, spiritual, social, emotional, intellectual, and occupational (Hettler, 1984). The framework serves as a visual tool providing a holistic view of overall wellness and helps individuals assess the various dimensions of personal well-being (Figure 8.2). It is important to recognize a much older and deeply spiritual framework—the Medicine Wheel, which has been used by generations of various people indigenous to the Americas for health and healing. Within the Medicine Wheel, also known as the Sacred Hoop, each compass direction on the wheel represents a different aspect of wellness that supports the development of a balanced individual (Aktá Lakota Museum & Cultural Center, n.d.; National Library of Medicine, n.d.). The East symbolizes new beginnings and the mental dimension, while the South represents growth and emotional well-being. The West embodies introspection and spiritual growth, and the North signifies wisdom and physical health. The circle itself serves as a reminder that everything flows in a circle. Both frameworks recognize the importance of remaining balanced at the center of the wheel while developing equally the physical, mental, emotional, and spiritual aspects of one's personality. School counselors can benefit from a more profound and comprehensive approach to self-care that enhances their personal well-being and their capacity for effective and sustainable leadership. Drawing from the Wellness Wheel, we focus on the six dimensions of wellness from a leadership perspective.

Physical wellness involves exercise, nutrition, sleep, and managing our stress and health. For school counselors, engaging in lifestyle practices focusing on prevention is essential for maintaining their physical health. There is a wealth of research showing how physical wellness can play an important role in our emotional and social wellness by relieving stress, anxiety, and depression and how poor health can lead to shorter lifespan (Mahindru et al., 2023; Reimers et al.,

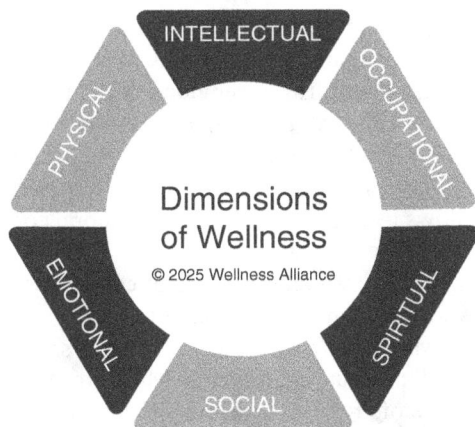

Figure 8.2 The National Wellness Institute's Six Dimensions of Wellness. Content Has Been Reprinted With Permission From the National Wellness Institute, Inc., NationalWellness.org.

2012; Schultchen et al., 2019). Yet, countless stories are shared by school counselors who have worked through lunches, skipped breaks, or worked extended hours and weekends to serve their administrators, students, and families. The Nap Bishop, Tricia Hersey (2022), maintains that this disregard for our bodies and physical health began early in our education. She makes a profound connection by highlighting how early schooling socialized us to ignore our bodies' needs in favor of productivity. Hersey provides examples such as the removal and diminishing of time for physical education, recess, restroom breaks, and nap time, which conditioned us from an early age to prioritize productivity over being in tune with our bodies' needs. As leaders, if we are disconnected from our bodies, how can we truly be connected with the needs of others? School counselors must monitor their physical health for common signs of distress (Centers for Disease Control and Prevention, 2014), including (1) changes in appetite, energy, and activity levels, (2) difficulty sleeping, nightmares, and upsetting thoughts and images, (3) physical reactions, such as headaches, body pains, stomach problems, and skin rashes, and (4) worsening of chronic health problems. Taking the time to meet our basic needs brings us back to our humanity. Prioritizing our well-being allows us to be more attuned to the needs of those around us, and leaders who maintain good physical health set a powerful example for others.

Spiritual wellness consists of understanding and tending to the beliefs, values, and ethics that guide your work. It involves connecting your inner and outer worlds to support living in your values and purpose. School counselors engaged in equity work are often asked to solve complex problems, offer a clear course of direction for their followers, and negotiate challenging situations. Tending to your spiritual wellness allows you to align your inner world (values, beliefs, ethics) with your outer world (actions, decisions, relationships). It involves creating space for rest, reflection, and reconnection to the morals, values, and ethics that guide us as individuals. Creating time to reconnect with nature, read inspirational books, engage in spiritual, religious, or cultural practices, or acts of community service are great ways to reconnect us to our values. If we are constantly moving on to the next task, the next goal, or the next issue, we may steer off course without realizing it and act in ways that are contrary to our principles. Spiritual wellness allows us to pause and check our moral compass as leaders to ensure we are heading in the right direction.

Social wellness includes developing a sense of connection and belonging and a strong social network that can provide support and guidance. School counselors, especially those who are the only counselors in a school building, benefit from having well-developed support systems. Mia Birdsong (2020) beautifully describes the importance of creating "a community of friends and neighbors that provide both a safety net and a spring board—support when things are hard and celebration when things are good." Her metaphor reminds us of the gymnast who is able to be more daring in their technique because they trust in the support of those around them. This support system is crucial in social justice work and allows school counselors to take bold actions and push boundaries with confidence. A strong support system can provide psychological safety, allowing individuals to take risks, express their ideas and concerns, speak up with questions, and admit mistakes—all without fear of negative consequences (Wanless, 2016). Our support circle reminds us that we are not alone in our efforts and can take charge when needed, enabling us to rest and recharge. They recognize when we need to step back and readily offer their assistance. More importantly, these individuals appreciate that we are more than our work, valuing us not for our status or achievements but for our human spirit. Alternatively, social wellness means creating boundaries with relationships that move us away from our values, humanity, love, and care. Leaders must invest time and energy in cultivating their support network.

Emotional wellness is about the overall state of emotional health and well-being. It includes the ability to understand ourselves and cope with the challenges that life can bring. School counselors who regularly check in on their emotions can process them more fully and ask for help when needed. Poor emotional health can contribute to lowered immunity, hypertension, relationship issues, and difficulty at work. In Chapter 6, we discussed the resistance school counselors may encounter in their advocacy work. Challenging long-held traditions and changing systems can be an emotionally charged process when they are tied to our values and communities we hold dear. Emotional wellness can provide school counselors the resilience to face these challenges. Leaders who prioritize their mental health engage in their day-to-day leadership actions grounded and focused, even in the face of adversity. In Chapter 3, we described the importance of emotional intelligence, which includes the ability to recognize, understand, regulate, and influence one's own emotions and the emotions of others. The relationship between emotional wellness and emotional intelligence is symbiotic, with each enhancing the other. High emotional intelligence can help school counselors develop better coping strategies, stronger relationships, greater resilience, and increased self-care. In turn, emotional wellness can provide a stable foundation for developing emotional intelligence skills.

Occupational wellness consists of the personal satisfaction, balance, and fulfillment one receives in life through employment, academic, or volunteer work. It encompasses various aspects of employment, including career development, job satisfaction, work-life balance, and personal growth. It involves balancing one's time at work and time spent enjoying leisure activities. Establishing health boundaries, seeking growth opportunities, embracing flexibility, managing stress, and celebrating achievements are all helpful strategies for achieving occupational wellness (Mahesh, 2024). Finding work-life balance can be particularly challenging for school counselors working in under-resourced schools and with large caseloads. Even if the recommended 1:250 ratio was rooted in evidence-based studies and implemented, the reality of school counselors' working environments includes increasing student needs, widening equity gaps, and decreasing resources. These structural limitations make it impossible to meet the needs of all students at the level you would ideally want to. We cannot stretch ourselves so thin that we become ineffective in our role, detracting our focus on students. While the drive to help others may tempt you to work extended hours or weekends, school counselors must resist the urge to sacrifice their personal well-being for professional responsibilities. You cannot do the work required of multiple people, no matter how skilled or dedicated you are. Recognize that this is not a reflection of your capabilities but rather the structural limitations imposed on educators by systemic inequities.

Intellectual wellness involves creating opportunities for your brain both for rest and stimulation for critical thinking. Essentially, it means staying curious and engaging in learning new things. Intellectual wellness can be nurtured through both personal and professional development. Activities can include reading books and articles, attending workshops and conferences, and creating your own professional learning communities. Don't forget we are moving beyond shallow wellness work. Engaging with information deeply involves more than attending events or reading the latest trending book. Exhaustion and disconnection prevent us from engaging in deep critical thinking with the information that is being provided to us. To engage in intellectual wellness, one must assess the quality and credibility of the presenters and authors as well as the information provided. Intellectual wellness involves considering an issue from multiple points of view, thinking about the broader consequences of ideas or actions presented, and acknowledging personal biases. They also recognize bias in the information encountered. School counselors must do more than passively absorb information. Avoid rushing to implement takeaways immediately, and take time to critically evaluate what you learned. Slowing down creates space for analysis, enabling leaders to dissect complex systems, understand underlying issues, and develop effective strategies for change. Table 8.2 provides examples of wellness activities within each dimension and questions for reflection.

Table 8.2 Wellness Activities

Dimension of Wellness	Sample Activities	Reflection Questions
Physical wellness	Prioritize quality sleep Engage in regular exercise Maintain healthy eating habits Get regular health screenings	Do you maintain a regular exercise routine that you enjoy? Are you consistent in taking breaks and lunch to ensure you rest and refuel? Do you avoid going into work sick to prevent spreading illness and allow yourself time to recover? Do you listen to your body and rest when you need to?
Spiritual wellness	Create space for reflection Connect with nature Read inspirational texts or books Talk to a spiritual mentor, counselor, or coach Engage in religious or spiritual practices Journal Practice gratitude	Do you allow yourself time alone? Do you put down your phone to just be? Do you practice activities that allow you to slow down?
Social wellness	Keep in contact with friends Spend time with loved ones Participate in community events Join a healing or talking circle	Do you actively seek out social activities that bring you joy? Do you feel supported by your social network? Do you have people who will freely celebrate your wins or gently correct you when you are wrong?
Emotional wellness	Practice progressive muscle relaxation Use guided visualization Perform yoga Listen to soothing music Engage in a hobby Talk to a therapist	Are you able to express your emotions in a healthy and constructive way? Are you aware of your emotional triggers and how to manage them? Do you seek help or support when you are overwhelmed or distressed?
Occupational wellness	Set personal and professional goals Pursue passion projects Schedule regular breaks and time off	How well does your work align with your values? Are you able to balance work life and personal life? How effective are you at managing your stress related to academic or work responsibilities?

(Continued)

Table 8.2 (Continued)

Dimension of Wellness	Sample Activities	Reflection Questions
Intellectual wellness	Read books and articles Seek out a mentor or coach Join professional organizations Conduct action research Engage in self-study research	Are you open to new ideas and perspectives? Do you make time for reading, learning, or educational pursuits? Are you willing to engage in topics outside of your comfort zone?

As you consider how you engage in self-care across the various dimensions, it is critical to recognize that self-care is not always accessible to everyone. Keep in mind, that commercialized models of self-care prioritize the welfare of the privileged (those with the time, access, and resources). At the same time, the well-being and care of marginalized groups is seen as less important. Leaders recognize that the individual has to be mindful of the collective, and the collective has to be mindful of the individual (Chew et al., 2016). Understanding the various dimensions of wellness can help you develop a more comprehensive practice of care and rest while also fostering an environment that promotes various forms of self-care among those you lead. What good is it if you, as the leader, are rested and well while others around you are struggling in the same fight for systemic change? Transformative and liberatory leadership recognizes that we are inextricably linked to each other and that our wellness and wholeness are interconnected. These forms of leadership acknowledge that individuals cannot self-care their way out of harmful systems and ensure that everyone is supported and empowered through community care.

Community Care

Community care involves individuals actively nourishing and sustaining each other's well-being within a community by using their relationships to foster collective wellness (Dockray, 2019). Meg Leach (2019) describes community care as "building networks of people who can help when community members need it…making self-care possible for those who cannot achieve it on their own." Ultimately, it means creating a network of people who show up for each other in times of need. Community care focuses on the connections, intentional actions, and efforts to mobilize individuals to support one another. Historically, systems shaped by racism have led to disparities in economic stability, education, food, healthcare, neighborhood environment (housing, transportation, safety), and social and community environment. These social determinants of health affect a wide range of health, functioning, and quality-of-life outcomes and risks (Johnson et al., 2023). Consequently, community care emerged as a workaround for systems that do not inherently support care, offering a way for communities to thrive. Community care requires all of us to step outside of our privileged identities, empathizing and standing in solidarity with those who experience different forms of marginalization and oppression. It involves listening and understanding their perspectives and taking concrete actions to support access to care and redistributing resources and opportunities in ways that address these inequities. Community care responds to existing inequities in resources by creating support structures to bridge these gaps, providing individuals and the broader community support through mutual aid and protection.

Community care has been the cornerstone of BIPOC and QTBIPOC communities for generations. It is grounded in the collectivistic principles and values of many of these communities, including collective responsibility, collective interest, and cooperation (Mental Health America, n.d.). White school counselors interested in moving toward a more collectivistic form of care are obligated to learn from the histories that have shaped the practices people of color embrace in times of crisis. Throughout history, these communities have created systems of support to sustain collective well-being. The Underground Railroad, with its network of safehouses, was used by enslaved Black Americans to escape to free states. The Free African Society was created in Philadelphia after the Revolutionary War to provide financial support, education, and community services to newly freed Black individuals to build community resilience (Zinn Education Project, n.d.), and in Chapter 7, we discussed the role of the Black Panther Party in supporting Black communities. Indigenous communities in the Pacific Northwest practice *potlatch*, marked by the redistribution of wealth and goods or sometimes the destruction of property to demonstrate generosity and community solidarity (Gadacz, 2024). In *Braiding Sweetgrass*, author Robin Wall Kimmerer (2013) references the work of Lewis Hyde. Hyde explains that indigenous communities established "gift economies" (p.30) in which food in particular was always given as a gift, not commodified, because it was about nurturing relationships; with each other and with the land. Among Latinx communities, *mutualistas* in Mexican-American neighborhoods provided social services, legal aid, and financial support critical in resistance against discrimination (Marquez & Jennings, 2000). Filipino migrant domestic workers in the San Francisco Bay Area, shaped by their shared identities and experiences, created supportive networks and forged bonds to navigate the US healthcare system and endure the harsh conditions of their labor, creating strategies of survival that make room for friendship, joy, mutual aid, and radical politics (Francisco-Menchavez, 2018, 2024).

Community care is also seen in less formal structures through small daily acts that build and maintain community resilience and support. In communities, this may include community check-ins, shared meals, carpooling, and community gardens. In families, this can involve shared responsibilities and elder care.

In online communities, this may consist of virtual support groups or resource-sharing platforms. While general resource-sharing platforms may focus on the distribution of resources, one rooted in community care prioritizes inclusive, equitable, and participatory practices. BIPOC school counselors have utilized various forms of community care to sustain the well-being of the individual and the community. The Facebook group Professional School Counselors of Color (PSCOC) is a great example of community care. Alicia Oglesby, high school counselor and administrator for the PSCOC group, states:

> As an administrator for the PSCOC Facebook Group, I felt that I was selected by Kisha, the founder, because of my skills and advocacy. I believe she saw a leader in me, and I was just beginning my school counseling career at the time. But that exemplifies the intention of this space. We are not a collective that just happens upon each other. There is thoughtfulness and honoring a historical context within the creation of this community. Other groups are shaped by what already happens in our society; how society is shaped directly influences how these more unintentional spaces form. They maintain the status quo. There is no rhyme or reason to the gathering. A group of similar-enough people all click join and do what they always do. PSCOC is committed to being different from that. For one, it's a space specifically for people of color who are current and former k-12 school counselors. That alone means we recognize the historical marginalization that impacts us as people and as professionals. Secondly, the topics are often seeking support we know we can offer in good faith. We lean on each other to advance in our careers, better assist students, confront racist systems, and so much more. Lastly, I think organizing is a key function of the group. We plan events to continue to network and help each other thrive. We know no one else will if we don't provide that ourselves. Yes, PSCOC is a special community where care is centralized, and that's why I've been an administrator for 10 years.

Kisha Hughes, PSCOC founder, describes why she created the Facebook group and describes how the group enhances individuals' ability to engage in various forms of wellness:

> PSCOC was partly born from a realization that the journey through a school counseling career can be isolating and challenging, especially in white spaces where seeking help isn't always comfortable. As a new counselor, I recognized the need for a supportive community to guide me, and I knew others likely felt the same. I jumped on my computer on July 4, 2014, and created PSCOC. During our early years, many of our white counterparts were disturbed that we did not accept white members. What they failed to see—or didn't want to see—was the mistreatment BIPOC school counselors often faced in other counseling groups. Comments or posts by BIPOC school counselors were

frequently ridiculed or shut down, causing many to become passive participants, merely lurking for resources without engaging. Recognizing this need, I created a space for us, by us, where we could truly be ourselves. PSCOC is that space, fostering a community where BIPOC school counselors can freely and authentically connect, share, and thrive. Our admin team (Kimberly Brown, Carletta Hurt, Alicia Oglesby, and myself), each bringing specialized skills, connect with members on a profound level—professionally (PSCOC Leadership Academy & virtual conferences), emotionally, socially, physically (PSCOC Fitness), and spiritually. Together, we foster deep, meaningful connections that transform our community into a family. Over the past 10 years, we have not only watched our members grow professionally, we have also seen their families grow! There are so many PSCOC nieces and nephews that we love dearly. We are able to do this by fostering a supportive and inclusive community by using surveys for climate checks, engaging posts to spark conversations, and creating opportunities for school counselors to present at conferences, regardless of their experience level. We build courage, enhance professional skills, and form new friendships. We aim to ensure everyone feels they have a seat at the table no matter where they are in their career. We celebrate our members, remind them of their amazing impact, and show up for them. This support is crucial for BIPOC school counselors, who often face isolation in various schools and districts. In the PSCOC Facebook group, counselors can be their authentic selves, knowing it's a space where they truly belong.

The California Association of School Counselors (CASC) offers healing circles as a way to bring care and support to their members. These circles provide a space for individuals to come together, share their experiences, and offer support to one another. Tiffany Le, a high school counselor, shares her experiences with healing circles:

Through my involvement in the CASC Social Justice, Equity, and Anti-Racism Committee, we have seen the need among California school counselors to have a healing space to process our thoughts and feelings related to the social unrest that emerged since 2020. We have hosted many virtual restorative forums, open to all school counselors and educators, to discuss topics and current events affecting marginalized communities. In these spaces, colleagues can share their concerns, offer support to one another, and provide ideas and resources related to these topics. Through facilitating these healing spaces, I have found connections with like-minded colleagues that I have not easily found in the workplace; these moments of connection have brought comfort in times of stress and helped recharge my passion for social justice causes that affect my students and marginalized communities.

The leaders in each of these examples recognized that the needs of individuals were not being addressed and came together to develop a network of people who could care for each other when needed, thus creating opportunities for various forms of care.

For white school counselors and those coming from more individualistic cultures, it is critical to shift one's thinking beyond self-care to collective care. This can be challenging for white school counselors especially those who have grown up in the United States with Western ideals of individual accomplishment. Privilege naturally puts a person in a position of safety, guarded against discrimination, prejudice, oppression, and other harmful societal forces. Many white school counselors may have learned they should be kind or respectful to others based on religious or societal principles. However, they may not have been raised with a collective mindset or learned that their well-being or success was interconnected to that of others. White people do not often experience feelings of solidarity related to their racial identity (Helms, 1990; Tatum, 1994).

Although many white school counselors may possess other marginalized identities (e.g., queer, disabled, low socioeconomic background) that do give them a sense of solidarity with others, it is important to remember that the dominant group in school counseling is still white women (ASCA, 2024). When experiencing hard times, white school counselors may default to self-care for themselves and others. While a one-time gift basket for someone who is grieving far away may be appreciated and check off a box for you, it may not be as helpful as group rotation of weekly phone/house calls to coordinate groceries, laundry, mail sorting, or emotional support. Learning to integrate collective care means investing intentional time and energy, not doing it alone, and it is often not monetarily driven. Within your school, instead of just writing a teacher a note of support for her cancer treatments, take her a simple homemade lunch, and along with a co-counselor, cover her classes for the afternoon. In your community, rather than sending meals during hard times, bring those in need to your house instead. Cook for them while other neighbors or friends go and tidy up their house, change bed linens, or mow the yard. Refer to Okun's characteristics of White Supremacy culture (1999) below as reference points for moving from a frame of self-care to community care.

Community care is an incredibly powerful form of holistic care because it recognizes people's inherent worth and humanity and centers on the belief that everyone has something to offer the community and that those in need remain equally valuable and worthy (Leach, 2019). This is uniquely different from transactional relationships and leadership approaches where exchange is based on the immediacy of mutual benefit. It recognizes that everyone has times when they can give and times when they need to receive. At its core, community care involves extending support selflessly without the expectation of reciprocation from the same person. An individual's value to the community isn't tied to their status, power, wealth, popularity, or professional success. Rather, community care focuses on bringing to the group compassion, humility, empathy, and love. One of the biggest challenges to engaging in community care is overcoming the expectation of a balanced exchange. The idea that we must always give as much as we receive creates a transactional mindset that is contradictory to liberatory leadership and community care.

For school counselors and those in helping professions, asking for help can be incredibly challenging. Needing assistance can stir up feelings of weakness and failure. Rather than ask for help, we attempt to go it alone to meet some unrealistic expectations. Yet, school counselors love to help and as such, are often very good at offering assistance. For so many of us, providing support to others can be incredibly fulfilling because it aligns with our values and mission. It is a paradox, the idea that others are deserving of help, but we are not. On the one hand, we believe in the value and worthiness of others to receive support and the recognition of their humanity. On the other hand, we deem ourselves unworthy of the same assistance, denying our own humanity and contradicting the very principles of compassion we so often advocate for others. Instead consider this, how does refusing help from others affect their opportunity to demonstrate their love and care for us? How might this lead to missed opportunities for deeper connections with those who care for us, especially at a time when we may need it most? Leaders who engage in community care model a form of leadership that prioritizes love, care, and generosity of resources.

Collective Action

Collective action extends the principles of community care by focusing on broader systemic issues within the outer circle. Defined as an action taken by a group of individuals to achieve a common goal (Wright et al., 1990), collective action requires joining forces to achieve something bigger than what one can accomplish alone. It involves critically examining and challenging systems and structures that perpetuate inequality and privilege. In Chapter 7 we discussed the importance of moving across the collaboration continuum for collective action through partnerships, alliances, and coalitions. According to Lizarazo Pereira and colleagues (2022), collective actions depend on at least three variables: identity, perceived unfairness, and perceived efficacy. Research has shown that disadvantaged groups are more likely than advantaged groups to challenge injustice through collective action (van Zomeren & Iyver, 2009). However, there are instances when members of advantaged groups will engage in collective action in favor of disadvantaged groups (Craig et al., 2020; Subašić et al., 2008). These conditions arise when members of advantaged groups perceive the disadvantages of others as legitimate or when they develop a moral connection to those being disadvantaged because they've witnessed or experienced actions that violate their sense of ethical principles (Harth et al., 2008; van Zomeren et al., 2011). Community care, the second circle in these circles of care, underscores empathizing, listening, understanding, and connecting with those around you, which can set the stage for these conditions. Engaging in a practice of community care fosters collaborative relationships with those who share a similar commitment to care and change, in doing so fostering a sense of belonging and identity among individuals. The heightened awareness gained from community care can motivate individuals to name and address these inequalities. Lastly, recognizing that there are others in your circle who are equally dedicated and working toward the same goals can increase the perceived self-efficacy of collective action. Given this, leaders can play a critical role in fostering environments that encourage advantaged groups to recognize the legitimacy of others' disadvantages and identify with those affected by injustice. Raising awareness about inequalities and injustices and connecting these issues to broader moral and ethical values, can help move people to take collective action.

Whether the goal is to change or defend the status quo, identity and perception of injustice are important predictors of collective action (Thomas et al., 2020). One of the greatest obstacles to engaging in this last circle of care is stepping outside of one's own privilege and recognizing the system that has benefited you for so long, could be harming others. Many individuals are willing to offer care, but their support is conditional upon maintaining existing systems. They may find it difficult to recognize that these systems could be causing harm to others, as they have not personally experienced such harm. Because their perspective is limited to their personal experiences, they vigorously believe that the systems which they have benefited from are inherently just and effective. Their circle of care extends as far as their own well-being. Their inability to envision the harm inflicted on others by these systems restricts their capacity to engage in care through collective action. Instead of standing in solidarity, they split sides choosing convenience over community. It is important for school counselors to recognize if they might be someone whose care for others is conditional on maintaining existing systems. It requires honest self-reflection and consideration of our attitudes and behaviors. How have you responded when someone has shared with you that they have been affected by a system that you value and believe in? Have you invalidated their feelings or experiences? Have you offered excuses for the system rather than acknowledging their feelings and concerns? Do you minimize your own role in the harm caused or the impact of the system on others? Earlier, we compared these circles of care to a beating heart radiating outward. To reach the outer circle of care and the expansiveness of our heart requires us to acknowledge our true feelings, reactions, and potential biases. While it may be easy to convince ourselves otherwise, those deeply ingrained in this work recognize the rhythm of a beating heart committed to justice. Authentic allyship demands consistent and meaningful action.

How Systems of Oppression Undermine Caring Environments

While an overview of the Circles of Care has been provided, we believe it is equally important for leaders to name and understand the traditional leadership principles that stand in opposition to these forms of care. Creating systemic change includes acknowledging the cultural practices that undermine our ability to engage in self- and community care. Values such as individualism, grind culture, and sense of urgency are all deeply rooted in capitalism, patriarchy, and white supremacy. These characteristics can seem very seductive to leaders and are qualities that have been historically celebrated in the world of leadership. From workshops and training to motivational posters, themes such as ambitious goal setting, hard work, and perseverance against all odds have long been glorified attributes of "successful" leaders. This mindset is an especially common trap to fall into if you are a school counselor with a large caseload or inadequate resources. The temptation to push through to do what little you can under the immense pressures of constant demands and excessive administrative tasks is strong. However, the pressure of unrealistic expectations on yourself and those you are working with can lead to increased stress levels, fear of failure, and in turn a fear of taking risks. The busyness of it all keeps us from recognizing how it harms our ability to create caring environments, engage in rest, and evaluate if the policies, practices, and systems we have created are truly best for our youth.

Furthermore, these values are often exploited by systems of oppression in a manner that is antithetical to the transformative and liberatory principles of leadership. In the context of equity and social justice work, these characteristics can lead to burnout, isolation, and psychological distress. In order to address this issue, let us examine how white supremacy culture, can negatively impact opportunities for self-care, community care, and collective action. By naming and recognizing how these systems influence our behaviors individuals can become more conscious of their actions and assess whether these align with their leadership values. As this understanding deepens, consider how these behaviors affect your relationships and leadership effectiveness and think about areas for improvement.

White Supremacy Culture and Caring Environments

Tema Okun (1999) asserts that

> white supremacy culture can be powerful because it is ever present, yet difficult to name or identify. Whether the group is white-led or predominantly white or people of color-led or predominantly people of color, these characteristics can become the norms and standards of an organization

and thus influence our leadership approach and our ability to create a community that values rest and care. As we examine each characteristic (Okun, 1999), the focus will be on how these traits impact our behaviors, relationships, and ability to engage in Circles of Care. Consider how these behaviors manifest in your school, district, or professional organization and their potential impact on students, colleagues, teams, and organizations (Table 8.3).

Key functions of effective leadership such as building relationships, creating a sense of safety, organizing, inspiring, and leading by example are deeply

Table 8.3 White Supremacy Cultures Impact on Caring Environments

Characteristic	Leadership Behavior	How It Affects Relationships	Impact on Rest and Care
Perfectionism	Leaders focus on inadequacies and mistakes, rather than learning from them. Show little appreciation for the work of others. Create unrealistic expectations and excessive workloads.	Can damage relationships by fostering a critical and unappreciative environment. Can lead to decreased morale and trust among team members.	Can lead to chronic stress and burnout as teams struggle to meet unrealistic expectations.
Sense of Urgency	Leaders prioritize immediate short-term gains over long-term results. Rush decisions, act quickly, and may neglect inclusive and democratic processes.	May cause strain in relationships by dismissing others' input, leading to a lack of collaboration and decreased team engagement.	The constant rush can prevent leaders and teams from taking breaks. Unsustainable pace harms well-being.
Defensiveness	Criticism of those in power is viewed as rude and threatening. New or challenging ideas are met with defensiveness. Significant energy is spent protecting power and managing the feelings of those in privilege or power.	Can create an environment where open communication is stifled. Team members may feel discouraged from sharing new ideas, feedback, or openly discussing challenges leading to a lack of trust and collaboration.	Defensiveness can lead to stress and anxiety as leaders and their teams navigate constant tension.

(Continued)

Table 8.3 (Continued)

Characteristic	Leadership Behavior	How It Affects Relationships	Impact on Rest and Care
Quantity over quality	Leaders prioritize quantity such as goals and outcomes over quality like relationships and decision-making process.	Devalue the relational aspect of work. Can lead to a lack of connection and engagement leading to a transactional environment.	Pressure to achieve and produce can lead to burnout.
Worship of the written word	Written communication is valued over other forms of communication.	Disregards other forms of information sharing and prior.	Increased pressure on those who struggle with written communication.
Only one right way	Leaders believe there is only one correct way to do things. Others are expected to conform to that one way.	Limits different approaches and perspectives. Can inhibit collaboration if everyone must adopt one approach.	Restrictions on flexibility and creativity can lead to frustration and stress as individuals navigate rigid expectations.
Paternalism	Decisions are made by those in power on behalf of others without considering their viewpoints and input.	Those impacted by the decisions may feel devalued and ignored.	Powerlessness can weaken a team's sense of agency and freedom leading to a diminished sense of self-worth.
Either/or thinking	Leaders view things in terms of black-or-white oversimplifying complex issues.	Leaves no room for understanding the spectrum of possibilities leading to reduced problem-solving.	Pressure to oversimplify complex issues can cause worry and tension.
Powerhoarding	Leaders are reluctant to share power. Suggestions for change are viewed as threats.	Collaboration is stifled and innovation is discouraged.	Burden of responsibility is unequally distributed leading to exhaustion.

(Continued)

Table 8.3 (Continued)

Characteristic	Leadership Behavior	How It Affects Relationships	Impact on Rest and Care
Fear of open conflict	Conflict is avoided and those who raise concerns are viewed as the problem. Leaders insist on politeness as term for conversation.	Limits honest and open communication. If conflict is left unresolved, can lead to ongoing tension.	Suppressing conflict and unresolved issues can impact emotional care.
Individualism	Leaders prioritize individual achievement over teamwork. Competition is more highly valued than cooperation.	Can lead to isolation as individuals prioritize their own success over collective goals.	Shouldering the responsibilities alone can lead to fatigue and exhaustion.
I'm the Only One	Leaders believe they are the only one who can do things correctly and struggle to delegate work to others.	Creates a sense of dependency and limits the growth of others.	Leaders bear the brunt of the work often taking on too much.
Progress is bigger, more	Leaders equate progress with doing more, rather than doing things well.	Focus on productivity over process can lead to strained communication and transactional relationships.	Constant pursuit of more can create little time for rest, leading to exhaustion.
Objectivity	Leaders believe in a neutral and objective approach ignoring potential bias and the validity of emotions.	Relationships can suffer when emotional needs are disregarded. Decisions based solely on metrics and data can be dehumanizing. People can feel unheard when their experiences are overshadowed by facts and logic.	Ignoring people's personal experiences can undermine caring environments.

(Continued)

Table 8.3 (Continued)

Characteristic	Leadership Behavior	How It Affects Relationships	Impact on Rest and Care
Right to Comfort	Leaders prioritize their own comfort and scapegoat those who cause discomfort.	Prioritizing only one person's needs in a relationship can lead to resentment and frustration.	Leaders who avoid difficult conversations may disregard the workloads of others or fail to address their team's needs.

connected to rest and care. A leader's behaviors within each of these aspects can foster an environment where rest and care are prioritized or contribute to their neglect. As such, the purpose of reviewing these characteristics is not to blame or shame anyone who exhibits any of these traits, but to help individuals understand how these traits can impact one's ability to lead effectively. While white supremacy culture affects everyone, it does not affect us all in the same way. As Okun (1999) states, "white supremacy targets and violates BIPOC people and communities with the intent to destroy them directly; white supremacy targets and violates white people with a persistent invitation to collude that will inevitably destroy their humanity." For BIPOC school counselors, this means finding ways to resist adopting these traits and reclaiming our right to caring environments. For white school counselors, this means recognizing the ways in which we may conspire with white supremacy through active participation. For all of us, it involves acknowledging how these characteristics ultimately harm our relationships and our ability to build Circles of Care.

Stepping into Your Ruby Shoes: Use of School Counseling Skills

As you conclude this journey down our yellow brick road, we hope you recognize that you've always had the power to lead, you just had to learn it for yourself. Relationship building, emotional intelligence, counseling microskills, group facilitation, and collaboration, are all tools that you have already been using in your role as a school counselor. The theories, frameworks, and strategies we have provided in this book are meant to enhance the skills you already possess. Leadership is not a title or status, but an ongoing daily practice and we hope you continue to seek opportunities to cultivate these skills. Now more than ever, your students, school, and community need leaders with brave hearts who can help them weather storms and build bridges to liberation. It's time to click those heels and get to work.

References

Aibing, X., & Xinying, H. (2020). Correlative study between self-care and psychological well-being of school counselors. *Proceedings of the 2020 4th International Seminar on Education, Management and Social Sciences (ISEMSS 2020)* (pp. 972–976). Atlantis Press https://doi.org/10.2991/assehr.k.200826.201

Aktá Lakota Museum & Cultural Center. (n.d.). Lakota Medicine Wheel. https://aktalakota.stjo.org/lakota-culture/lakota-medicine-wheel/

American Counseling Association. (2014). *ACA code of ethics.* https://www.counseling.org/docs/default-source/default-document-library/ethics/2014-aca-code-of-ethics.pdf?sfvrsn=55ab73d0_1

American School Counselor Association. (2022). *ASCA ethical standards for school counselors.* https://www.schoolcounselor.org/getmedia/44f30280-ffe8-4b41-9ad8-f15909c3d164/EthicalStandards.pdf

American School Counselor Association. (2023). *ASCA member demographics* [PDF]. American School Counselor Association. https://www.schoolcounselor.org/getmedia/9c1d81ab-2484-4615-9dd7-d788a241beaf/member-demographics.pdf

Asante, S., & Castillo, J. (2018). Social connectedness, perceived social support, and health among older adults. *Innovation in Aging, 2*(Suppl 1), 737. https://doi.org/10.1093/geroni/igy023.2719

Baumeister, R. F. (2012). Need-to-belong theory. In P. A. M. Van Lange, A. W. Kruglanski, & E. T. Higgins (Eds.), *Handbook of theories of social psychology* (pp. 121–140). Sage Publications Ltd. https://doi.org/10.4135/9781446249222.n32

Berg, M., & Seeber, B. K. (2016). *The slow professor : Challenging the culture of speed in the academy / Maggie Berg and Barbara K. Seeber.* University of Toronto Press.

Birdsong, M. (2020). *How we show up: Reclaiming family, friendship, and community.* Hachette UK.

Birkeland, M. S., Nielsen, M. B., Hansen, M. B., Knardahl, S., & Heir, T. (2017). Like a bridge over troubled water? A longitudinal study of general social support, colleague support, and leader support as recovery factors after a traumatic event. *European Journal of Psychotraumatology, 8*(1) 1–10. https://doi.org/10.1080/20008198.2017.1302692

Bowlby, J. (1973). *Attachment and loss: Separation, anxiety and anger.* Basic Books.

Carpini, M. X. D. (2000). Black panther party: 1966–1982. In I. Ness & J. Ciment (Eds.), *The encyclopedia of third parties in America* (pp. 190–197). Sharpe Reference. http://repository.upenn.edu/asc_papers/1

Chew, L., Jayaseelan, L. V., Ayo'dele, A., Mukonambi, M., Mina-Rojas, C., & Hernández, A. M. (2016, November 3). *Webinar summary: Self-care and collective wellbeing.* https://www.awid.org/news-and-analysis/webinar-summary-self-care-and-collective-wellbeing

Cohen, S., & Wills, T. A. (1985). Stress, social support, and the buffering hypothesis. *Psychological Bulletin, 98*(2), 310–357. https://doi.org/10.1037/0033-2909.98.2.310

Council for Accreditation of Counseling and Related Educational Programs. (2009). *2009 CACREP Standards.* https://www.cacrep.org/wp-content/uploads/2024/04/2024-Standards-Combined-Version-4.11.2024.pdf

Craig, M. A., Badaan, V., & Brown, R. M. (2020). Acting for whom, against what? Group membership and multiple paths to engagement in social change. *Current Opinion in Psychology, 35*, 41–48. https://doi.org/10.1016/j.copsyc.2020.03.002

Dockray, H. (2019, May 24). *Self-care isn't enough. We need community care to thrive.* Mashable. https://mashable.com/article/community-care-versus-self-care/

Gadacz, R. (2024, June 6). Potlatch. *The Canadian Encyclopedia.* https://www.thecanadianencyclopedia.ca/en/article/potlatch

Harth, N. S., Kessler, T., & Leach, C. W. (2008). Advantaged group's emotional reactions to intergroup inequality: The dynamics of pride, guilt, and sympathy. *Personality and Social Psychology Bulletin, 34*, 115–129. https://doi.org/10.1177/0146167207309193

Helms, J. (1990). Black and white racial identity. Greenwood Press.

Hersey, T. (2022). *Rest is resistance: A manifesto.* Hachette UK.

Hettler, B. (1984). Wellness: Encouraging a lifetime pursuit of excellence. *Health Values, 8*(4), 13–17.

Hofstede, G. (1980). *Culture's consequences: International differences in work-related value.* Sage.

Francisco-Menchavez, V. (2018). *The labor of care: Filipina migrants and transnational families in the digital age.* University of Illinois Press.

Francisco-Menchavez, V. (2024). *Caring for caregivers: Filipina migrant workers and community building during crisis.* University of Washington Press.

Fye, H. J., Cook, R. M., Baltrinic, E. R., & Baylin, A. (2020). Examining individual and organizational factors of school counselor Burnout. *Professional Counselor, 10*(2), 235–250.

Johnson, K. F., Kim, H., Molina, C. E., Thompson, K. A., Henry, S., & Zyromski, B. (2023). *School counseling prevention programming to address social determinants of mental health.* Journal of Counseling & Development.

Kennedy, M., Kreppner, J., Knights, N., Kumsta, R., Maughan, B., Golm, D., ... & Sonuga-Barke, E. J. (2016). Early severe institutional deprivation is associated with a persistent variant of adult attention-deficit/hyperactivity disorder: Clinical presentation, developmental continuities and life circumstances in the English and Romanian adoptees study. *Journal of Child Psychology and Psychiatry, 57*(10), 1113–1125.

Kim, N., & Lambie, G. W. (2018). Burnout and implications for professional school counselors. *Professional Counselor, 8*(3), 277–294.

Kimmerer, R. W. (2013). *Braiding sweetgrass: indigenous wisdom, scientific knowledge, and the teachings of plants.* Milkweed Editions.

Jones, A., & Pijanowski, J. C. (2023). Understanding and addressing the well-being of school counselors. *NASSP Bulletin, 107*(1), 5–24.

Leach, M. (2019, January 3). *How community care makes self-care a social justice act.* The Tempest.

Lizarazo Pereira, D. M., Schubert, T. W., & Roth, J. (2022). Moved by social justice: The role of kama muta in collective action toward racial equality. *Frontiers in Psychology, 13*, 780615. https://doi.org/10.3389/fpsyg.2022.780615

Loades, M. E., Chatburn, E., Higson-Sweeney, N., Reynolds, S., Shafran, R., Brigden, A., ... & Crawley, E. (2020). Rapid systematic review: the impact of social isolation and loneliness on the mental health of children and adolescents in the context of COVID-19. *Journal of the American Academy of Child & Adolescent Psychiatry, 59*(11), 1218–1239.

Lorde, A. (1992). *Burst of light.* Women's Press.

Mahesh, L. (2024). Recognizing occupational wellness: Finding balance and fulfillment in work. *International Journal of Multidisciplinary Research Studies, 6*(1), 31–37.

Mahindru, A., Patil, P., & Agrawal, V. (2023). Role of physical activity on mental health and well-being: A review. *Cureus, 15*(1), e33475. https://doi.org/10.7759/cureus.33475

Markus, H. R., & Kitayama, S. (1991). Culture and the self: Implications for cognition, emotion, and motivation. *Psychological Review, 98*(2), 224–253.

Marquez, B., & Jennings, J. (2000). Representation by other means: Mexican American and Puerto Rican social movement organizations. *PS: Political Science & Politics, 33*(3), 541–546.

Masi, C. M., Chen, H. Y., Hawkley, L. C., & Cacioppo, J. T. (2011). A meta-analysis of interventions to reduce loneliness. *Personality and Social Psychology Review, 15*(3), 219–266.

Mehreen, R., & Gray-Donald, D. (2018, Aug. 29). Be careful with each other. *Briarpatch Magazine*. https://briarpatchmagazine.com/articles/view/be-careful-with-each-other

Mental Health America. (n.d.). Community care. https://www.mhanational.org/bipoc-mental-health/community-care

Mullen, P. R., Blount, A. J., Lambie, G. W., & Chae, N. (2018). School counselors' perceived stress, burnout, and job satisfaction. *Professional School Counseling, 21*(1). https://doi.org/10.1177/2156759X18782468

Mullen, P., & Crowe, A. (2017). Self-stigma of mental illness and help seeking among school counselors. *Journal of Counseling & Development, 95*(4), 401–411. https://doi.org/10.1002/jcad.12155

National Library of Medicine. (n.d.). *Medicine ways: Traditional healers and healing*. U.S. Department of Health and Human Services, National Institutes of Health. https://www.nlm.nih.gov/nativevoices/exhibition/healing-ways/medicine-ways/medicine-wheel.html

Nelson, J. (2015). *More than medicine: A history of the feminist women's health movement*. New York University Press.

O'Halloran, T. M., & Linton, J. M. (2000). Stress on the job: Self-care resources for counselors. *Journal of Mental Health Counseling, 22*(4), 354.

Okun, T. (1999). White supremacy culture. https://www.whitesupremacyculture.info/uploads/4/3/5/7/43579015/okun_-_white_sup_culture_2020.pdf

Oyserman, D. (1993). The lens of personhood: Viewing the self and others in a multicultural society. *Journal of Personality and Social Psychology, 65*(5), 993.

Oyserman, D., Coon, H. M., & Kemmelmeier, M. (2002). Rethinking individualism and collectivism: Evaluation of theoretical assumptions and meta-analyses. *Psychological Bulletin, 128*(1), 3–72.

Pressman, S. D., Cohen, S., Miller, G. E., Barkin, A., Rabin, B. S., & Treanor, J. J. (2005). Loneliness, social network size, and immune response to influenza vaccination in college freshmen. *Health Psychology, 24*(3), 297.

Reimers, C. D., Knapp, G., & Reimers, A. K. (2012). Does physical activity increase life expectancy? A review of the literature. *Journal of Aging Research, 2012*, 243958. https://doi.org/10.1155/2012/243958

Schultchen, D., Reichenberger, J., Mittl, T., Weh, T. R. M., Smyth, J. M., Blechert, J., & Pollatos, O. (2019). Bidirectional relationship of stress and affect with physical activity and healthy eating. *British Journal of Health Psychology, 24*(2), 315–333. https://doi.org/10.1111/bjhp.12355

Singelis, T. M. (1994). The measurement of independent and interdependent self-construals. *Personality and Social Psychology Bulletin, 20*(5), 580–591.

Skovholt, T. M., & Trotter-Mathison, M. (2014). *The resilient practitioner: Burnout prevention and self-care strategies for counselors, therapists, teachers, and health professionals*. Routledge.

Sonuga-Barke, E. J., Kennedy, M., Kumsta, R., Knights, N., Golm, D., Rutter, M., ... & Kreppner, J. (2017). Child-to-adult neurodevelopmental and mental health trajectories after early life deprivation: The young adult follow-up of the longitudinal English and Romanian adoptees study. *The Lancet, 389*(10078), 1539–1548.

Subašić, E., Reynolds, K. J., & Turner, J. C. (2008). The political solidarity model of social change: Dynamics of self-categorization in intergroup power relations. *Personality and Social Psychology Review, 12*, 330–352. https://doi.org/10.1177/1088868308323223

Surmitis, K. A., Fox, J., & Gutierrez, D. (2018). Meditation and appropriation: Best practices for counselors who utilize meditation. *Counseling & Values, 63*(1), 4–16. https://doi.org/10.1002/cvj.12069

Taras, V., Sarala, R., Muchinsky, P., Kemmelmeier, M., Singelis, T. M., Avsec, A., ... & Sinclair, H. C. (2014). Opposite ends of the same stick? Multi-method test of the dimensionality of individualism and collectivism. *Journal of Cross-Cultural Psychology, 45*(2), 213–245.

Tatum, B. D. (1994). Teaching white students about racism: The search for white allies and the restoration of hope. *Teachers College Record, 95*(4), 462–476.

Thomas, E. F., Zubielevitch, E., Sibley, C. G., & Osborne, D. (2020). Testing the social identity model of collective action longitudinally and across structurally disadvantaged and advantaged groups. *Personality and Social Psychology Bulletin, 46*, 823–838.

van Zomeren, M., & Iyer, A. (2009). Introduction to the social and psychological dynamics of collective action. *Journal of Social Issues, 65*, 645–660.

van Zomeren, M., Postmes, T., Spears, R., & Bettache, K. (2011). Can moral convictions motivate the advantaged to challenge social inequality? Extending the social identity model of collective action. *Group Processes & Intergroup Relations, 14*, 735–753. https://doi.org/10.1177/1368430210395637

Wanless, S. B. (2016). The role of psychological safety in human development. *Research in Human Development, 13*(1), 6–14. https://doi.org/10.1080/15427609.2016.1141283

Wickramaratne, P. J., Yangchen, T., Lepow, L., Patra, B. G., Glicksburg, B., Talati, A., Adekanattu, P., Ryu, E., Biernacka, J. M., Charney, A., Mann, J. J., Pathak, J., Olfson, M., & Weissman, M. M. (2022). Social connectedness as a determinant of mental health: A scoping review. *PLOS One, 17*(10), e0275004. https://doi.org/10.1371/journal.pone.0275004

Wright, S. C., Taylor, D. M., & Moghaddam, F. M. (1990). Responding to membership in a disadvantaged group: From acceptance to collective protest. *Journal of Personality and Social Psychology, 58*, 994. https://doi.org/10.1037/0022-3514.58.6.994

Xiong, Y., Hong, H., Liu, C., & Zhang, Y. Q. (2023). Social isolation and the brain: Effects and mechanisms. *Molecular psychiatry, 28*(1), 191–201.

Zeanah, C. H., Egger, H. L., Smyke, A. T., Nelson, C. A., Fox, N. A., Marshall, P. J., & Guthrie, D. (2009). Institutional rearing and psychiatric disorders in Romanian preschool children. *American Journal of Psychiatry, 166*(7), 777–785.

Zinn Education Project. (n.d.). *April 12, 1787: Free African Society founded*. Zinn Education Project. https://www.zinnedproject.org/news/tdih/free-african-society-founded/

Resources

Chapter 1 We're Not in Kansas Anymore: Leadership and Liberation

Podcast: Dreaming in Color
Offers leaders of color space to share how they have leveraged their unique assets and abilities to embrace excellence, drive impact, and more fully define what success looks like.
https://open.spotify.com/show/0iEF9goc2wBAYmwTAHVTh9?si=a0ae323 50f55476b

Values Card Exercise
Help individuals identify and prioritize their core values.
https://www.think2perform.com/values/

Chapter 3 Leading with Heart and Brain: Emotional Intelligence and Leadership

The Insight Quiz by Tasha Eurich
Dr. Tasha Eurich provides this 5-minute quiz on self-awareness. You take it, and a friend takes it about you to provide a more comprehensive score.
https://www.insight-book.com/quiz

Podcast: The Leaders Journey Podcast-Beyond fight/flight: The fawn response, people-pleasing, and peacekeeping.
Dr. Chuck DeGroat discusses the natural reactivity we have to anxiety and how fawning behavior can lead to people pleasing.
https://sites.libsyn.com/119718/beyond-fightflight-the-fawn-response-people-pleasing-and-peacekeeping

Chapter 6 The Wickedness of Resistance

Influencing Style Questionnaire
Self-assessment tool designed to help individuals identify their preferred influencing style.

https://www.ipcinfo.org/fileadmin/user_upload/webcasting/documents/
Influencing%20Style%20Questionnaire.pdf
Influencing Style - Push and Pull Questionnaire
  Tool used to assess an individual's preferred approach to influencing others.
  https://view.pagetiger.com/leadershipframework/pillars/PushMePullYouDi-
  agnosticTool.pdf
The Harvard Negotiation Project
  https://www.pon.harvard.edu/category/research_projects/harvard-
  negotiation-project/

Chapter 7 Somewhere Over the Rainbow: The Power of Collaboration and Coalition Building

Video: How a 1968 Student Protest Fueled a Chicano Rights Movement
  This video explores the pivotal role of a 1968 student protest in shaping the
  Chicano Rights Movement.
  https://www.youtube.com/watch?v=GWWWPW7I0iU?si=ibbmtXJ3EQpY8
  LiK
*Podcast: Codeswitch (2023, January 23). How the Rainbow Coalition was
  formed and its legacy. NPR.*
  Discussion on the Original Rainbow Coalition formed in the late 1960s in
  Chicago.
  https://www.npr.org/sections/codeswitch/2023/01/23/1150867899/how-the-
  rainbow-coalition-was-formed-and-its-legacy

Chapter 8 There's No Place Like Home: Finding Rest in Community

Quiz: Find Your Balance
  An assessment tool to learn which areas of your life you've been neglecting,
  what you've been paying too much attention to, and the specific areas you
  can improve on.
  https://wheelofwellbeing.com/quiz/

Index

For Product Safety Concerns and Information please contact our EU
representative GPSR@taylorandfrancis.com
Taylor & Francis Verlag GmbH, Kaufingerstraße 24, 80331 München, Germany

www.ingramcontent.com/pod-product-compliance
Lightning Source LLC
Chambersburg PA
CBHW050651280326
41932CB00015B/2870